HANGRY

HANGRY

A STARTUP JOURNEY

MIKE EVANS
THE FOUNDER OF GRUBHUB

LEGACY
LIT

NEW YORK BOSTON

Legacy Lit, an imprint of Hachette Books
Hachette Book Group
1290 Avenue of the Americas
New York, NY 10104
LegacyLitBooks.com
Twitter.com/LegacyLitBooks
Instagram.com/LegacyLitBooks

First Edition: November 2022

Grand Central Publishing is a division of Hachette Book Group, Inc.

The Legacy Lit and Grand Central Publishing names and logos are trademarks of Hachette Book Group, Inc.

The Hachette Speakers Bureau provides a wide range of authors for speaking events. To find out more, go to www.hachettespeakersbureau.com or call (866) 376-6591.

The publisher is not responsible for websites (or their content) that are not owned by the publisher.

Library of Congress Cataloging-in-Publication Data
Names: Evans, Mike (Entrepreneur), author.
Title: Hangry : a startup journey / Mike Evans.
Description: New York : Legacy Lit, [2022]
Identifiers: LCCN 2022026038 | ISBN 9780306925535 (hardcover) |
    ISBN 9780306925559 (ebook)
Subjects: LCSH: Grubhub (Firm) | Food service—United States. | New business
    enterprises—United States.
Classification: LCC HD9981.9.G78 E93 2022 | DDC 338.4/7647950973—dc23/eng/
    20220727
LC record available at https://lccn.loc.gov/2022026038

ISBNS: 9780306925535 (hardcover); 9780306925559 (ebook)

Printed in the United States of America

LSC-C

Printing 1, 2022

*For Christine and Evie, who make pizza night
the best grub of the week.*

Make no little plans. They have no magic to stir men's blood and probably will not themselves be realized. Make big plans, aim high in hope and work.

—Daniel Burnham

If more of us valued food and cheer and song above hoarded gold, it would be a merrier world.

—Thorin's last words to Bilbo Baggins

HANGRY

Prologue

I'm done.

All-day meetings. All-night coding sessions. Midnight outages. Software bugs. Patent lawyers. Employees. Investors. Thousands of angry customers. Millions of happy ones. And pizza. So. Much. Pizza.

I'm done with all of it.

This fills me with equal parts relief and outrage. I say it out loud: "I'm actually done." I'd been trying, quite unsuccessfully, to quit the company I started for a solid three years. I finally managed it (hence my relief). Unfortunately, they slammed the door so hard it hit me in the ass on the way out (hence my outrage).

Be careful what you wish for. You just might get it.

So here I am, in Virginia Beach, sitting gingerly on the threadbare paisley covers of a too small bed, in America's shittiest motel room. Lights from the parking lot shine weakly through beige curtains, so faded that it's impossible to tell if they share the same pattern as the bedspread. The bottom of the "door" sports a four-inch gap. This muddies the distinction between whether this room is indoors, or just a partially obstructed partition of outside. Every few seconds, a car passes by on the busy road just past the parking lot, the headlights sweeping in and all over the walls of the room. The room smells strongly of cleaning products and cigarette smoke. Underneath that is a miasma that permeates all of Virginia Beach: a hint of salt spray and diesel fumes.

I'm not here because I'm broke. Quite the opposite. GrubHub, the company that I founded twelve years ago at my dining room table, just had its IPO. I could have paid for a suite in one of the waterfront hotels. Hell, I could have bought one of the waterfront hotels. But that would be missing the point of this ill-begun adventure. I'm trying to get grounded. Learn patience. Find the smile that I lost along the way. And figure out how to fix some of the damage I caused.

Turns out, I might have created a Frankenstein.

It started small. I just wanted a pizza. Did that. Yum.

Then, I wanted to quit my job. Yep. Did that too. Nice.

Then I wanted to pay off a crushing pile of school debt. Job done. Woohoo!

After that, I just wanted to make it bigger. So, it grew. It got big. Too big. It got away from me. Now, I worry that Wall Street's insatiable appetite for profit will turn the company I founded into a trap. Will GrubHub stay true to its roots? Or will it become a necessary evil for restaurants? Will it level the playing field for mom-and-pop restaurants against the big chains, or will it become just another vendor, trying to take a piece of the pie?

Whether it becomes a Frankenstein or not, it was a grand success for a lot of people, including me. An IPO, so I've been told, is the dream of every entrepreneur.

Like I said, be careful what you wish for. You just might get it.

So. Now what?

I'm going for a ride. A long one. I'm going to ride my bike over four thousand miles, right across the United States, Atlantic Ocean to Pacific. I'm going to unwind the twelve years of insane work that almost killed my marriage and left me utterly spent. Now free, I plan on passing three glorious months meeting amazing people, drinking in sweeping vistas of this grand country, and, maybe, learning how to smile again.

Ironically, now that I am free of thinking about pizza all day long, my stomach won't let me stop. I'm desperate for the one that I ordered to get here. Now that all the board meetings, fancy Wall Street dinners, and hobnobbing at Michelin-starred restaurants are done, I can get back to eating comfort food again (especially since I can spare the calories on this bike ride!). It's funny that now that I don't need to entertain investment bankers, my GrubHub order is late. But I don't laugh. I'm hangry. And getting hangrier by the second.

As I sit in this crappy motel room, I feel like quitting this adventure before I even start it. I worry that if I go through with the ride, I suspect that I will discover that this is not the shittiest motel in America. (Turns out I'll be right about that.) I miss my wife, Christine, in our Chicago home, probably reading a book in our infinitely more comfortable bed, snuggled up with our dog, in a house where the doors go all the way down. Back home, there is food in the refrigerator. Or, if not, at least there, pizzas arrive in less than two frickin' hours.

But I'm not at home. I'm here, hungry, lonely, and not quite so sure I've made great life decisions lately. This trip sounded like a positive way to start a new chapter of my life. It seemed like a good idea at the time.

Finally, there's a knock on the too short door and the long-awaited pizza arrives.

My grindingly empty stomach doesn't allow the luxury of waiting for the 'za to cool. I don't even slow down to add the pepper flakes. About half the still-melty cheese from the first piece remains stubbornly stuck to the pie as I pull it off too quick and take a bite.

Glory! Taste buds erupt. Saliva flows. Angels sing.

This might be the best slice of pizza I have ever had!

Oh! How the mighty have fallen!

Most people think a Chicago-style pizza is a monstrous, two-inch-thick wheel of cheese, embedded in a thick cornmeal crust, more akin to a birthday cake than a pizza. But most people are wrong. Chicago-style has nothing to do with the thickness of the cheese. Any true Chicagoan knows that giardiniera is the key to a great pie. It's an unassuming ingredient: pickled peppers or vegetables in oil—spicy or mild, as you like it. This Virginia Beach–style pizza is sadly devoid of spicy pickled peppers. But necessity being the mother of invention, I have substituted bell peppers and garlic. So, really, it's not too bad. But "best pizza ever." Pshaw! Hardly!

Still, I eat.

And eat.

And eat some more.

As I eat, I'm interrupted by an incoming text.

"Your pizza is about to leave the restaurant," it reads.

Oh, for fuck's sake. Seriously?

I presume they're referring to the mostly eaten pizza sitting here on my crappy motel bed. Clearly, the system I patented at GrubHub four years ago, the one that is supposed to increase the accuracy of these texts, still hasn't been implemented correctly. A decade of habit has me opening my email to write a feisty note to the product team about it…and then I remember.

I quit today. It's over. It's not my problem anymore.

Be careful what you wish for. You just might get it!

I put down my phone and work through the final delicious garlicky piece. I stuff a towel into the gap between the door and the floor. I lie down, too excited about what comes tomorrow to settle. But before long, the pizza in my belly drags me down into a food coma and I sleep.

When I wake up, I will leave my old life behind and ride west.

PART ONE

I create a thing.
It is very hard.

1

Old Spice, New Hobby

GrubHub is born in an armpit.

As it turns out, armpits don't really feature heavily in most startup origin stories. Usually, they go something like this: some wunderkind goes to Harvard, or Stanford, or MIT. They spend a couple years furiously thinking about how to get rich by changing the world in some small (but highly profitable) way. After some kind of divinely inspired eureka moment, they quit school, raise a crap ton of cash from venture capitalists, and then, magically, two years later have an IPO, and start buying islands and planes and shit.

This is not that story. Mostly, this is a story about how I'm cranky. And that crankiness turned into a hobby. And then that hobby turned into a business. I realize I probably need to learn something about running a business. So, I figure out some stuff as I go along by listening to my customers. And then, over a decade later, I have a huge business. I make a metric shit ton of cash when it goes through an IPO. After that, I'm *still* cranky. At this point, I could have bought an island, I suppose. But what good would that do anybody? So, I punt everything and go on a bike ride, trying to figure out where I went wrong (oh, by the way, the business went way off the rails and became brutally exploitative), and how to do it right the next time. This story will be disappointingly uninspiring for the Silicon Valley crowd. It isn't glamorous and doesn't fit into how the business schools teach entrepreneurship. But, if you're a bit of a couch potato, pay attention.

The year is 2002. Tech startups are in the doghouse. Just two years earlier, the dot-com boom, and subsequent bust, cost investors *trillions* of dollars. So, having recently graduated from MIT, I've taken a stable, if boring, job at an early internet mainstay, homefinder.com. I've just finished work, and I'm heading home. It's one of those drizzly fall days, the ones that serve as a harbinger of Chicago's coming winter, with its polar vortexes, potholes, and mystery black slush. I rub my arms and stamp my feet at the bus stop.

Two buses have already sped by, too packed to let anyone else onboard. My stomach clenches—I haven't eaten since midmorning. Work was so boring that I only made it to 10:45 before skipping out for lunch. Now, dinner is a long way off—with traffic, I'm looking at a solid hour of creeping home along Michigan Avenue toward Chicago's Edgewater neighborhood (also known, vaguely, as "up toward Canada" to the froufrou, downtown crowd).

I'm cold, hungry, and tired. I'm looking forward to finally nabbing some dinner, but I'm also really tired. Maybe I'll cook something easy tonight? Grilled cheese?

A third bus arrives, also packed, but the driver is willing to let us fight for a couple of spots. I find my way aboard in the wake of a sharp-elbowed MMA fighter, who moments before was cunningly disguised as a kindly grandmother.

The heater on the bus is turned up to the max. The huffs and sighs of a hundred commuters has coated the windows with condensation. A trickle of sweat rolls down my back. Within minutes, drowsiness overwhelms me, my head nodding as we make excruciatingly slow progress north. Grilled cheese is too hard. Three ingredients. Ugh. Maybe quesadillas? That's only two.

Bam! The bus slams to a stop.

My face makes contact with the armpit of destiny. I have no idea whose armpit it is. It belongs to a perfectly well-groomed man. It doesn't smell bad. In fact, it smells good. Too good. Like it suffered through too many strokes of cool-fresh-evergreen deodorant.

Nope. Not going to do it. I can't cook tonight.

We've all had this moment. Stomach clenched, tired, hungry, and lacking all possible motivation. Mostly, we just shoulder through it, head down, trying to get dinner on the table. But nobody has that much stamina at the end of a long day. It's exactly this feeling that makes delivery so appealing. But it's also true that nobody wants to call a pizza place, get put on hold, and then read their credit card numbers over the phone to a teenage kid. But unfortunately for Mike with his face in dude's armpit, GrubHub won't exist until tomorrow. Actual online ordering is still years away.

I didn't come to the idea of making delivery better out of the blue. Delivery food has always featured heavily in my life. Being raised the youngest, feral child of a single mom, we were on a first name basis with the Domino's driver. When she *did* cook, mom rotated through three or four key dishes, chief among them being "taco salad." Taco salad consisted of crumbled Old El Paso taco shells, browned ground beef, tomatoes, and pinto beans. As an adult, I call this dish "nachos"—but somehow back then, naming it "taco salad" transformed it from a snack to a meal for the whole family. Taco salad was always served in the same bowl, one of the few wedding presents that survived my parents' marriage. It had the word *Munchies* written on it in a thick, skating-rink font. (The bowl was such a fixture that it was actually one of the ingredients.) Mom could whip up taco salad in ten minutes. I don't judge her. In fact, I'm impressed she was able to pull this meal off, while also holding down her third-shift, second job.

I'm not tired, like mom was tired. But I was running on fumes before the armpit, and now there's nothing left. Unfortunately, even if I am willing to go without dinner myself, I'm not the only one at home who needs to eat. It is my task to keep Christine, my wife, alive by getting fuel into her face. She is in the final months of law school, leading up to the bar exam. She hates it in the same way that Hermione Granger hates tests—which is to say, loudly and falsely. She is actually deeply enthralled by her academics, even though she complains about them. I know that when I get home, she will be studying, and when I go to bed, she will be studying. Sure enough, when I wake up, she will be studying. When she is *not* studying, she is thinking (and complaining) about studying. She is the happiest I've ever seen her. (She, by the way, does not appreciate this observation.)

But with all this studying, she can forget to eat, so it falls on me to get her food.

Because the apple does not fall far from the tree, my methods for getting dinner on the table closely mirror my mother's: simple and easy above all else. But it's hard to get much simpler than quesadillas, and that already seems like a stretch.

This leaves delivery. I bring to mind my drawer of menus awaiting me at home. It has a few decent options: Calo Pizza, Andie's, Carson's Ribs. But we had all three this week already, so we need something new. That means one thing: the Yellow Pages.

Here's the cranky part that eventually turns into a billion-dollar business: I loathe the Yellow Pages.

Sure, there are a bunch of restaurants in there, along with ads and coupons. If a restaurant exists, it stands to reason that it's listed, meaning the Yellow Pages are comprehensive at least. But this enormous trove of information is presented alphabetically, with emphasis sold to the highest bidders. This is a shockingly poor way to present delivery restaurants because it doesn't answer the only two questions that I care about when I'm hungry: Do they deliver to me? And are they any good?

So, why couldn't I just create a website that lists all the restaurants that delivered to my zip code? It wouldn't be hard—I could code it up in one night. Tonight, even.

This is not the first time that this particular thought has gone through my head. I never feel like cooking, so I face this problem—and daydream this solution—a few times a week. Plenty of bus rides home, I have thought, "Hey, maybe this time I'll start coding up a delivery guide when I get home." But every time, that motivation has given way to reading a sci-fi novel, or playing *Halo* on Xbox, or watching reruns of *Buffy the Vampire Slayer*.

But this is the first time that I've thought about it with my face smashed into a stranger's overscented underarm. Apparently, this was the missing ingredient—the thing that has finally motivated me to take the first step of turning an idea into an actual hobby.

I arrive home. The steep stairs to our second-floor apartment always feel like an extra kick in the teeth after a long day. I'm greeted by an inferno blast as I open the door. The boiler driving our ancient radiator heat has one setting: roast humans. One of the enormous steel registers is gurgling with the first use of the season.

"I'm home!"

"In here, studying."

(See? Told you so.)

I make my way to the kitchen/dining room. It's just barely big enough for a table and chairs. OK, that's a lie—it's just barely big enough for *our* table and chairs. When we moved in, we treated ourselves to our first grown-up present, an enormous dining room table. It's big enough to host a feast for twelve. (Have I mentioned we don't cook?)

Christine has appropriated every bit of space on that table for books and notes. There are piles two and three volumes high in places. At some point, she started using that too big legal-size yellow paper that all lawyers use. The bigger paper has not helped the situation.

"You know, when we bought that table," I say, "I'm pretty sure we were thinking it would be for sitting at to eat, at some point."

"That would require one of us cooking, at some point," Christine says, not unreasonably.

"So, pizza?"

"Again?"

"Any other ideas?"

"Um. Lucky Charms?"

"Again?"

She shrugs and I go to fix her the Lucky Charms. She flashes me a sincerely grateful smile, happy that she didn't need to pause her studies, overlong. She goes back to reading about federal jurisdictions, or some such, all the while munching away on blue diamonds, green shamrocks, and purple horseshoes.

I get myself a bowl of deliciously empty calories and carve a little work-space on the table, hoping she's too engrossed to realize I've moved some of her stuff. Time to get started on this delivery guide website.

I open my laptop and start coding. First step is to create a map of Chicago. Once that's done, I trace in all the zip codes. I want a user to be able to click on the one in which they live. Then, once they've committed to that ballpark location, it should be a simple task to look up which restaurants deliver in that proximity. This simple innovation is, honestly, already at least one million times better than the Yellow Pages.

Storing restaurant names, phone numbers, operating hours, and so on, requires the use of a database. I like a free one called MySQL, an open-source database system created by a trio of Scandinavians in the mid-1990s. In the database, I set up the various tables of data, along with defining the relationships between them. I then invent a theoretical test restaurant and load it. It works, but it's uglier than a DMV website. Midnight has come and gone. Christine is still studying, so, I keep at it too.

"I'm headed to bed," Christine finally says, sighing and yawning.

"Good night," I say. And then I remember to ask her how her day went.

"Good," she says, "exhausting. I read two hundred pages today, but I still don't feel prepared for class tomorrow. Not that it will matter—the lectures are just personal anecdotes from the professor's greatest hits, rather than having anything to do with the actual subject matter. Still, I need to learn this stuff if I'm going to pass the bar. What are you working on?"

"Oh, I figured I'd make a website to store menus, instead of the drawer." When I say it out loud, it doesn't sound all that useful.

"That's cool," she says, kissing me on the cheek. "It will be good to have something more than three restaurants to order from. Have fun. Good night."

Determined to get something working before I join her, I continue. I'm still absorbed, tinkering with this cool new delivery guide I've made for hours.

Eventually, the sun comes up.

I take a shower, eat some Lucky Charms, and head back out to work.

2

Quitting Is All the Rage

"Food," I say.

"Spot," Holly says.

Holly Maloney is sitting in the cubicle across from mine, at my day job. It's early evening, and the only two employees here at the office are myself and Holly's husband, Matt. Holly doesn't work here. She wandered up here because she's hungry and got sick of waiting for Matt and me to finish playing video games on the company network. While Matt is off in the bathroom, she has been helping me think of a name for my delivery information website.

"Food," I say.

"Finder," Holly says.

"Delivery."

"Finder."

"Grub."

"Hub."

Naming businesses is hard. Usually. This one wasn't.

Matt and Holly leave. As do I. When I get home, I snag the domain name grubhub.com. It is the first change I've made to the website in months. In fact, it has been half a year since that all-night Lucky Charms–fueled coding frenzy. The website has been a once-a-month kind of background hobby, sandwiched in between all the other excitements and frustrations of life.

But even though I haven't put a ton of effort into it, the website works. There is no online ordering. Just menus and phone numbers. I can find dozens of restaurants that deliver to my address. Whenever I get bored of the selections, I spend an hour making calls and adding a few more options. Once I call in an order to this new restaurant, the food usually shows up with a full menu. I scan it and put it on the website.

More months pass. I vaguely suspect this delivery guide might be something I could put some more effort into. Maybe even make it a business. On occasion I get motivated enough to actually drive around and pick up a few menus.

Now it is Monday, 9:14 a.m. Exactly one hour ago, it was 9:12 a.m. Minutes take hours in cubicleland. I already know that this is going to be a long day in a long week in what will be a short life.

I work at the laziest startup on the planet, homefinder.com. The site, which lists homes for sale, has been designed to mimic the real estate section of a newspaper. HomeFinder is owned by a company called Classified Ventures, which also owns apartments.com, cars.com, and auction.com—each does what it says on the label. Classified Ventures is, in turn, owned by Gannett and Tribune, two usually adversarial newspaper conglomerates. This unholy mingling is, on its face, their attempt to adapt to the emerging internet, which is rapidly destroying their classifieds revenue. The reality is darker: Classified Ventures is little more than a smoke screen. As long as it appears that Gannett and Tribune are at least doing *something*, that is good enough. They don't want us to be actually profitable—that would make their local papers unhappy. (I know, it is *shocking* that newspapers fared poorly at the dawn of the internet age helmed by such enlightened leadership.)

Classified Ventures has provided me with a perfectly pleasant cubicle, if also a totally sterile one (is there any other kind?). The beige fabric walls are tall enough that even though I stand over six feet tall, I need to perch on tiptoes if I want to annoy my neighbors. I presume it is meant to feel like I'm in a cozy den, but it feels more like being at the bottom of a deep well. I've got a fancy Herman Miller chair, with all sorts of levers. Tucked under the desk is an overpowered computer, the size of a small bear.

My bland workspace is situated within a bland office that itself resides within the most central part of Chicago's central business district. All in all, I work in a perfect cubicle farm—replete with constantly jamming printers, slightly worse than Starbucks coffee, and a finely curated selection of paper clips. It is so utterly inoffensive that it manages to be deeply offensive.

Exactly one hour later, it is 9:15 a.m.

Matt barges into my semiprivate (but officially, definitely, not private) space and takes a seat on my side desk, forcing me to lean far enough back that the chair's spring groans in protest. Like me, Matt is a couple years out of college, and somehow manages to be a Midwest version of a California surfer: He drinks PBR instead of Pacifico; he's got dreamy blue eyes and a mane of long curly hair pulled back into a ponytail—in California it might be described as a mullet, but here in the Midwest it's surely not the worst haircut. He is a cheery guy and always has one story or another about his epic weekend.

I am ready for him today, armed for small talk by virtue of looking up the scores of the most recent Bears' game.

"My weekend was awesome," Matt says, unprompted. "Holly and I went over to Holland, Michigan, this weekend. Stayed near the beach. Too cold to go swimming. Oh man, I got so drunk. You should come with us next time."

"Yeah maybe," I say, meaning definitely no. "Let me know next year when you're getting it set up and I'll let Christine know." Also untrue—there is zero chance that Christine, a committed introvert, would willingly choose to go within one hundred miles of such a boondoggle.

Matt pops his head up above my cubicle wall and looks around.

"I'm dodging Nancy," he says, in a stage whisper. "She's bound to give me crap for leaving a little early on Friday."

"A little? You left in time for brunch. I'd be annoyed too if I was your boss."

"I'll be fine," Matt says, chuckling at himself. "Besides, you're one to talk, you take some epic lunches yourself."

Well. He is not wrong.

"Nancy likes me because I actually fix problems when the site goes down," Matt says. "It's not fair that she gets crap from her overlords because I don't put in as much face time as the other useless sys admins. I get all my work done in half the time everybody else does. No point in just sitting around."

"You could ask for more work," I say, understanding that this is bound to be a nonstarter.

Matt laughs. Somewhere in the awkward silence that follows, he realizes I was not joking. He quickly changes the subject before I press him on my suggestion.

"So, what did you do this weekend?"

"I tinkered with the GrubHub website a little bit," I tell him. "It was pretty fun. Not guzzling-beers-in-Michigan fun, but what can I say? I'm a nerd."

Matt doesn't mock me for this. He is a nerd too—in fact, he's wicked smart. He just prefers to be a lazy nerd, as opposed to a workaholic, like me. We nerds come in different flavors.

"We used it last night," Matt says, getting excited at the memory. "We were too wiped out from our trip to cook. It worked great. But you know it looks like crap, right?"

"I'm an engineer, not a designer, Matt. I will worry about making it look pretty at some point. Mostly, I've been focused on getting all the neighborhoods listed so it ranks higher on search engines."

"Has that worked? Is it getting a lot of traffic?"

"About a thousand visitors per day," I tell him.

"That's pretty good! Have you thought about selling ads or anything?"

"I put up some banner ads," I say, "but they only make about a dollar a day. That's fine, though—it's really more of a hobby right now. Maybe someday it will be something more. I doubt there's all that much money in food delivery. Definitely not enough to stop working for the man and pay off my debt."

(I am shockingly wrong about this.)

"Maybe you should sell premium listings or something?" Matt says.

"That is the obvious next step, but I haven't gotten around to pitching a single restaurant yet. Besides, like you said, it still looks like crap."

Matt perks up. "I could try and sell one for you."

I shrug.

"There's nothing to sell. Don't get me wrong, it would be easy enough to create a premium restaurant listing—I could just change the background color and sort it to the top of the results. But I suspect restaurants won't buy just a color change—they'll want actual orders."

"Still, I could sell one," Matt says. This is not the first time he has suggested himself for this particular gig. He asks about GrubHub just about every day. He obviously wants to be involved somehow. Matt is smart, persuasive, and when he gets around to doing work, it's top notch. But he's also very Matt-forward. What this means is, beyond working together, I'm not even sure that I am actually his friend nor he mine. It's more like I'm an effective resource to achieve the goal of having fun with someone. Whenever we hang out, I come away feeling like a supporting actor to the lead. With that in mind, sharing GrubHub with him might be a mistake. But some paying customers would be great, and I dread the idea of waltzing into a restaurant trying to sell ads. Maybe I should let him have at it.

"Let's talk about it tomorrow."

"Cool," Matt says. "Crap—there's Nancy. I'm outta here."

Absent of any further distractions, I am free to get some actual work done.

I line two pieces of paper next to each other—a clean sheet and last week's not-so-clean sheet. Glancing through the older version, I make note of any unfinished tasks—which honestly amounts to nothing significant.

To create my task list for the coming week, I consult the lengthy specification document. It reveals, in excruciating detail, the next version of the website. Every question has been answered, every navigation specified, even the color scheme has not been left to chance. There are no decisions for me to make. My job is to simply translate this aspirational document into code.

It takes about twenty minutes to get warmed up. I begin by reviewing the front end of the website, then the database structure, and finally everything in between. In total, there are four or five different systems that contain the logic and rules for how the website works. Holding all this stuff in my mind requires intense concentration. In industry jargon, this is called entering flow state. Most developers use some kind of music to get into it—my current playlist features Offspring and Rage Against the

Machine. Pounding through my headphones, this music serves to put a barrier between myself and the susurrus of chatter flowing around me in the office.

Once I am in flow, I add a text box to the website for the user to describe the property they've listed. This is a required field. To the end user, this appears simply as a little red asterisk. Behind the scenes, though, the users' input must be verified, and the website must reject any submissions that have been left blank. Also, since some of this information shows up on real estate listings, it needs to comply with equal opportunity housing requirements. We had a meeting last week where we discussed the importance of filtering any possible word that could be racist, profane, or discriminatory. I suggested we just filter out all words in the dictionary. (My boss was not impressed with my snark.) Still, the rules exist for good reason, so I spend the better part of an hour trying to get it right—Googling lists of profanity and copying them into the database to protect any would-be home buyers from salty language.

Flow state is the opposite of mindfulness—there's no emptying out to observe. Not watching how my mind works, I don't have the presence of mind to realize just how happy I am as I code. There's more buttons and fields to add. More navigation. More fiddling with the database. Eventually, I finish. Coming out of flow state is faster than entering, but not instantaneous. It takes me a few minutes to come back to the present.

And then it hits me—I have to pee.

Before I leave my desk, I want to see how far I got. Honestly, this is the best part of my job—who doesn't love checking boxes off a to-do list? I get a shock: every single item that I wrote down three hours ago is crossed off the list.

I'm done for the week. And it's only Monday. This job is too damn easy.

I watch as my career unhinges its jaw, ready to swallow me whole. It unfolds in terrifying clarity: short bursts of frenzied coding alternating with weeks of mundane meetings. Turf battles. An extra week of vacation when I hit my ten-year anniversary. Hooray.

A couple of weeks pass by, but it's still only Monday, and only just time for lunch.

Today is a good day for the fast-food cafeteria a few blocks over in the federal building. It features about a dozen restaurants, a mix of chains and independents. But for all the plentiful choices, I always end up at Panda Express.

Is there a more perfect lunch than Panda's orange chicken? It is tangy, sweet, crispy, and savory. The texture is unyielding, at first, but then gives way with a satisfying crunch. Sticky rice drenched with the contents of about a million soy sauce packets offers a salty, carb-loaded counterpoint.

With a succulent bit of orange goodness poised on my bamboo chopsticks, I open my book. It is volume number eighty-three, or some such, of Robert Jordan's epic fantasy series, *The Wheel of Time*. I lose track of my surroundings for the second time that day. Four chapters later, I return to the land of the living, noticing my sore back and aching shoulders from being hunched over the table. The orange chicken is gone. Half of this double order was supposed to go home to Christine. But when you've finished your week's work by noon, the subsequent three-hour lunch is not conducive to leftovers.

Back at the office, I sheepishly creep back to my desk. After about twenty minutes, it becomes obvious that nobody noticed my extended absence. At around four o'clock, my boss comes by.

"Thanks for getting that project done so quickly last week," he says.

"Yeah, no problem. It was easy."

"Do you think you'll be able to get the next version done by the end of the week?"

Is he joking? He is not.

"Uh, it's already finished," I say.

"Really? You just started today."

"Yeah, do you have anything else for me?"

"No, the release schedule is backed up, so there's no point."

"I'll go talk to the guys in R&D, then, and see if they have anything for me to pick up." I've got to find *something* to do.

"Great idea," boss man says.

Eventually, he wanders off, and the clock on my computer screen hits 4:31. That rounds up to 5:00. My iPod's playlist is "Breakup Songs" as I head for the exit.

"I Quit," by the all-girl Brit band Hepburn is the first track. Nice.

———

I am pretty good at quitting things.

My first year at college, I quit the crew team when I saw ice float past me during an early morning practice on Boston's Charles River. In year two, expectations around conformity in the fraternity I joined chafed me badly. Rather than work it out, I abruptly quit, causing terminal damage to all my relationships there. In year three, I got an internship at Ford, and lasted just four weeks. It would have taken the better part of a decade, probably, to earn any real responsibility there, so the internship seemed pointless.

My unhappiness at work runs deeper than just boredom and a well-liked cubicle. It's not this job—it's *any* job. Jobs are limiting. Because jobs are specialized, with different workers complementing each other's work, everyone pretty much stays in their lanes. Sure, I can peek over a cubicle wall into marketing, strategy, or sales, but ultimately, those jobs are done by somebody else. As far as the organization is concerned, I'm *just* a coder.

But there's a deeper issue: I hate people telling me what to do. I'm not sure anyone loves that, but with me, it rises to a kind of pathology.

What I come to understand while working at Classified Ventures is that all these negative feelings—daydreams of quitting, crankiness at being pigeonholed as "just a coder," and hating being told what to do—they're all just symptoms of something much deeper: discontent. This is simply an intrinsic quality of who I am. I am not content; I have never been content. I will never be content. Being content is not who I am.

In fact, discontent is a feature, not a bug. Entrepreneurs aren't happy people.

Discontent is my driving force, my animus. I look around and say, "This is not right. It is crap." I say this about everything—friendships, businesses, the TSA line. But if it was just that, I'd be just another grumpy asshole. But I don't stop at "this is crap." After the complaining, I add another impulse: "It should be better—I can make it better." This final piece is the difference between a miserable grump and a driven entrepreneur.

This is precisely why Henry Ford built a car instead of training a faster horse. (Sorry about quitting on you, Henry. But I'm sure you understand.)

Down at the bottom of the well, I feel the pressure to leave building in me. I know it won't be long now before I just storm out of here.

Don't get me wrong. I love me a good quitting. Quitting is great.

But this wouldn't be quitting. This would be giving up. What's the difference? A good quitting comes hand in hand with a goal. It's abandoning a thing in favor of something better. Giving up is just frustration and apathy.

I don't have any discernible goal, so I better figure out what's next. And quick.

———

It is a meteorological mystery of Chicago that the wind blows strongly into a biker's face at all times—doesn't matter if I'm heading north, south, east, west, up, or down—I always face a gale.

This is especially true the next day, a Tuesday in early December. The air is frigid. To my left, the wonder of the city is accented by Christmas lights festooned across the bare branches. The multicolored lights bathe Lake Michigan to my right, illuminating the ice forming along the sand. It's beautiful. It's peaceful. It's cold as balls. The kind of cold that freezes up *inside* my nose. I cycle on—I'm excited to get home and work on GrubHub and get warm.

It's time to do something about the terrible "pick your zip code by clicking on a map" situation. The piece of software I need is called a geocoder, a bit of kit that turns an address into usable latitude and longitude coordinates (for example, 111 West Washington becomes 41.883, –87.631 [that's GrubHub's future corporate headquarters if you're scoring at home]). There is commercially available software to do this—in fact, I use MapQuest at the day job—but it costs six figures per year for the license.

No problem—I'll just brew my own.

The raw US census geography data is hidden deep in the bowels of a government website. It includes all of the address locations in the US, along with their map coordinates. Downloading the enormous data set, which I started four days ago, just finished. The backup copy fills twenty CDs. It takes half a night of tinkering to write the software on top of the government info that actually converts an address into a lat/long.

With that done, I now need a way to store delivery boundaries, instead of just zip codes. This is not a simple thing to work out. The boundaries of a restaurant's delivery don't tend to be simple rectangles or circles—more often than not they follow major streets, which means they have lots of weird angles jutting out. Still, any shape, no matter how complex, can be broken down into lines, and lines can be described by the point at either end. Therefore, any delivery boundary can be specified with a series of latitude and longitude coordinates.

Late into the night, I work through the technical details. I'm happy. When I finally come out of my programming flow, I hear the predawn chirping of birds in the big tree outside my apartment window. My happiness fades as I take stock.

What the hell am I doing? Technical solutions are fun and easy to solve (for me, anyway). But what is the point? How many nights have I spent working into the wee hours of the morning, messing about with this stuff? The website is getting snazzier, but it certainly isn't changing my life. Really, it's just an unpaid extension of what I do on a normal workday.

If I want to get out of my day job, this website is my best bet. But a hobby isn't going to change my life. It needs to be something more. It needs to become a bona fide business. The difference, I realize, is that a business actually *makes* money. So, I guess it is time to sell some restaurants on advertising.

There is a world of difference between a website that makes zero dollars and a website that makes one dollar. In the thousands of mentoring sessions I have had with would-be entrepreneurs in the decades since this realization, I've tried to underline the importance of this moment. Get a customer. A real customer. One that pays actual money, rather than saying that they would *probably* pay for something. This is the difference between a hobby and a business. It is the difference between a wantrepreneur and an entrepreneur.

Earlier that day I had told Matt that I didn't have anything ready for him to sell. But is that really true? With a little more effort, all those eyeballs on my website could conceivably be converted into orders. Orders are valuable, ergo, eyeballs are valuable, therefore, I've got something to sell. Probably. Maybe.

The next morning, I head straight for Matt's desk.

"Hey, you want to try selling a restaurant?" I announce before I even say good morning.

"Yeah, sure," he says, eagerly. "What am I selling?"

This is a good question.

"See if you can get them to prepay you for a few months of premium listing on the website," I say. "If they bite, tell them I'll sort them to the top of the listings and change the color. It would be great to figure out a way to track orders, but I'm not sure exactly how to do that yet. Coupons, maybe? I don't know. Let's worry about that later."

As I say it, I realize that something about this sentiment rings true. The best way to start is to *start*. A business comes into being with the first sale. Anticipating the first sale has got me thinking in new directions—coupons, premium placement, color schemes, and so on. I'm not just thinking about what I want a website to do for me. I'm thinking about what I want a website to do for a paying restaurant.

"What if they want something else beyond that?" Matt is a salesman, that much is clear.

"Go ahead and promise it to them. Whatever it is, I'll code it up over the next week or two." Again, there's something here that rings true. Getting the business is the hard part. Building features is easy. So easy, in fact, that I spent a year aimlessly doing just that.

"Nice! What should I be charging them?"

"I don't know. It's not important. I care more about proving that I can get somebody to pay something right now than I do about getting the pricing just right. Let's try $100 per month. See if you can get a $300 check."

"That seems cheap," Matt says, looking dubious. "Didn't you say the site was getting a thousand visitors per day?"

"Yeah. Most of it comes from the top listing for 'food delivery' on Google. Also a few links from Citysearch and the *Sun-Times*."

"That's probably enough to sell a restaurant, right?" Matt says, getting his confidence back. "I can bring a laptop and show them how they would be featured on search engines. Heck, I'll give it a try during lunch."

Back at my desk, I'm nervous and distracted. I don't have any actual work to do today—I finished it all the day before, of course—but even if I did, I don't think I'd be able to concentrate on it very well. A long lunch at Panda Express allows for calls to a few restaurants, collecting data for the website. When I finally get back to my desk, I make a token effort to be productive, but my heart isn't in it.

Late in the day, Matt appears in my cubicle.

"Here you go," he says, triumphantly holding out a check for me to see.

"What's this?" I ask.

"A check from our first customer."

Huh. Just like that GrubHub has gone from a hobby to a business. A year of tinkering was fun, I guess, but this feels more *real*.

"How'd you do it?" I ask, beaming.

"I went down to Charming Wok and sat down at the bar. I ordered lunch and got to talking to the owner. I told him that we had this cool new website called GrubHub. We can send him tons of delivery orders if he's interested in premium placement."

"And just like that he paid you?" I can't believe it.

"Well, it wouldn't have been a two-hour lunch break, then, would it?"

Two hours? If Matt is admitting to a two-hour lunch break, this means it was probably closer to four. He continues his story.

"The guy tells me to wait until the lunch rush is over and he'll talk to me. So, I have a couple of beers. He eventually wraps up the lunch service and pulls up the website. He's not exactly impressed, to be honest—you know it looks like crap, right? Anyway, I tell him to search for 'Chicago Chinese delivery' on Google. GrubHub comes up as the first ranking."

"It does?" This is news to me. I knew it ranked first for "Chicago delivery," but I never checked for a combination of "cuisine and city."

"Oh, I thought you told me it did. I guess I got lucky. At any rate, it does, and it worked. He was impressed. He asked me how much it costs. I let him know and he says, 'sounds great.' And then just sits there. I ask him check or cash. He tells me he isn't the owner."

"Ha! That sucks."

"Yeah, I just spent two hours selling the bartender," Matt laughs. "Then he tells me that I need to talk to his *mom*. His mom! She owns the restaurant. He goes and gets her, and I go through the whole thing again. Except instead of sitting there waiting and drinking beers, she's *grilling* me the whole time. Then she finally agrees it's a good idea."

I finally look at the check. It's made out for $140.

"The owner is a pretty good negotiator," I say, surprised. "One hundred forty dollars for three months of advertising?"

"That's for six months, not three."

And this concludes my first lesson in pricing, negotiation, and the unquenchable desire of salespeople to hand out discounts. Still, while $140 isn't $600, it's a hell of a lot more than zero.

"Fine by me. It's a start! Thanks!"

That $140 was the first money GrubHub ever makes. From this moment on, it is a legitimate business, not a hobby.

Immediately, I'm hit with a wave of anxiety.

If discontent is the entrepreneur's first muse, then anxiety runs a close second. This isn't fear about what might happen if I jump headfirst into something new. It's the opposite. This anxiety is FOMO (fear of missing out)—what will happen if I *don't* make the jump? What if somebody else gets there first?

In its current state, the best I can say about GrubHub is that it is marginally better than the Yellow Pages. And if I can see that, then somebody in Silicon Valley can probably see it too. If I don't pounce soon, I might miss my shot.

With the check in hand, leaving my current job magically transforms from giving up to quitting. It's no longer a vainglorious abandonment of corporate America in a blaze of glory (actually, that's exactly what it is, but it's not *just* that). Now, there's something pulling at me: a new business that I've created.

For the second time in two days, I queue up "I Quit" on my playlist. I enjoy the music so much more today.

———

About a week after Matt's first sale to Charming Wok, I am at home on my couch nursing a beer. This couch was the first thing that Christine and I bought after we got married while I was a graduate student at MIT— back then, we were still sleeping on a futon. This thing offers virtually no support, instead swallowing me in an excess of microfiber. Chilidog, our bony puppy, is curled up in a tight ball on my left hip, completely buried by blankets, happily ignoring the January weather. She'll stay until spring if I let her.

Christine comes bustling in the front door, all hats, scarves, gloves, and parkas.

Without even a hello, I say, "I'm going to quit my job."

My wife looks at me like she's a moose in headlights. I say moose, not deer, not to exaggerate her stature, but because you can keep driving if it's just a deer. If you run into a moose, the moose will always win.

She puts down her grocery bags with exaggerated slowness, removes her jacket and hangs it up in the closet. Then, she gently takes off her shoes and puts on her slippers. It's all very Mister Rogers. Eventually, she comes to join me on the couch.

"Is that a good idea?" Christine asks, finally.

"No. Definitely not. But I think I want to do it anyway."

"OK…"

I plow on.

"Look, the way I figure it, we can… Wait, what?"

"OK. You should quit your job," she says, just as calmly as the first time she said it.

"Really?" I can't believe what I'm hearing.

"You seem miserable there," she says, compassionately. "Honestly, I'm surprised you lasted this long. I know you were just doing it to get me through law school—well, I'm through. I'm sure I'll get a job soon. There's no point in you waiting until I get something definite lined up."

Christine had finished law school at Northwestern and then passed the bar a few months back. But, unlike most of her classmates, she didn't have a job to go to. It wasn't because she was a bad student—in fact, she was at the top of her class. But she's focused on public interest work, rather than going to a big law firm. Unfortunately, no job offers materialized.

"I'll get a job eventually," Christine says, with admirable certainty. "Heck, I can work at Starbucks or something if nothing comes up."

Then, she gets practical for a moment.

"What about the loans? Won't there be penalties and interest?"

Now that she has passed the six-month mark after graduation, our loan payments have started up again. Between Christine's undergrad degree at Boston University, her law degree from Northwestern, and my undergrad and graduate degrees from MIT, we are $236,000 in debt.

"The loan payments are thirteen hundred bucks a month for thirty years," I remind her. "That's *2033*. They'll have flying cars and lightsabers by then. What's the worst that could happen? Penalties? Interest? Sure, I guess. So, what? We're paying off the loans until 2037 instead of 2033? It's hard to get worked up about the difference."

But the loans are not the only issue. There's daily life to consider too.

"It would mean getting very tight with our budget," I admit. "No eating out, no travel. If we really tighten our belts, we could make it two months on savings. If I cash in my 401(k), we could make it another two months after that. The penalty isn't that big. Just ten percent."

"What about your bonus from work?" she asks, looking a bit less certain now that I've laid out the financial situation. "They give a pretty huge one in February, right? That's only a month away. Seems like it's worth sticking around for that, at least."

"That's a good idea—it would be another ten grand or so, probably. Maybe I can take Matt on as a partner for some additional cash too?"

"You should quit. Definitely. Who cares about the money? I just want you to be happy."

I'm flabbergasted by her support. Not *surprised*—she is a very selfless person. But still blown away because supportive is not a reasonable thing to be, given the circumstances.

Her backing makes my decision that much easier.

"I should do it," I say, letting one last hint of doubt bubble to the surface. But then, I'm over it.

"I'm gonna do it," I announce.

Christine smiles. "Great!" she says.

This isn't idle daydreaming anymore. I'm getting revved up to quit my software job, the one that pays $100,000 per year, so I can pitch restaurants to sign up for a website that helps them schlep pizzas.

Just to make sure I'm not crazy, I consult a few family and friends.

"Is this a good idea?" I ask.

The response is unanimous.

It is not.

I'm going to do it anyway. Christine and I tighten our belts and do our best to stick to our new strict budget. I cash in my 401(k). I'm hoping that by the time the tax penalties roll around next April, I'll be able pay them. With that shot of cash, I've got a buffer of about six months, assuming we cut coupons and shop clearance at the grocery store.

When it comes, my bonus is big: $11,000. I deposit it into a freshly minted GrubHub bank account. Matt decides to chip in as my business partner—his $11,000 check goes in there too. Now, we've got a whopping $22,140 in our business account.

By 2018, the company will be worth $13 billion. That's a 58,717,253 percent increase. But let's not get ahead of ourselves here. At this point, GrubHub has a single customer.

3

Pizza. And RC Cola

The back room at J.B. Alberto's pizza restaurant, on Morse Avenue in Chicago, is like a portal to another time. Cigarette smoke stains the ceiling from decades of crusty old Italian guys running a business. In one corner sits a computer that rivals my old Commodore 64 for age. Papers are strewn everywhere. An aluminum box of olive oil serves as a stool. The cardboard table looks better fit for a poker game than a desk.

The smell, though, is amazing. Pepperoni. Pizza dough. Fennel.

It is a good thing I never tried J.B. Alberto's pizza before now—I doubt I would have bothered starting GrubHub. Their pizza is *that* good—in fact, it's the best pizza in the nation. I am uniquely qualified to make this claim. In my twelve years at GrubHub, selling restaurants across the country, I ate more pizza from more restaurants in more cities than anyone else in America.

But I had to travel all around the United States to discover that J.B. Alberto's, situated less than a mile from my house, is number one.

Tony Troiano bought the place at the age of fifteen in an effort to stave off his family's return to Italy. Tony is never alone—there are always a few older guys hanging out in the back room. Anybody who wants to sell Tony something submits to the interrogation of this motley crew. They are merciless.

Tony directs me to the chair next to the desk. The chair is tiny. I am so low to the ground that my knees hit my chin.

I imagine the hundreds of delivery boys who have been hired and fired in this chair. But it is not my turn yet, so I am to wait and watch the show.

Currently, Tony and his gang are listening to a young sales rep. The kid is trying to sell them frying oil. Poor guy cannot be much past twenty years old. Probably his first real job.

Tony says, "You tellin' me this is high-end peanut oil? It's no better than the soybean stuff. After four days it goes off and I have to throw it out. I want my money back."

The guy says, "If you filter it twice a day it'll last a week."

Tony gives him a withering stare.

"Tell me, kid. Do you think that I have been running this place for over twenty years, and suddenly, today, you've revealed to me the great unknown technique of filtering our frying oil? Is this supposed to be some kind of secret technique that only peanut oil salesmen know? Were a dozen of your predecessors just holding out on me? Filtering isn't the problem. We're talking about the fact that you said this oil would last a week, and it didn't."

"You must not be filtering it right," the kid doubles down, but he is less sure this time.

"Get the hell outta here. And take your damn peanut oil with you."

"But I already delivered it," the kid says, his voice now a register or two higher than before. "My boss will *kill* me."

Tony says, "Maybe you'll think next time before you blame your customers for your inferior product."

The kid is beaten, and everybody in the room knows it. He angrily loads up cans of peanut oil on his dolly and pushes them out of the room, all the while muttering to himself but not loud enough that anyone can hear him.

Then, it is my turn.

"What did you say you wanted?" Tony asks, exasperated and clearly with better things to do with his time.

"Thanks for having me," I say, lamely. "I'm here to talk to you about my website, grubhub.com."

"We've already got a website," Tony says.

"And it probably doesn't help much, right? You probably had a nephew code it up for you, yes?" He glances at one of the old guys, and I can see I've hit the mark.

"The thing is, a website doesn't help at all—it only matters how many people use it. We've done more than just create a delivery guide—GrubHub has the top ranking on Google, Microsoft, and all the other search engines. When people are searching online for takeout, most of them end up on our website."

"I don't think it's for me," Tony says. "Listen, we've been around for decades. If somebody doesn't know about us by now, I don't think your HubGrub or whatever is going to make a difference."

"But what about new people moving into the neighborhood?" I ask. "Especially yuppies. All they—we—do is use the internet to find stuff."

Tony continues to look skeptical, but at least he has not kicked me out yet.

Plowing forward, I praise the wonders of the internet—especially my little corner of it. Printouts of the website help me paint the picture. Tony and his cohort ask tons of questions—they actually start to get interested. As they grill me, even before I finish one answer, someone else asks a new one. This feels like a good sign. I shovel as much information into their brains as I can, trying to cover all the benefits of GrubHub before I get interrupted.

Just when I am thinking I might be headed for my first sale, Tony shuts me down.

"Well kid, you sure talk fast," he says. "Let me get you a couple of pizzas. And an RC Cola."

He calls out to the kitchen, and one of the chefs appears with a couple of pizza boxes and pushes them into my chest. Tony places the one-liter bottle of soda on top, and ushers me toward the door—I'm forced to focus on keeping the bottle from rolling off onto the ground. But I am not giving up that easy.

"Well, I'll be back next week," I say, unable to shake his hands as mine are full.

Tony laughs and looks at the old guys.

"OK, you can give us another try, I guess," he says, and closes the door behind me.

———

In the two weeks since I quit my job, I have yet to sign up a single restaurant. Already, I am starting to wonder if this thing is going to work. But

I'm not ready to give up just yet. Maybe the problem isn't the website. Maybe the problem is me.

I head to Borders bookstore.

I want to learn everything I can about selling, and because I am completely out of my depth, I pick *Selling for Dummies* off the shelf and head to the café. My tight budget—and total failure at selling any restaurants—prevents me from actually buying the book unless the advice inside is pure gold. I need to give it a test drive over a cup of coffee and a deliciously sweet and crunchy sugar-crusted blueberry muffin.

The book starts gently, with a bit of philosophizing. Sales gets a bad rap, it explains. Most people think it is the act of convincing someone to buy something they don't need. Or, slightly better, convincing them that they need something they didn't know they needed.

But neither are correct.

True sales start with listening. (Who knew?)

Once you have discovered what the client needs, you smoothly transition to revealing how your product meets those needs. Then, and only then, ask for the money. Repeat until rich: First, discover needs. Second, meet needs. Third, ask for money.

Apparently, I've been doing this all wrong. When I pitch GrubHub, I've been starting with solutions, and then going on to price. But I've been missing the *needs* bit. And according to *Dummies*, I am supposed to discover needs, meet needs, then ask for cash, and only in that order.

Of course, it is not quite that simple. The book is very clear that it's important to not linger too long on the first step—the "finding out needs" bit—especially if I find out that their needs and my solution don't fit. Everybody has needs, but my product can only solve a tiny portion of them for a small group of people. For example, there's no point to me selling a fine dining establishment if that restaurant doesn't do delivery. Also, there's no point in trying to sell to a restaurateur who doesn't want new customers (let's not even pause to wonder why a business wouldn't want new customers—which, even after all this time, I've never been able to comprehend). So, before I ever set foot inside a restaurant, I should make sure that there is a chance I'll be meeting with someone whose needs I can meet—this is called "qualifying" sales.

Three coffees later, the lights are going off as one of the employees suggests I either buy the book or put it back. Could I, perhaps, make that choice quickly? You don't have to go home, but you can't stay here. I take a calculated risk and buy the book.

Back at home, it turns out the book is filled with useful gems, such as most sales are about relationships; listen before talking; only sell products you believe in; disciplined scheduling is superior to charisma; *no* might mean "not yet"; find the decision-maker; rejection isn't personal; and once someone is sold, stop selling.

And then there is the gemmiest gem of all, the most important rule of sales: *Ask for the money.*

If you don't ask for the money, it's just a friendly chat.

Armed with my newfound insights, I head the next day to Clark Street in Andersonville. A-ville is a Chicago neighborhood dense with third-generation neighborhood gems, trendy restaurants standing shoulder to shoulder. With my new sales education, I know that walking down a street, going into businesses is called "canvassing." Because it's face-to-face, it's a lot more nerve-wracking than cold-calling over the phone. It is not for the faint of heart; it involves a lot of rejection, and even, sometimes, *ejection*. I'm nervous, but I'm ready.

It is a total failure.

JB's Deli, Kopi, Calo, Reza's, Andies, Svea, Middle East Bakery, Taste of Lebanon—at every stop, I don't get more than two feet past the door. Sometimes it's a host, sometimes a waitress, and once even a dishwasher who each stop me before I can even get a dozen words out.

Back at home, fixing some bugs on the website makes me feel better as I get into the flow of programming. But when I emerge, I realize that what I have been doing on the technical side doesn't matter—a shinier website isn't going to help me *sell*.

I do a quick postmortem on my day. What went wrong? The answer is obvious. In all cases, I had failed to find the decision-maker. Decision-makers set up screens that keep salespeople from being able to talk to them. There is a joke in the *Dummies* book about how good salespeople do things like walking into businesses through the alleyway, rather than the front door where you can be easily intercepted. It was meant as a metaphor for doing whatever it takes, but I wonder if it might be taken literally.

The next day I try again, walking down the alleyway on the east side of Clark.

There's an old, torn notice from the city plastered to a telephone pole warning about rat poison. The dumpsters emit a funk that is two parts curdled milk and one part pasta. Cigarette butts make a springy carpet just outside the back door of Calo restaurant—lots of half-smoked sticks hint at a busy night and flustered servers from the previous shift.

I pull open the back door and walk in.

The owner is right there, tapping away at a computer. He looks at me, first surprised, then angry.

"Who the hell are you?" he sneers.

"Hi, I'm Mike, I'm here to talk to you about my website, called grubhub.com..."

But before I can get any further, he shouts, "Get the hell out of here!"

Trying to stay positive, I consider this interaction progress: I was ejected by the owner of the business, rather than screened by his staff.

I go from restaurant to restaurant, learning as I go. It turns out that restaurants really don't like it when you bother them during their lunch rush. But there is a chunk of time from 2:00 p.m. to 4:00 p.m. when things calm down and everyone has more time to listen to me. I don't make any sales, but I learned something. Progress point number two!

I try all sorts of different pitches in all sorts of different restaurants. I try arguing passionately that the product is going to bring in droves of orders. I try live demos. I try printouts. Every time a restauranteur suggests a feature, it gets coded up that same night, and then I am back to show them the next day.

None of it works.

Three weeks into this misadventure, I am at Pizzano's Pizza and Pasta, just north of downtown. This meeting was supposed to happen the previous day, but the owner had forgotten, and I went home having wasted three hours in bad traffic. At least the guy felt bad enough to reschedule. I am hoping I can trade on that guilt to get my first sale. Progress point number three?

I swing into my usual pitches—droves of customers, demos, printouts, my whole repertoire. Ten minutes in, though, the familiar sense settles over me that this is not going to end well. I know I'm losing him—he's looking at his watch, trying to figure out how to let me down easy and get me out of his restaurant.

I throw one last Hail Mary.

"Look," I say, putting the computer demo away and stuffing the print-outs into my bag. "You're an entrepreneur. I'm an entrepreneur. Take a chance on me."

The man thinks for a minute, disarmed by my direct appeal. He looks at me, taking his time, sizing me up. Eventually, just as I think he's about to wish me a nice afternoon, he breaks out into a smile.

"OK," he says. "What do I need to do?"

I leave with my first check.

I take the money and get out of there, remembering the exhortation from *Selling for Dummies*: Once they are sold, stop selling. Shut your mouth. Take the check. Walk away.

I'm equal parts annoyed and relieved. After getting kicked out of dozens of restaurants and schlepping all over the damn city, all it took was "Take a chance on me"?

Good grief.

But here's the thing: It wasn't just that. It was creating a product, getting out there and facing rejection, thinking about what was wrong, reading about what to do right, leaning in on building a relationship first instead of listing features for a product, learning to listen, showing up at the right time, and maybe, just a little, trading on shame and guilt. And somewhere in all that mess, *something worked*.

"You're an entrepreneur. I'm an entrepreneur. Take a chance on me."

I decide this is my new closer. I head back to J.B. Alberto's on Morse Avenue—I really want to lock this place down for GrubHub. Or maybe I don't—maybe it's just a good proving ground for my sales pitch. Either way, the new killer closing line has been working—seven restaurants have signed up since I started using it, and I have cleared two grand in sales. This is a huge relief after my lackluster start.

At J.B. Alberto's, the usual motley crew of guys are hanging out in the back room. Tony hears me out once again, and then I hit him with the line: "Look, you're an entrepreneur. I'm an entrepreneur. Take a chance on me."

"What else you got, kid?" he asks, unimpressed.

I should have known it wouldn't be this easy.

I need to try something else. I might as well try my fancy new sales knowledge out on Tony. What was it the book said? Discover your customer's needs. Listen before talking.

"How do you grow your business?" I ask. "What works for you guys?"

"You really wanna know? The back of the receipts at grocery stores have been good for us. I also really like the Val-U-Pak neighborhood guide—you know, that packet that you get in the mail that has all the coupons?"

"How many customers does that get you each month?"

"Twenty. Maybe thirty."

"Out of how many, total? How many pizzas do you bake in a month?"

"Twenty-five hundred or so. Maybe three thousand in January."

Oh. They get less than 1 percent of their business from their "best" advertising. This matches with what I have been learning over the last couple months: Independent restaurants aren't growing their business with fancy advertising techniques—there's no NFL prime-time slot for them. What ads they do buy are little things: park benches, grocery store receipts, coupon mailers.

The most successful restaurants thrive simply by surviving. The restaurant industry has horrific attrition rates. Nearly a quarter of all restaurants close every year—even in good years. I am beginning to suspect that good restaurants aren't good because they're run well, have great food, or have figured out service to perfection. More likely, they are just stubborn. *Which is not great for sales!*

So, if I am going to help restaurants, the thing I need to do is make them more likely to survive past that third or fourth year. Get them enough chances to be the business providing pizza for the kid's birthday party, the church bingo game, or the school fundraiser; simmer over time; and then, one day, they are a neighborhood gem, by virtue of being the last one standing.

I am not actually sure I can help J.B. Alberto's. GrubHub won't make a dent in their orders—not at its current size, anyway. So, I decide to fall back on the lessons from the *Selling for Dummies* book and just try listening and learning.

"Do you put your menus on people's doors?" That seems like a standard, if annoying, restaurant move.

"No, that doesn't really work for us," Tony says, dismissing it with a wave of his hand. "Our menu isn't complicated. People usually know what kind of pizza they want. When they are looking for a good pie, they pick their favorite place. A long fancy menu doesn't really help."

"What else works?"

"The Yellow Pages."

"Aren't calls from the Yellow Pages a pain in the ass for you? Doesn't it just bring in a ton of calls from outside your delivery area?"

"Yeah, it's a pain," Tony confesses, "but they bring in a trickle of new customers pretty reliably. Hanging up on a few people from the South Side doesn't bother me too much. That's just the price you pay. Besides, they're just Sox fans. Right?"

I decide to not press him on what a waste of time and effort that is.

"What else have you tried? Park benches?"

"Yep."

"TV?"

"Yep."

"Radio?"

"Yep."

"So, you've tried just about everything, and given up on all of it except store receipts and the Yellow Pages. Have you tried any kind of internet advertising?"

"Look, kid," Tony says, starting to get exasperated. "Yes, I've tried everything, OK? Almost nothing *actually* works. At some point, I sort of gave up on messing with all this stuff, and just fell back on making good pizza. After a few decades, the food speaks for itself."

"Your pizza *is* amazing..." I concede.

"You want a couple pies?" Tony says, brightening. Nothing really gets him excited apart from the chance to share his delicious 'za. I tuck this away as another tip for selling restaurants—every owner thinks their food is the best. A useful thing to know if I ever want to resort to flattery. I resort to flattery.

"Why do you think I came back?" I ask.

"I thought you were trying to sell me advertising!" Tony booms, laughing.

"Nah," I say, "you're wayyyyy too grumpy to buy anything. I'm just in it for the pizza at this point."

Tony doesn't argue about the grumpy bit; instead, he gets me two delicious pies, shakes his head at me—still laughing—and sends me on my way once again.

As I walk out, he puts another RC Cola on top of the pies.

———

It is high time for a business plan.

It's *past* time for a business plan. The internet tells me, in no uncertain terms, to create a plan *before* I quit my job and start my business. Oops.

Fortunately, I already had an inkling of how to start GrubHub. I learned in a very strange place: my acoustics engineering class in grad school.

Acoustics was, by far, the hardest class I took at school, and that's saying something, because MIT is no joke. The class was taught by a Dr. Amar Bose, as in, the founder of the speaker company. It combined the most advanced areas of materials engineering (how to vibrate stuff to make sound), electrical engineering (how to use electronic gizmos to record and playback sound), and fluid dynamics (how the shape of a room changes sound).

What was most fascinating to me was that the answer to most questions about how sound waves behave is "Erm, well, we don't exactly know." Or, in more precise engineering terms, "It is simply too complex an undertaking to accurately predict how materials, electronics, and volumes of air combine to make sound." What is measurable, though, is the results of all those things *after the fact*. Once those measurements have been made, only then can we make educated guesses about how to improve sound quality. This approach focuses on empirical observation in the real world, as opposed to theoretical prediction on a piece of paper. It's probably not how most people imagine advances in technology take place, but you'd be surprised how much trial and error is involved in things like rocket ships and nuclear bombs.

Put simply, the only real way to make a great speaker is to just go ahead and make a bad one, knowing it won't be perfect. Then you can measure its performance, model it, and improve it. Then, make another speaker; then, measure and improve, and so on.

The final class in acoustics (and, coincidentally, my final class at MIT) had nothing to do with sound or speakers, though. Instead, Dr. Bose put down his chalk and talked for two hours about how he created a company. Based on his research, Dr. Bose at first built an incredibly unconventional system that pointed a series of speakers *away* from the listener, to simulate the environment of a concert hall. The system was a commercial failure— but in more crucial ways, it was an important success, because by making a bad speaker, he figured out how to make a *better* speaker.

Every cycle Bose went through resulted in a better product and new research ideas. Then, he explained that he did the same kind of experimental process with the company itself. He basically just started it, and *then* figured out how to make it work, after the fact. There's a phrase for this in startup circles—"building the airplane while it's in the air."

The real secret behind Bose was *financial* engineering, not acoustic engineering. In that last class, Dr. Bose wrote a bunch of formulas out on the chalkboard. *How much does a speaker cost to make? How much can he sell it for?* As he went along, the questions got more sophisticated as he iterated the business. *What percentage does the retail store get? How long does it take to transport the product to the store? What impact do materials costs have? How much revenue needs to be fed back into research?*

There are no clear mathematical answers to these questions; this is not science. The answers he came up with were guesses, but they were useful anyway because guesses can be tested. This method *does* yield science: mathematical formulas that get refined over time. Eventually, a predictive model emerges.

The punchline of the lecture was this: Eventually, after years of trial and error and testing of guesses, Dr. Bose knew almost exactly which numbers drove growth. This can be true of any business: Iteration and observation eventually shows a business owner how to tweak numbers to drive growth at a company. For Bose speakers, this meant they needed to focus on a single directive: *Minimize time in inventory*. The longer a speaker sits on a shelf, the longer capital the company used to put it there is tied up. This realization drove Bose to create direct-to-consumer sales in a pre-internet era—something that none of the other high-end speaker companies did (who instead relied on high-end dealers). It is also what drove Bose to pioneer the outlet store concept.

The initial launch of Bose required investors, but after its second speaker system and some moderate commercial success, the company was able to continue growing for four decades *without any additional investment*. The money for growth came entirely from revenue, extracted through financial engineering.

I remember sitting in Dr. Bose's class completely blown away. It is impossible to overstate how much this lesson meant to me. In my head I found myself saying, "I'm going to do that, someday." And to think I almost skipped this last lecture to take one of the school's sailboats out on the Charles. It turns out that showing up is important. Well, for this class, anyway. I regularly punted my Policy of Nuclear Weapons class to go sailing, and that was *also* a good decision.

But I did not miss that class—I heard Bose, and today I am going to use what I learned to crack the code on this GrubHub thing.

But how to get started?

It turns out that while the internet is very insistent that every entrepreneur needs a business plan, nobody actually knows what exactly comprises this magical document. I can't find a reasonable definition of what one is, or how to get started making one.

The answer pops up in a very unexpected place.

Scrolling through the templates in Microsoft Word, I find one titled, "Microsoft Business Planner," with sections like Introduction to Sales Forecasting, Credible Projections, and Customers. I shit you not—that's how I made my business plan. Somebody at Microsoft had decided to write a primer on starting a business and bury it deep in the bowels of the program, and I happened to happen upon it.

Looking back on those documents (twenty years and a couple billion dollars later), I'm really impressed with the advice I found in those templates. It is written in a down-to-earth and homey way, comparing the journey of a business to a long car ride: "The prudent traveler gets in touch with the Automobile Association of American and orders a map, then sits down at the kitchen table with a highlighter."

It was a narrative from the dark ages. 2004, Microsoft. They hadn't discovered MapQuest printouts.

I use a spreadsheet titled "Sales Forecasting." One of the key concepts here is that there is a cost related to every sale, driven by how long it takes to make, and the hourly rate of the salesperson.

I reflect on my real-life experiences: How long did each of my ten sales take? Superficially, it was around two hours. But it is not just the time I spent in the restaurant—it's the time it took to set up the meeting, the time it took to drive to and from the place, and sometimes there was more than one visit. But here is the tricky bit: I only succeeded with a fraction of the restaurants I attempted to sell—and all that effort into the failed attempts *also* counts. If I am brutally honest with myself, tallying up every minute, it took about two hundred hours to sell ten restaurants.

My target wage is about $20 an hour. Some quick math reveals that each sale is generating about $300 but costing $400 to make.

So, how do I make this work? I fiddle with numbers and play with the spreadsheet, thinking through different scenarios. Do I increase the price it takes to get listed? No, that would only make sales *harder*. Do I decrease the time per sale? But how would I do that? Do I pay myself less? There isn't much blood left to squeeze from *that* stone.

Finally, I crack the code.

It might take twenty hours to sign up a new restaurant, but it takes a lot less time to *renew* a restaurant that is already a customer. Sometimes it takes no time at all, I just run the credit card again.

It's all about *renewals*. If most of my restaurants renew, then it doesn't matter if I lose money on the *initial* sale. The renewal meetings take less time, and don't need to average in all the failures that are an inherent part of new sales. I play with that number in the spreadsheet, and sure enough, if I can get an 80 percent renewal rate, I'll be clearing $10,000 per month in just over a year.

Something about this insight on renewals feels vaguely familiar to me, but it takes me most of a week before I realize what it is: This is how J.B. Alberto's operates. New customers are expensive. Getting them to notice you takes a lot of work. But repeat customers are cheap, and they already know who you are. That's how J.B. Alberto's gets 95 percent of their business each month for free. Renewals.

———

I'm back at J.B. Alberto's. At this point, it's unlikely that I'm going to get them signed up on GrubHub. But, the great food and better advice are reason enough to keep coming back.

"Assume for a moment that you're already a customer," I start.

"Stop right there, kid," Tony says, "I don't have time for mind games, and that's a pretty smarmy sales pitch."

"Oh, I don't want you to sign up anymore," I say. "You've made it clear you don't want to. I just need some advice."

For the first time, he doesn't say anything. I'm not sure he's ever had a salesperson actually *listen* to him.

"Assume that you've been a customer for three months," I go on, "and I come back to you for a renewal. What would it take to get you to buy the product a second time?"

"It depends on if it worked the first time."

"How do you know that?" I ask.

"Coupons, usually. We put different types out there for different types of advertising we do. You know those coupons on the back of the grocery store receipt? That's our best bet—we've been doing them for years."

"How many people use those? How much does it cost?"

"We get about a hundred on a good month." He points to a box by the phone where he collects them. "We change up the designs pretty frequently, so we can track how long the customer holds on to them before they get used. Sometimes it's years. We've been paying about six hundred a month for those coupons for the last few years."

"So, you budget about six bucks per customer."

"For *new* customers. We get repeat customers because our pizza is good. We don't need to pay for advertising for them to order."

Tony has clearly gone through the exact same math I have. Is every restaurant owner in the country just as smart as Dr. Bose?

"If I could get you new customers for say, three bucks each, you'd renew with me, right?"

"Yeah, of course," he says, but then he hits me with a reality check. "But it only works if you could figure out a way to track it without using coupons. I don't like the idea of printing coupons off the internet. That's too easy to fake. Somebody might decide they want our pizza, and then just go to your site to get the coupon. There's no way to guarantee they found out about us from you, even using coupons, which really just means I'd be discounting existing customers, rather than paying for new ones."

"What if I could guarantee the customer came from GrubHub?"

"How would you do that?" he asks, leaning in a little.

"I'm not sure yet, but I have an idea. I'll be back in a couple days."

———

At home, as I work through the pizza and RC Cola, I build a voice-over-internet telecom server. That's a fancy way of saying I write some software to use my computer to mimic an old landline telephone. Telephones, plural, up to a few hundred, in fact. It is surprisingly easy to rent phone numbers from a wholesaler—each number costs about a buck a month. I put in my computer's internet address, and voilà, I now have a dozen unique phone numbers in the Chicago area code that all ring the computer in my apartment.

Next, I assign each inbound number to a specific restaurant, and put this new "fake" phone number live on my website. When a call comes in on one of these rented lines, I then forward the call on to the restaurant using its normal phone number. The system allows me to track how many calls the restaurants are getting, and even *record* the call—which is way more accurate than using coupons and doesn't require the restaurant to offer a discount. Christine, a bona fide attorney, suggests adding a "this call may be recorded" message. Good idea.

At this point, I have no inkling that this phone system will eventually become the subject of several lawsuits, the ire of the New York attorney general, angry demands from a US senator, price limiting ordinances by multiple city councils, and the hatred of the restaurant industry as a whole.

But hey—it seemed like a good idea at the time.

This new phone system is a hit. Renewals become easy. At the end of each restaurant's three-month premium contract, I deliver a CD with the recordings. It justifies their advertising spend in a tangible way that they've never experienced before. The restaurant owners also like it because they can quality check their employees on the phone too.

By July, thirty restaurants are live. By October, I'm up to fifty restaurants and I take in $6,403.81. Christine gets her first legal job. We start paying our school loans again. During the gap in payment, with the accrued interest and penalties, the final payment moved from 2033 to 2037. I raise my salary to $4,000 per month, which is a huge relief.

But that does not stop me from taking home free food. And RC Cola.

Ten Years Later

"See you in six weeks," I whisper, kissing Christine's cheek.

Christine grunts, her eyes flutter, and she mumbles something, which is fair enough—it is, after all, 2 a.m. I had imagined that this moment might be pregnant with the gravity of a sailor headed out to sea, saying farewell to his beloved.

Alas.

I will be driving a van from my home in Chicago to Virginia Beach—eighteen hours and nine hundred something miles—to start my bike trip. I'm going to ride into the sunset, and my starting point is the northernmost viable option that doesn't involve starting in a big city. On the street in front of my house, the rented van is stuffed like a Chicago pizza. Bike, bags, and gear were tossed in last night with the customary chaos of last-minute packing. My ridiculously large bike has been shoehorned inside.

The bike's front wheel is jammed between the driver and passenger seat, resting on the console between them. As I settle in to drive, it gets in the way of my elbow and no amount of shoving can dislodge it. I briefly consider rearranging things, but it's past time to be moving.

I point the car along Lake Shore Drive. To my left, Lake Michigan looms. Dusk is a forgotten memory, and dawn is hours away yet. The windows of the high-rises facing the lake are heavy-lidded—slumbering—though the city's never quite darkness casts a purple-yellow light on overcast skies.

Starting this drive reminds me of another road trip I took years before. Just hours after I finished finals during my junior year at MIT—I made a mad dash home to Georgia. Totally drained and desperate to get away from the stress and burnout, I seriously considered quitting school. (Not so different from having recently rage quit GrubHub as it turns out.)

MIT Mike was hardworking and driven, but still a nice kid. That youngster didn't have the angry beast inside his chest, just between his heart and his stomach. He didn't snap at people. He didn't smack the side mirrors of cars in bike lanes (especially GrubHub deliveries).

I want to get back to being him.

Where did that kid go? Working eighty plus hours a week for twelve years will change you, even if those eighty hours are satisfying, successful, exciting, and challenging.

Was it worth it?

My bank account is bursting at the seams. I'm told I need a bigger one. (It hadn't dawned on me that checking accounts could be too small.) It was probably worth it. But most days I'm not so sure. For all my newfound wealth, in more fundamental ways, I'm bankrupt. I've got a lot of work to do to reclaim my marriage. I've got a lot of work to do on myself. Time will tell if I'm successful. I know. Poor me, right? That sound you hear is the world's smallest violin. I'm a rich guy up to his lending limit with privilege. I get it. Fuck this guy.

And what about the world? Is it better for what I've created? It's definitely more convenient for hungry, tired people all over the country. But what about for restaurants? Again, I'm not so sure. But maybe that doesn't matter, since it's out of my control, now, anyway. The best I can do is do better with the next thing. There will be a next thing. But I'm not sure what. Partly, that's what this bike trip is about. If I learned anything creating GrubHub, it's this: be intentional. Think about what you're trying to accomplish before setting out to do it. Be thoughtful what you ask for, because you'll probably get it.

I've got three months at ten miles per hour ahead of me to reflect on what I've accomplished since that fateful night with the armpit. More importantly, I can figure out what I'm going to do next.

4

Back of the Napkin

It's been almost a year since I quit my job at homefinder.com, and so much has changed...not least of which, Calo—the pizzeria where I was once yelled at for coming in the back door—is now a customer.

Once again, I slip into the place via the alleyway. This time, I have a CD full of phone calls in hand. It's proof that their advertising dollars are well spent—they got over sixty orders last month. I think, *This renewal is going to be a piece of cake... or a piece of pizza, I suppose.*

The back room at Calo resembles the one at J.B. Alberto's, only this one is more like a command center. There is the same random collection of filing cabinets and tins of olive oil, but it's also crowded with monitors showing closed-circuit camera feeds from all over the restaurant. There's not much activity on the black-and-white screens right now during the afternoon lull. A few servers do side work; a booze rep is hard selling the bartender. And even though I don't know much about restaurant management, all this surveillance seems over the top.

Sure enough, when I hand over the CDs with the phone orders recorded on them, the manager gets way too excited about listening to the calls. It's pretty obvious that he doesn't really care about tracking orders—he just wants another way to surveil his employees. I notice that as he prepares to slip the CD into the computer, the delivery manager and a couple other employees linger within earshot, looking busy but clearly listening intently.

The CD compartment whirs and swallows the disc. Windows Media Player launches automatically. Generally, I would expect that Media Player just plays the CD, but it doesn't do that—instead, it unpauses whatever had been running in the background.

Which, unfortunately for all involved, is some freaky hard-core porn.

"What the hell are you trying to pull, handing me a CD with porn on it!" the owner yells, desperately trying to cover his tracks. The delivery manager moves further out of earshot—she's heard enough.

"What? No! It's just phone orders," I say, incredulous that he'd try to blame me. "It must have been running on the computer already. Windows Media Player will sometimes…"

"Get the hell out!" he yells, starting to push me out the back door.

I'm back in the alleyway. Again.

Calo becomes an ex-customer.

And they aren't the only one. An increasing number of restaurants have canceled recently, making it harder to get ahead. GrubHub has plateaued.

The dollars aren't enough. Not for all the hard work. I'm taking in about $7,000 every month, total. It's not nothing—especially as it came *from* nothing—but after expenses, I pocket about half of that as my salary. It's not even half of what I made before. I'm frustrated, I'm underpaid, and I'm overworked.

In theory, Matt is my partner, but the truth is, he hasn't actually done anything to help start the business. I need to get him to start pulling his weight, or he needs to hit the road, and I'll find someone else. Unfortunately, Matt and I never signed any documents about the two checks we put in, so the legal ramifications of this are going to be messy. I'm desperate to get some help to get this thing off the ground, and I'm frustrated that I'm saddled with a partner that isn't doing anything.

Dejected from Calo's cancellation, I head north a few blocks to meet Matt at Moody's Pub.

The interior of Moody's is as close as you can get to being in a Dungeons and Dragons tavern. There are no lights on, ever, and the dirty windowpanes let in barely a trickle of winter sun. Adding to the gloom, three huge fireplaces emit as much smoke as they do heat. On the walls there is a cattle skull, an old rusted French horn, and a pickax.

Despite the odd ambience, the food is amazing. Matt and I each order the Moody Bleu burger and a Berghoff beer.

The ambiance at Moody's may be suboptimal, but their burgers are works of art. The Moody Bleu is laid upon a foundation of fatty ground beef, cooked pink in the middle and charred to perfection on a greasy skillet. On top of the patty, a quarter pound of crumbled blue cheese softens and slides down onto my plate. It's the perfect amount, with half of it ending up heaped onto my hand-cut fries. A sliced red onion adds just enough kick to complement the funky blue cheese perfectly. My first bite is hot, savory perfection and Matt and I give each other a thumbs-up. Each bite that follows builds on the first, and we work through our monster burgers in silence. Eventually, I find the final fry and the bottom of my beer stein.

It's time to get down to it.

"GrubHub is getting old," I complain, wiping burger grease off my chin.

"I thought the business was doing well," Matt says, sitting back in post-burger bliss. "Didn't you figure out that the secret was renewals?"

"The problem is that I'm on a hamster wheel," I say, scanning for the server to get a second beer. "That first month, I was fine—I signed up ten restaurants, and nobody canceled. But a certain percent of the restaurants cancels each month, so by month six, I was at fifty restaurants, but then ten canceled. Not great, but not terrible: five steps forward, one step back. But, as we're approaching one hundred, nearly half my time is just replacing the ones that cancel. It's growing slower the bigger it gets."

"Why are they canceling?" Matt asks. "Aren't they getting lots of orders? I thought they loved the CDs with the phone calls."

"Most cancellations aren't by choice. The places just go out of business."

"Really?" Matt asks, barely believing me. "That many?"

"Yeah, about a quarter of all restaurants close every year. It's nuts. Nobody in their right mind would decide to be a restaurateur."

"Well, can you just pick restaurants that won't go out of business?" Matt asks.

No shit, Sherlock—if only *I'd* thought of that.

"How the hell am I supposed to do that?" I ask, letting my frustration at my situation, and Matt's cluelessness, rise in my gut. "I can't predict the future."

"Track record has got to count for something, right?" Matt says, not unreasonably.

"What is it that stockbrokers always say? Past performance doesn't guarantee future results?"

"True, to a point," Matt concedes. "But what about this place? It's probably been around since the Chicago fire."

"Right—this one has survived a long time, and probably will continue, so yes, I could just focus on places like this. The problem with old restaurants, though, is that most of the owners are grumpy cheapskates. In fact, that's probably one of the chief reasons they are still around. The cranky ones handle the tough side of the business just fine. It's the fancy chefs that never get ahead."

We pause over our beers. I need to get through to him that I can't do this all alone.

"It's not just sales, anyway—there's the delivering of the CDs, collections, coding, marketing. The work is endless. I need help. You're not helping out at all. If you want to be a part of this, that needs to change."

"Hold up. You're taking home a paycheck from GrubHub. I'm not."

"A small one, yes, but that's only because I'm putting in eighty-hour weeks. I'm making half as much money as I used to, but I'm working twice as hard. If you're not going to pull your weight, then you don't get to keep half the company."

"To hell with that. We both put money into this business. You don't get to just decide that didn't matter. Besides, you chose to leave your job. Don't whine about it to me now."

"Yes, we both put cash in. But I'm investing more now. Every paycheck that I take home from GrubHub is smaller than the one I would get in corporate America. The gap between those two is called opportunity cost. And I'm essentially investing those dollars into the business every month. So, we need to update our ownership percentages to reflect that investment."

"Hell no. Opportunity cost isn't equivalent to actual cash. There's no way I would agree to that."

I take a deep breath, cooling my nerves so I don't get dragged into trying to win an argument. This conversation isn't about winning. It's not about fairness. It's about reaching my goals. I've got a very clear goal in my mind with GrubHub: I want to pay off my student loans. That's easier with Matt engaged than without him. Besides, the specter of a legal battle scares me. In the end, he might get half the business, even if I kick him out. It's better to get the benefit of his brain and labor than go down that path.

"Look, I want you as a business partner, but you've got to show up. You're out unless you start doing more."

Matt doesn't have my equanimity. He isn't trying to bury his frustration to reach a goal. He's just angry. He shoves his empty plate to the side and gestures angrily with his hands.

"I've done a lot of work too. I signed up the first restaurant, and I called a couple hundred restaurants to get their information too. I've delivered CDs to restaurants too. All without getting paid. No way."

This line of argument threatens to have me seeing red. It's true that Matt did some work, but it's not one hundredth the part of what I've done. Trying hard to keep my blood from boiling, I tell myself not to try to get an A in history.

"Look, whatever's in the past, let's wipe the slate clean. But going forward, my eighty hours a week on the busines—even with a paycheck—needs to be balanced out by something on your end. Just start at ten hours a week," I say, trying to think of a number small enough that he really can't say no. "Help with the CDs. Handle the marketing on Google."

"Fine," Matt says. He's still pissed, but he sees the ten-hour offer as an olive branch. And I imagine he's got no more desire to get into a full-time legal battle than I do.

I'm still annoyed. The arrangement is still unfair, and that is a hard pill to swallow. But I do swallow it, focusing instead on my goals, rather than trying to win an argument. This technique becomes an important pattern, one that I use again and again as I grow the business: suppressing some negative emotion for a greater goal. I lose count of how many times I suppress frustration at an unfair partnership, annoyance at disrespect from employees, or even something so mundane as boredom at a meeting. And it works. It's ugly, but it works. Goals trump frustration, annoyance, and boredom nine times out of ten.

Now content with our partnership and a full belly, I fall into a more lethargic kind of whining.

"The churn isn't the only problem. Collections are a disaster. About one in ten restaurants is late in paying their bills. About half of those never intended to pay at all."

"You've got to pester them," Matt says, "until it's easier to *pay* you than it is to *deal* with you."

"Sure, that might work, but it just means that I'll have less time for sales. Besides, it's not like I can just cut bait and cancel them. If I do, it makes the website worse."

It feels good to talk through the problems out loud. Maybe we can crack this nut.

"Why does it make the website worse?" Matt asks.

"Diners come to find options. The more options GrubHub has, the more valuable the site is for them. Whenever I remove a restaurant, the service is less valuable to diners, and then to make matters worse, it hurts our search engine ranking."

"Just taking down one restaurant hurts us with Google?"

"Yeah—it's the restaurant row effect," I say.

In just about every town in America, there's a street where there are a bunch of restaurants all jammed up next to each other. But, instead of cannibalizing each other's businesses, as you might expect, they actually help each other. Customers gravitate toward the area, rather than to a specific restaurant. So, instead of the competition hurting each other, the sum is bigger than the individual parts. (Some might call this synergy. But I'm allergic to business jargon, so let's just say they are mutually embiggening.)

"It's really important to have lots of different cuisines represented. Somebody might search for Thai food, and then find a Mexican restaurant they realize they prefer. We lose that halo effect if we remove a restaurant. But, without a consequence for unpaid bills, it's impossible to do collections."

The basic problem is this: Right now, I need to double the number of customers to double my revenue and it's a slog. And because of churn, every successful sale makes the next bit of growth that much harder. I just don't see a way out of it.

"How about this, then?" Matt says after we've sat in silence for a minute or two, both of us taking long sips of beer. "Why can't we just charge the restaurants *per order*?"

Mind.

Blown.

The solution is so simple that I can't believe I haven't seen it before.

Charging per order would shift my focus to working purely on website traffic to increase revenue. Heck, even if a restaurant cancels, their orders will just go to other restaurants.

"So, instead of schlepping around town signing up restaurants, I can focus on getting people to use the website..." The light bulb over my head is flickering to life; I'm talking slowly like the kids in Scooby-Doo right as they work out that the monster is really just a cranky old janitor.

"Is that easier?" Matt asks.

"Hell yeah." Now I'm fully excited. "Doubling eyeballs means writing software and I can do that all day long. Have I mentioned that sales sucks?"

"You'd still need to sign up restaurants," Matt says, bringing me down to earth a bit.

"Sales might actually be easier, though," I counter. "Instead of shelling out cash for a listing on a website that might not even work, if we charge per order, all the risk is on GrubHub. I can tell them that they don't pay anything unless they get orders."

"You don't pay a dime unless you make a dollar," Matt says.

I already know that line is *gold*. It will get me more sales than the "take a chance on me" line I've been using. I can go back to all those restaurants that I failed to sign up and try this strategy. Maybe I can even get J.B. Alberto's on board and walk away with more than a pizza and RC Cola.

Matt and I get two more beers and come up with two other key ideas. Matt jots them down on a napkin. That mustard-stained document is much more the business plan for GrubHub than the thirty pages of stuff I wrote up in Microsoft Word. It becomes a big part of our lore. (Unfortunately, my dog ate it, so all I've got left are pictures.)

In addition to the concept of charging per order, we come up with two key ideas. First, it's got to be only credit cards, no exceptions. Saying no to restaurants who want to pay with cash is going to be hard, but collecting cash just takes too much damn time. Let alone checks, which always manage to be "in the mail" for months on end.

Second, put the menus up for every restaurant in the city, not just those who are paying GrubHub for a listing. This will create a ton of traffic from Google. The restaurants that *do* pay are spending their money to get the extra exposure of the top rankings. Taking the idea further, instead of it just being two prices: free and premium, we can have a spectrum of prices, with the highest-paying restaurants bubbling up to the top.

This new version of GrubHub that we're talking about—per order charges, credit card only, and every menu online—will be a much better version of the business. The difficulty of slogging through the first hundred customers without these rules makes me appreciate them all the more. I'm going to stick to them, come hell or high water.

I'm excited about getting away from a subscription business. Subscriptions are a lot like broken clocks: right twice a day, but mostly wrong. Sometimes they are too cheap, when I'm sending way more orders to customers than makes sense for the fee, for example. Or they are too expensive: A customer might only get a couple of orders—clearly not worth the hundred bucks—causing them to cancel.

On the other hand, charging per order is extremely flexible. Better yet, it aligns interest: Restaurants want tons of orders, and now I'll get rewarded for making that happen.

Matt and I say goodbye and I head home, excited at these new plans, but a bit snoozy with a food coma. After a siesta, I'm ready to get to work on GrubHub 2.0, which turns out to be disappointingly anticlimactic. There's nothing to code—the phone system already tracks and records calls.

The only thing I'll need to do is figure out which ones are actually *orders*. After listening to a few hundred calls, it's pretty clear that if a call lasts longer than thirty seconds, it's more likely than not an order. At forty-five seconds, the probability of no order goes up to about 90 something percent. If I just bill for those calls, then I'll be giving away more free orders for short calls than I will be charging for the long calls that aren't orders. Or, in engineering terms, statistically, there will be more false negatives than false positives, which is to the restaurants' benefit. Mathematically, it's on the generous side of fair.

Remember that thing I said about several lawsuits, the ire of the New York attorney general, angry demands from a US senator, price limiting ordinances by multiple city councils, and the hatred of the restaurant industry as a whole? Yeah, it's this part, only a few million calls later.

It seemed like a good idea at the time.

That evening, a dozen restaurants switch over to a per order fee at three dollars per order. Our new system requires them to switch to a credit card for billing, I tell them, apologetically. No problem, they say, reading the numbers over the phone. I scribble them on a piece of paper, with the intent of figuring out how to charge them through QuickBooks by the end of the month.

There's a weird emotion that comes with all this. It's sort of a simultaneous combination of elation and frustration. On the one hand, it's very exciting that this new version of the business is going to grow faster and be easier to run. On the other hand, it's disappointing that I had to bang my head against the wall on sales for a year before some of these insights came to me.

But that's one of the realities of startups. The innovations look blindingly obvious in retrospect, and easy for everyone on the outside looking in. But it can take months, or even years, of doing things the wrong way before the right path forward crystallizes.

———

It's not about sales anymore. It's about marketing.

How hard can it be?

Oh, honey. Bless your heart.

I've already had some success with search engine optimization (SEO). *SEO* is a catch-all term for all the stuff a website does to impress Google. The goal of it is to get the first search result when people search for "food delivery," or "Chinese delivery," or "Edgewater pizza delivery," or a million other terms. SEO is a winner-takes-all strategy—the first ranking drives about five times more traffic to a website than the second listing. The second listing drives more traffic than the rest of the listings combined.

There's no medal for third place.

There's no guaranteed and clear playbook on SEO (though plenty of snake oil salesmen will tell you they have it figured out). Getting it right is not so much different as being a druid chanting around Stonehenge, hoping the Google gods grant my website abundant fertility. Unfortunately, these deities are fickle. Their provenance is granted or withdrawn on a whim. When acolytes are consulted for the whys and wherefores, they mysteriously refer to "The Algorithm" in hushed tones.

That's OK, I speak Algorithm.

SEO has a plucky younger brother: search engine marketing, or SEM. It's like SEO, but with the important distinction of costing lots of money. SEM are those ads that show up on the top of Google labeled "sponsored." Much like SEO, these are winner takes all—the first listing gets the lion's share of the clicks. If SEO is the august leader of the digital advertising pantheon, then SEM is the trickster. While the organic search listings are sacrosanct, above demeaning themselves to business concerns, these paid listings are all about taking the bribe money. They are built on an auction system. The more the advertiser pays, the higher they are in the ranking. The system is genius. (For Google, at least.)

Marshaling these two strategies takes a ton of work. It's not like I can just get the top ranking for the word *delivery* and then sit back and relax. The approach instead is to cast a wide net. People might type "Chicago Chinese delivery," or maybe, "Lakeview chicken wings." Hell, even "Drunk 4AM tacos" is a cry for food (or for help, or both). I need to create sections on the GrubHub website that contain those phrases.

Every combination of cuisine, food item, neighborhood, and time of day are candidates for SEO phrases. There are millions of permutations of these different terms; in fact, it would be impossible to create all those web pages by hand. But it isn't hard for a *program* to generate them automatically—the one I build churns out about one hundred pages in an hour. After a month, I've got over one hundred thousand phrases—every conceivable combination of geography, restaurant cuisine, and menu item gets its own page.

I'm good at this. Sales? That was hard. Marketing? Hard. Legal? Hard. But this? This is easy. I love programming. It's impossible to be good at everything that a business requires to thrive. Heck, that's why I hope to hire employees someday. But it's important to be good at something. Harvard Business School, Stanford, and UChicago all churn out a good percentage of business leaders that think of all businesses as interchangeable.

The theory goes that if they are good at online e-commerce businesses, then that necessarily transfers to sports, hospitals, or publishing. But it isn't that simple. Specific skills matter. It's incredibly important to become good at some specific aspect of a business. And for me, that's software development.

The huge volume of search term pages that my program has minted is a good start, but it doesn't change anything overnight. Google is skeptical of content until it has been around for a few months, so I need to let them bake for a while.

OK, so what's next? What else could I do to market this thing?

For a start, a concept has been making the rounds on the internet called guerrilla marketing. It's scrappy, and unscalable, and it's all the rage. I look at a bunch of the ideas central to it: flyers, yard signs, street teams, that sort of thing. They live in the fringe of the marketing world, even more than the park benches and grocery store receipts that restaurants typically use. They also tend to produce a lot of litter. Being a successful convert of the "give a hoot, don't pollute" messaging of my childhood, this doesn't appeal to me. There's also the pragmatic consideration that a flyer in the garbage isn't going to produce any new customers.

The answer? Fridge magnets! People hold on to them for decades—they're useful for holding up pictures of the kids or pets. Space on that big white rectangle in the kitchen would be a little micro temptation every night, right? Salad? Heck no! Let's order a pizza!

Also, fridge magnets are cheap, about five cents each. So, I order twenty thousand as a test batch.

Two weeks later, a semitruck pulls down my one-way residential street. I guess I had been expecting a UPS delivery or something. But it turns out, fridge magnets weigh a ton. No, tons, actually. Almost three.

The delivery driver informs me that he doesn't get paid to unload freight, and that if it takes more than thirty minutes, he needs to charge me. Schlepping hundreds of boxes up to my second-floor walk-up is no joke. Because I'm an engineer, I understand the need to distribute the boxes around the outer perimeter of the walls throughout the apartment. My downstairs landlord would probably not appreciate me and 20,000 fridge magnets crashing into his living room.

The magnets are a seemingly great idea but distributing them turns out to be nigh on impossible. I can't find anyone willing to deal with the weight, for a start—even people I try to hire off of Craigslist balk at the heavy boxes. In the end, I just take a few hundred every day and walk down the street putting them on cars.

Yeah. I'm that guy, aka, asshole.

The magnets help, but they aren't a game changer (in fact, it eventually takes me more than two years to get rid of them all). This is something I learn again and again: There are no silver bullets in marketing. The answer is to try everything—always keep experimenting; and when you find stuff that works, do more of that. (Until it stops working, then try something else.)

Subway ads, direct mail, flyers, postcards, billboards, radio, door hangers, grocery store receipts, street teams. It all works a little bit, but no one thing stands out. Part of this is because *attribution* is the holy grail of marketing. Figuring out what works is hard—this is why everyone from dentists to jewelers ask customers how they found out about their business. But even the most exact tracking will never fully answer the question because marketing works best when customers see a brand in multiple places over a short period of time. It's not an individual thing that works, but a combination of everything that really moves my financial graphs up and to the right. (Again, it's not synergy. It's mutual embiggening.)

It turns out that the other thing that matters with marketing is *time*. Growth doesn't happen overnight. Marketing a startup is better thought of as how a glacier grinds down a mountain: Steady pressure over time.

Revenue takes a big hit when I switch everyone from subscription fees to per order fees. I drop off the plateau of seven thousandish a month, to about half of that. But it's worth it, because now the revenue will grow a little bit every month, even if I just sit on my couch.

And it does. (And I don't.)

Inexorably, the number of people visiting the site grows. Week after week. Month after month. The phone orders increase along with the traffic.

Now, I just need to wait.

———

So, marketing works. Slowly, but steadily. Over the course of six long months, Chicago winter grudgingly gives way to spring, which lasts what seems like two weeks, and now it's suddenly too hot, too humid summer. In all, it's been two and a half years since I coded up version one, and eighteen months since I quit my job to do this full time.

The switch to per order billing has taken a lot of the pressure off sales, but it's still a necessary evil. It is midafternoon, in that space between the lunch rush and prep for dinner when restaurant staff takes a break and catches up on side work—the golden hour for sales.

I'm headed to BB's Bagels. BB's would be a great win for GrubHub because it serves kosher food, which will really benefit my plan to list a wide variety of cuisines. BB's is situated on Touhy Avenue, at the junction of four ethnic neighborhoods: Swedish, Mexican, Jewish, and Indian. Few restaurants cater to all four groups, but everybody loves a good bagel.

The pinnacle of the bagel pyramid is, of course, the everything bagel. The perfect recipe is elusive. It is rare to find a place that gets the mix of poppy seeds, sesame seeds, salt, garlic, and onions just right. Too much sesame and it tastes like General Tso's chicken. Too little garlic and it falls flat.

Eric Berkowitz, the owner, meets me with a friendly wave. He offers me an everything bagel with cream cheese, which I take gladly. The bagel is outrageously good. Eric cheated—he used a lot of sea salt. Delicious, but dangerous, perhaps—it works great as a stand-alone baked good, but it would be overwhelming if used for a sandwich.

Two minutes into explaining GrubHub's phone system to him, Eric doesn't seem interested at all. I'm losing this sale before I really get started. This is the end of Eric's day, which started well before the sun came up; clearly, I'm the last thing that he needs to deal with before he goes home. He wants to make this meeting as short and painless as possible.

"There's no risk," I tell him, munching on my bagel, "because I don't make a dime unless you make a dollar."

"No, it won't work," Eric says. "You see, I hate getting phone calls when we're busy. And that's exactly when people call. I'd need to hire somebody just to answer the phones."

"But with a high-overhead business, with rent, heat, electricity, employees, and everything, more orders means more margin, right?"

"Most of our business comes from big catering orders," Eric says. "We just do the counter service to keep the lights on."

"But you want to grow the business, right?" This seems a basic question with only one answer—but I am frequently surprised that I am wrong on this point.

Eric shrugs and flips the demo pages closed.

Well damn—there's not much I can do here. It's hard to sell advertising to somebody who doesn't want more business.

"Sorry," he says, "but it's not for me. But, let me send you home with something tasty."

Eric shoves a random selection of baked goodness—bagels, bialys, you name it—into a bag. At least Christine and I are going to have a great breakfast tomorrow. Maybe I'll start late; maybe I can take a day off.

But I should make one more attempt to close the deal.

It's then that I notice the fax machine behind Eric. There's nothing special about it, and it's certainly not the first time that I've seen one on a sales call—in fact, there's pretty much *always* a fax machine somewhere in a restaurant.

"Do a lot of your orders come over fax?" I ask.

"Yeah, catering orders," Eric says, "but not the small deliveries." With that, he hands me the bag of baked goodies, and practically shoves me out the door.

You can't win them all, I think.

It wasn't a sale, but the conversation with Eric has me deep in thought as I walk back toward my car. Eric wasn't the only entrepreneur who didn't love the idea of getting a bunch of phone calls. Could I send the order over that fax machine instead? How hard would it be to just let a customer enter their order online, and then fax it to the restaurant?

Facepalm.

People say, "facepalm," but I *actually* did it—I literally smacked myself on the forehead as I stood rooted to the sidewalk, foot traffic flowing around me like I was some kind of boulder in a raging river. I'm equal parts excited about the possibility of online ordering and chagrined that it took me this long to figure this out.

It is a testament to just how big my blind spot was that it took eighteen months of full-time hustling and sales, combined with the difficulty of delivering CDs by hand, topped with the logic that a paper trail from fax machines might decrease cancellations, before I finally considered the possibility of online ordering.

Surely everyone would prefer typing and pressing a few buttons over arguing who is going to call, being put on hold, repeating their credit card number a dozen times, being put on hold again, losing the connection, and then calling back.

The facepalm, lightning bolt of inspiration is followed by the thunderclap of shame: Why didn't I start with online ordering, instead of building A FUCKING TELECOM SERVER?

It is blindingly obvious to me in that instant that I should have started with this. This is blindingly obvious to everyone. I've never met a person who said, yeah, starting with phone orders was a great idea. Because it wasn't. It was a truly terrible idea.

There's a concept in the startup world that a company should not shoot for perfection before building a business. There's a related belief that ideas should be tested on the go, iterating based on customer feedback. The feedback drives little corrections. If a correction is big enough, then it's called a pivot.

This is not what happened in my case. I didn't start with a good idea and then pivot into a slightly better idea. No, I just started with a shit idea, and then I spent years on it. Seriously, *phone orders*?

Entrepreneurs need to be good at quitting things. This is why.

I think about what I've already built. Most of the menu information is already in the database because I used it to create thousands of SEO pages (again, facepalm). All I'd need to do is add the prices, but that shouldn't be too hard. I have the scanned menus already too. This next bit is just data entry, and as a penance, it's the very least I could do for two years of wasted effort.

In the end it takes three hours—three hours to write the first version of online ordering.

Over the next week, most of the restaurants go live with online ordering. Orders triple. TRIPLE.

Facepalm. I really should have started with this.

My revenue jumps to over twenty thousand in the month following the visit to BB's Bagels.

All that stuff I said about glacial growth and steady pressure over time? Yeah, forget that. Instant growth is way better.

Nine Years Later

A long damn car ride, and it's approaching 5:00 p.m. back in Chicago.

Even though I already had my send-off, technically I am still employed by GrubHub until the end of the workday. This is significant, because, according to my employment contract, by finishing out the quarter I will vest my final options, earning more in *one day* than the school loans I was trying to pay off when I started this thing.

It's time for me to do my final act of work for GrubHub, justifying the fiction that I still have a job.

I make the call.

"Hey Matt. You want the password for the GrubHub domain?"

He is more than a little annoyed.

"I can't believe you managed to *not* tell the password to anyone, through the merger, or the IPO. The new CTO is annoyed."

"Best way to keep a secret is to keep a secret," I say, stating the shockingly obvious truth that almost nobody believes.

"So, what's the password?" Matt asks.

"You remember the lamp you had on your desk back at Classified Ventures in 2002? The model was called Eclipse. Which, when you think about it, is a *terrible* name for a lamp. Anyway, do you remember I used that when I registered the domain name?"

"Oh yeah. I remember that lamp. And the password. Wasn't it 'Eclipse12345'?"

"Yep."

It dawns on Matt slowly.

"You...never...changed...the...password?"

"Nope," I say, triumphantly.

"Over twelve years, through six financings, acquisitions, a merger, and two IPOs, and all the while creating a multibillion-dollar company, you never changed the password? You're ridiculous, Mike."

I can't tell if he's impressed or horrified.

"Yep," I say. (I'm impressed, for the record.)

Hopefully, by the time you read this book, Matt will have changed it. Otherwise, let me just say, for legal reasons: you definitely should not fire up GoDaddy, type in that password, and then point the GrubHub domain to a porn site or something. No, seriously, don't do it. We'd both get in a lot of trouble.

"It's been a pleasure, Matt," I say.

"Yeah, good luck on your trip," he says.

"Good luck running a multibillion-dollar company."

I hang up and chuckle. Which is a bit of a letdown, honestly. I had expected an earth-shattering moment of mirth as the realization dawned that I was done—or, barring that, at least a solid guffaw as the tension released.

But no—the end of my time at GrubHub elicited just a single LOL.

I did it. I'm done.

5

Failure to Launch

I expected San Francisco to look shiny and new and startupy but the whole city looks old to me, more European than American. It's got big ol' trees, winding roads, stately homes, and hills. Lots of hills.

I meet up with my old college dorm mate, Ryan, at a Starbucks on Geary Boulevard, in the Richmond neighborhood of San Francisco. An area sandwiched between Golden Gate Park and the Presidio that's usually smothered in dense fog. "Let me get this straight—you want me to join you in walking the entire city, going to every restaurant, picking up their menus?" Ryan looks perplexed, he's standing with arms folded over his hoodie. "That's going to take forever."

"Probably more like a week," I say.

"The *entire* city?"

"Not just San Francisco, actually—I want to get coverage for the whole Bay Area. That doesn't necessarily mean every single restaurant—if I can get three out of four, that will be good enough. Restaurants tend to clump together, so that might mean I need to walk or drive down about a quarter of the streets."

"How many menus is that?"

"I'm not sure. About fifteen hundred? Maybe less. Hard to say until it's done."

"I don't think this is how you're supposed to do startups," Ryan says, laughing at the scope of the quest.

"I'm not into glorifying hustle—that's not what this is about. I just don't see any other way to do this. I already tried to get them more efficiently:

faxes, self-addressed envelopes, workers from Craigslist. Nothing has worked. Do you have a better idea? If you do, by all means, lay it on me."

"Well, all the startup bros talk about scaling, and product market fit, and guerrilla marketing. They don't talk about huffing it all over the city."

"Well, maybe bad ideas are just genius in disguise. I mean, if nobody else is going to try this, then I'll have something unique."

This seems to be enough for him.

"Well, I'm happy to help," he says, stretching his legs, ready to walk. "You know me—the more ridiculous the plan, the more I'm excited about it."

Ryan has always been game for a poorly conceived plan—he really likes ideas that everyone else thinks are terrible. I've had the opportunity to learn this by leading him on several of my dubious adventures: learning to windsurf in the Charles River, skipping the green and blue runs on our first day of skiing, opting for the expert trails from the first lift, and exploring behind various locked doors on MIT's campus. This menu idea is bad enough that it appeals to him. (As I knew it would.)

We set off on our quest.

———

Turns out, San Francisco is hilly—who knew?

We make our way north from the intersection of Haight and Ashbury, strolling along whichever road looks to have restaurants, picking up menus as we go. It's a typical San Francisco fall day—damp and chilly ("the coldest winter I ever spent was a summer in San Francisco"—Mark Twain). And despite wearing only a thin hoodie, pretty soon I'm sweating, as I make my way from peak to peak keeping a sharp lookout for take-out restaurants.

We make our way through the Richmond district, continuing toward the ocean. The city disappears in the deepening fog. Ryan walks the south side of Geary Boulevard as I walk the north. I can barely see him through the thick fog. We stop in Chinese, Thai, and Siamese restaurants. As I had suspected, this personal approach works far better than faxing, calling, or badgering restaurants from a distance. Over the course of four hours, we manage to score about thirty menus.

Eventually, I figure we've run into the Pacific Ocean—I can't actually see it beyond the cliff. But it has definitely gotten a lot colder, and my sweat- and dew-soaked hoodie is no longer offering any warmth at all.

Ryan shouts from across the street.

"Should we stop for lunch?"

Though I'm sorely tempted, I'm crunching the math in my head. We've just spent half the day trudging around, and between the two of us we've collected only a fraction of the menus I was hoping to get out of this trip. It's already clear how much I have underestimated this task.

"Let's just do one more road, Ryan—down Balboa and back to where we started," I shout back across the street.

"That's, like four or five miles, Mike," Ryan calls, aggrieved.

"Suck it up, Ryan."

I head south, looking for whichever road runs parallel to Geary that looks likely to have restaurants. Ryan follows along—he's clearly grumpy now, but at least he hasn't given up.

And then he gives up.

"Enough, Mike. It's three o clock, and we haven't eaten since breakfast. There's a buffet place, just over here. Let's stop and eat."

I can see the poor guy is shivering. He has zero body fat and I've caused Ryan to get hypothermia several times over the last seven years from skiing, windsurfing—and he's so skinny that even a walk on a cold day feels like I'm exposing him.

"Fine, we can stop," I say, not wanting to have his premature death on my hands. "But let's make it snappy."

In the Chinese restaurant there's one of those smiling plastic cats on the hostess stand, the one with its little hand waving back and forth and its eyes roving side to side. The pillars are painted red, with scrolling Chinese lettering up and down in faux gold leaf. Ryan and I slide into a booth and take off a few of our sopping layers. Steam rises both from us, and from the orange duck at the buffet. It smells citrusy and sweet, not unlike Panda's orange chicken. A tiny mug of green tea warms my cupped hands, seeping in through my pruned fingers.

"That was brutal," Ryan says, stating the obvious. "I walked more of the city today than I have in the last year. Why is it so important to get all these menus?"

"There is no way to attract diners to the website unless I have restaurants," I explain. "And there's no way to get paying restaurants until I can offer them diners. How else can I start?"

"So, it's the chicken or the egg?"

"Exactly. My kind of venture is hard to get going. EBay had this problem. Amazon too. StubHub. Any business where there's a group of buyers and a group of sellers and the value comes from bringing them together... getting something to jumpstart one side of that network or the other is absolutely essential."

"I get that. But what do menus have to do with it?"

"The menus are my jumpstart. By putting up all the menus on the website, I can offer something of value to the diners without having to sell restaurants first (which would be impossible, because there's nothing to sell without the diners). And it's doubly valuable, because the menus also force search engines, like Google, to notice the website and send traffic in our direction."

"You sound like my startup friends," Ryan says, and not entirely warmly. "Pretty soon, you're going to start telling me about competitive differentiators."

"As in, how do I avoid Google or Yahoo, or some other eight-hundred-pound gorilla coming in and copying my business?" I ask. "Hard things are good differentiators. The harder they are to copy, the better."

Of course, this will only ring true *after* I've finished doing the hard thing. Which today, in dank and chilly San Francisco, basically sucks.

"At the rate we were going today it will take you a month to get all of the city's menus," Ryan says, fearing, I imagine, that he'll have to come along with me.

"Yeah, this is slower than I thought it would be. We've got less than fifty menus; I need to change my expectations. Maybe I should focus on hot spots instead. If I can get ten menus for each residential neighborhood, that will be enough. The number of menus matters a lot less than having at least a few for each household to peruse."

Once we've eaten and warmed up, it's clear Ryan's done for the day. I can't let it go, though. I head back out to walk, eventually crashing at his apartment, two dozen menus richer.

Over the course of the next week, I hit Soma, the Tenderloin, and Mission. I take a cab to Alameda and discover that Alameda doesn't have many delivery restaurants and getting a cab *out* of Alameda is a pain in the ass. I eventually make my way to Oakland; I walk it—all of it. Back in the city, I head to Chinatown. I walk Berkeley. I walk the whole of the San Francisco metro area.

The whole damn thing. Have I mentioned that it is hilly?

Over the course of the next few years, this question of the chicken and the egg comes up a lot. At a startup competition I enter at the University of Chicago, one of the judges pushes me on the point of how I get all the menus in a city. I tell him that I went and picked them all up. He laughs, content to let me have my secrets—nobody actually believes I did it. Other entrepreneurs, too, laugh at my "joke." Reporters wink, understanding that I'm being coy. Venture capitalists assure me that if I'd only sign on with them, they'd easily help me find a *scalable* way to make this happen.

Whatever. I'll say it again for the kids in the back: Hard work is a competitive differentiator.

Picking the menus up fills my days, but that isn't the entirety of the task. Each evening, they need to be scanned and photoshopped and loaded on the website. The basic listings—which are now just full listings that don't have online ordering yet—come together over the course of a couple weeks. It didn't take a big paycheck from venture capitalists. It just took hard work. But hard work is easier with a goal in mind, and those school loans aren't going to pay themselves.

I still need to get the delivery boundaries.

Some of the menus list them, clear as day—bless them. The rest I'm going to have to call one by one, and that is going to suck. Not only is it going to be time consuming but I already know the calls aren't going to go well. If I call a restaurant in the evening and ask where they deliver, quite reasonably their only possible answer—given that they're trying to make a sale—is, "Where do you want your food to be delivered?" When I explain what I'm doing—making a free delivery guide—some restaurant owners are going to say that's a cool idea and happily give me their info, but the rest, and the most, will get frustrated, tell me I'm wasting their time, and hang up. I get on the phones anyway, and my best strategy becomes to call back each restaurant at least a dozen times and give them specific addresses about where I'm located, trying to guess their service area by the process of elimination. It's like a gargantuan game of battleship.

On the best days I get the info I need from two, maybe three restaurants per hour. This clearly is whatever the opposite of scalable is.

And then I have another eureka moment: I try to think of people who move around a lot, day to day, week to week, and who might reasonably need to know the boundaries. Putting aside the idea of pretending to be a Mormon missionary, I hit on the perfect front: I've got a construction crew that goes from site to site, and I want to know where the restaurant delivers so I can order lunch for twenty or thirty always hungry people.

Bingo—it works like a charm. Within three hours, I've finished over one hundred listings.

Though it's a clever ruse, it's also in bad faith. These restaurants are potentially going to be my customers. I shouldn't be lying to them. I lean into a few lame justifications—it was a white lie, it didn't hurt anyone, it saved everyone a ton of time, it's fundamentally for their benefit. Mostly, I convince myself it's fine. (It's not fine.)

Regardless, even with my morally questionable time-saving techniques, endless days of walking, followed by tedious evenings of data entry make one thing crystal clear: I need to hire a salesperson.

A single Craigslist post gets me fifty applications. Some have decent résumés—others are more…unconventional (one person tries to sell me Amway products). My engineering brain is pulling at me to create a system to filter them. Ergo, I need some way to cut out everything but the serious applicants.

I settle on a simple question via email: "Thanks for applying to GrubHub. Why are you interested in this position?"

Nine out of ten of my emails *don't even get a response*. Of those that *do* respond, only two out of three answer the actual question as posed. These ratios have remained true since that day, across four thousand hires—only about 4 to 5 percent of all job applicants will respond to a single question via email. It turns out it's a good, if depressing, filter.

I meet up with the first candidate, Tyler, in the Marina district. My questions are super basic: "Are you good at sales?" or "Do you like food?" Interviewing really isn't my strong suit. Fortunately, Tyler, my first ever interviewee, is an absolute gem. *He* isn't awkward at all, carrying the conversation with meaningful answers and a light tone that makes me warm to him immediately.

Tyler is a super laid back SoCal guy, transplanted to San Francisco. He seems solid. After talking for fifteen minutes, I'm out of questions, so there's only one thing left to do.

"It seems like you might be a good fit," I say. "Let's go sell a restaurant."

He looks confused.

"Here are all my sales materials," I say. "GrubHub provides online ordering, and more importantly, new customers, to delivery restaurants. We don't make a dime unless they make a dollar. Let's go sell. If you get stuck on details or facts, I'll jump in. But sales isn't really about details and facts. To be clear, I don't want you to work for free. I'll pay you fifty dollars to make the attempt and one hundred dollars if you close the sale."

Tyler still looks perplexed.

"If you don't want to do it, I get it," I say. Suddenly this is the most useful filter of all—if you want the job, why not go do it right now?

"No, it's cool," Tyler says, "let's go give it a try."

At a nearby pizza place named Pizza Orgasmica (yes, really), Tyler introduces himself, makes eye contact, and nails a firm handshake. He politely asks if we could have ten minutes of the owner's time. Tyler gets down to business, asking about what kinds of needs the restaurant has in terms of getting new customers. The owner rattles off a few of the advertising things that he has tried. Then, Tyler jumps in and explains that our advantage is that we offer actual, real-to-goodness new customers. And then Tyler asks for the money.

It's a perfectly executed, classic sales conversation. Listen. Pitch. Close.

It fails spectacularly—we are both shown the door with little ceremony. Tyler shrugs.

"Can't win 'em all," he says, smiling. "Let's try another one."

Which is exactly the right thing to say.

I decide to hire him. I talk him through the details of pay and commissions. Tyler isn't very interested in all that—instead, he wants to know about stock options. This is a sign of just how familiar the denizens of San Francisco are with startups. I hadn't given it any thought, so I improvise, offering about one-tenth of 1 percent ownership in the company. He negotiates me up to about double that. I've probably given away too much. But perfect is the enemy of good enough, and now I've got a salesperson. Job done.

And just like that, GrubHub has one employee in San Francisco.

Tyler helps a bit with collecting the menus over the course of his first week, but mostly he's focused on selling restaurants.

After a month total of hard work, it's time for me to head back to Chicago. I have managed to collect and scan about six hundred menus—it's a respectable start, but well short of the fifteen hundredish the website would need to be comprehensive. Between myself and Tyler, we've signed up eight restaurants for online ordering. Again, it's not great, but better than nothing.

Rather than reinventing the wheel on marketing, I repeat the suite of paid advertising efforts that worked in Chicago: transit ads, online ads on websites, Google keyword searches, and a random collection of other small things. Between hiring a salesperson and paying for these ads, about $5,000 per week will now be flying out the door.

A week passes.

Orders trickle in, but way too slowly. Most days the entire city gets just one or two—even on a good day we don't even hit double digits. Accordingly, I get my first cancellation from a restaurant that's gotten zero orders. Even though the service doesn't cost them *anything*, they have been anxiously checking the fax machine, and are skeptical about keeping a phone line free to accept the orders.

Week two passes.

Tyler signs up no new restaurants.

Another week passes.

The sales tally hits the anemic total of three. But even that tiny piece of good news is mitigated by the fact that two more restaurants cancel, so I'm still stuck at just eight customers.

The two-month mark comes and goes. Things aren't much better.

The total costs of the San Francisco launch come to over $25,000. The debacle has drained the reserves that I struggled to build over the first two years in Chicago. There's less than six weeks of cash left in the bank.

Well, crap. That didn't work.

I'm more surprised than disappointed. I'm not inventing this playbook from scratch. I've done it before. It's supposed to work. Frustrating. And more than a little bit confusing. What went wrong?

I reduce marketing spending to the barest trickle of life support. In the absence of any better plan, I decide to give search engine optimization time to simmer. Traffic from Google is free, but takes a long time to ramp up.

But I can't quite bring myself to fire Tyler. His attitude is unflappable, and he's getting better—signing up two restaurants in the first week after I've reduced marketing spending. If I cut back on my salary, I can keep him around for a year, while I figure out what magic combination of marketing tactics generate orders in San Francisco. I guess I'll need to step up sales so I can score more free food from restaurants. Ugh. Again.

I spend sleepless nights turning my wheels on the same questions: Why was the launch a failure? How different is Chicago from San Francisco for GrubHub? Did it fail because I'm not in San Francisco full time? Does it just need more time? More money?

I don't know.

Up to this point, I'm just making things up as I go along. Try something. Watch the results. Change things and make them better. But I have no idea what to change in San Francisco, or how to make it better.

Having no idea *is* my answer. Creating a startup means living in an uncomfortable tension. It requires having the arrogance to assume that a thing that I invented—with no prior experience in the industry—is going to *revolutionize* that industry. I have the gall to go ahead and try it, throwing ideas on the wall to see what sticks. But it also requires humility. It requires listening to customers. In my case listening to restaurateurs and diners and recognizing that I have blind spots—big ones.

That's the change I need to make. I need help.

At four o'clock my eyes snap open.

Day one. A new thing. Finally.

It's time to get the bike ready.

It takes a while to pack everything, which isn't all that much fun at 4 a.m. Once the bike is fully laden, it's simply too heavy and awkward to lift. It takes a fifteen-point turn to even get it out of the already too short hotel door.

But then, the two-wheeled contraption I'll be using to cross the United States only vaguely resembles what most people think of as a bicycle.

A typical bike—technically the style is called a "safety bike"—has two wheels which are the same size, situated between a frame of two triangles. There are variations, of course, but the basic idea is pretty much the same from brand to brand. About 99 percent of all bikes are this type.

But not mine—I'll be on a _recumbent_.

A 'bent, as they're known, doesn't look much like a safety bike. The idea behind them is that cyclists' torsos are in a reclined position as they cycle. In fact, it looks a bit like a lawn chair on wheels. The seat is enormous. My whole ass sits nicely atop it. It's padded and comfortable. It has a mesh back. (Like I said, _lawn chair_.) My legs extend out in front of me, and the pedals lie just below my hip. This means that the neutral position for my head is level. I chose this 'bent for this very reason. I want to see the country. The idea is to look at the horizon, not the stripes on the road.

Connected to the front-wheel axle, rising in front of the handlebars, is a huge, curved windshield. The aerodynamics of this thing will increase my average speed by about one mile per hour—that's the equivalent of cutting about four days off the trip to the Pacific. (I don't know this yet, but in a couple thousand miles, I'll discover the best part about it is that it actually keeps my feet dry in heavy rain. And at that point, I'll have yet to discover that the worst part about it is that it acts as a sail during a tornado. The sail-in-a-tornado situation will somewhat overshadow the dryness benefit.)

The whole bike, made from titanium, weighs just over twenty pounds. It cost four times the price of my first car. But hey, I just succeeded in making the country 1.2 percent fatter, so I deserve to splurge a little. Also, my first car was a beater that cost $1,500.

I'm feeling like this bike trip is going to be an epic thing. The bike needs an equally big fancy name. Like a Greek goddess or something. Artemis, Athena, or some such.

Pushing the 'bent eastward is super awkward—even more awkward than pushing a regular, upright bike. At one point, the pedal catches my calf, drawing blood before I've even hopped on. Passing a phalanx of motels and ice-cream stands, the ocean stretches before me. It's too dark to make out much of it except the whitewater surf, but I know the ocean is out there—all brooding, and infinite, and implacable. A late spring breeze raises goosebumps on my bare arms. The smell of salt fills my lungs. I can taste adventure on the wind.

Behind me stretches the United States. In a few minutes, I'm going to turn around, hop on my bike, and ride across it.

Heck yeah!

As the light of the day grows, I see that the water is a dull iron gray and meets the horizon at an ever so slightly *less* dull iron gray. Laughing gulls wail and swoop. The natural beauty of a slow ocean sunrise is jarred by a military helicopter flying overhead, presumably en route to one of the army or navy bases nearby.

The sky brightens by degrees, slowly. The cold seeps deeper into my skin. And then I realize: I'm *bored*. I shouldn't be bored. This is the beginning of a *big thing*. Why am I bored? Probably because I've been pushing so hard for so long that I've forgotten how to be still, even for just a few minutes. Maybe that's one of the things I need to think about on this trip.

I scoop some water and a little bit of sand into a vial (there are two more empty vials in my bags—one for the Mississippi and one for the Pacific). I plan to display the three vials on my desk at home when I'm done, as a reminder to myself that I did a *big thing*.

I haul the bike into the ocean to "dip the wheel," to use the vernacular of the TransAm riders. It takes a few tries to get a good shot with the camera timer. At one point, the whole setup overbalances and buries itself in the sand. By the time I'm done fretting over the lens, I'm thoroughly shivering.

Time to begin.

I ride west.

6

Help Wanted

"The whole thing is shit. Absolute shit."

Professor Waverly Deutsch, the clinical professor of entrepreneurship at the University of Chicago Booth School of Business, is one of the most beloved and hated teachers I've ever had the pleasure and misfortune to know—intense, and brutal in her feedback. She's also *always* correct. This does not make her ungentle correction any easier to bear. After all, the only thing more annoying than a know-it-all who's wrong is a know-it-all who's right.

And damn it. She's right.

Professor Deutsch's office is what you'd expect out of a University of Chicago professor. Books everywhere, shelves and more shelves of books, desk, table, and couch. There's a cleared-out spot on half of the circular table, but the advancing library could make a push to take over this final patch of real estate at any moment.

Matt and I visit her to go over our final presentation for the U of C New Venture Challenge business plan pitch competition. With GrubHub's bank reserves wiped out by the failed San Francisco launch, there's not a lot of cash to go around. Our hope and plan is that we can win the competition, bag the $50,000 in prize money, and bring him on full time.

Little did we know that we'd learn a thing or two along the way.

Painfully.

It's winter semester, early 2006, three and a half years since my first efforts, and a few months since San Francisco. The company is limping along, back to that glacial growth again. I'm clearing expenses and taking a salary that affords nicer meals than dehydrated ramen noodles, but not by much. I'm desperate for this GrubHub thing to work.

"Uh, what specifically, is wrong with it?" I ask.

"First, it's too long," Professor Deutsch says. "You've got twenty something slides here. The presentation is nine minutes. You'll be nervous. You've got time for seven, maybe eight slides if you talk fast."

"But then there's no way to get all the info across," Matt protests.

"That leads us to the second problem," the professor says. "None of the judges are going to write a check at the end of your nine-minute presentation. The point is to *intrigue*, not inform. You want to tease them with a small glimpse into a billion-dollar opportunity. You want to tell a believable story about why the business model really works. But most of all you want to induce FOMO, fear of missing out. Say less. Tease more."

"OK…" I start.

"I'm not done," she interrupts. "The structure is *terrible*. You're just cramming data down their throats with no preamble. Tell them what you're going to tell them. Then tell them. Then tell them what you just told them."

"But that leaves even less time for the content," I say.

"You're catching on," Waverly says. "Also, everything in the presentation is low contrast. Don't you dare ever put red lettering on a black background or use three fonts in a slide ever again. Come back tomorrow and try again. If you don't make a marked improvement, I'm pulling you from the finals."

Professor Deutsch shows us the door. Matt and I make our way to an empty classroom to edit and practice the pitch.

"Let's get back to basics," Matt says. "We're supposed to start with the problem. So, what problem are we trying to solve?"

"Well, there's two," I say. "Problem number one is that it's hard to find the restaurants that deliver to my address. Problem number two is that calling by phone is a pain."

"Maybe we need to think bigger," Matt says. "The bigger problem is that it's hard to get good food delivered at home."

I pick up on the thread and riff on it.

"Maybe it's even more than that. We don't grow our own food. Heck, we don't even go to farmers to buy our food. We buy it from a supermarket. They get a premium for collecting all the food in one place. So, in a sense, we pay grocery stores for convenience. But we don't stop there. We go to restaurants instead of a grocery store to enjoy their cooking. That's also about convenience, but there's another element—the quality of the food is more refined."

Matt sees where I'm going.

"So, GrubHub isn't just a place to find delivery restaurants. It's an evolution in how we eat. We double down on the quality that a single restaurant can provide by enabling access to *all* restaurants. And we take the next logical step in convenience from farm to grocery store to restaurant by extending the convenience all the way to home."

"Yeah, now we're talking. How do we say that more concisely?"

"Getting food at home is hard. We make delivery better."

We noodle on that idea a bit, leaning in on the idea and proof points behind the idea that delivery, as it currently exists, is hard. A lot of people won't get this—they don't think of making a phone call as difficult. But people didn't think horses were slow before the invention of the automobile either.

I've got a few thousand recorded phone orders proving this point. Countless diners get put on hold, repeat themselves four or five times, and then fumble through reading the credit card over the phone. But it's not hard proof we need. It's an emotional connection. We need to relate it to something everyone has experienced. For example, whenever someone asks, "Should we order a pizza?" in a group of people, never once in the history of humanity has anyone jumped up and said, "Let me make the call!" In fact, it's like a reverse musical chairs: everyone scrambles to leave the room so they don't get stuck calling the restaurant. If we can relate the problem to the "not it" debate that happens once someone needs to call a restaurant then we'll have the audience hooked.

We edit the slides to reflect these ideas over the course of a few hours.

We bring it back to Professor Deutsch, who promptly deems it "shit" again and sends us packing with more advice. This back and forth happens four more times before she grudgingly agrees it's "not terrible."

During the semester-long competition, we learn more than how to make effective presentations and emotionally manipulate investors. We learn how to balance a balance sheet. We are introduced to the idea of unit economics—what it costs to get a single customer and provide service to them, and in return, how much revenue they generate. We learn that many founders are surprised at how hard launching a second city is (well, *Matt* learns that; I discovered this already, the hard way). We learn about competitive differentiation and barriers to entry.

I personally learn one of the most valuable lessons of my life: to say "thank you" when someone gives me advice, even bad advice. I find out that it's important to appreciate the effort that it takes for someone to share their opinion, and it's equally important to stop trying to win (or, for that matter, *start*) arguments when people are just trying to help. This has been hard for me because many people give me unsolicited advice, and it's frequently dead wrong. But it's usually coming from a place of being helpful. I try to focus on the positive intention and leave off the arguing.

A lot of the lessons stick, though. We get better at talking about the business. Heck, we get better at *running* the business. Most importantly, the relentlessly honest feedback of the New Venture Challenge (NVC) forges Matt and me into a functioning team.

We win the $50,000. Matt joins full time. For the first time since I started the business nearly four years earlier, I have a real partner.

———

One advantage of winning the NVC is the access it grants to the startup illuminati. During the competition, I had the opportunity to meet Chuck Templeton. Chuck founded OpenTable back in 1998, which makes him an elder statesman in dot-com years. Since then, he has moved to Chicago and helped tons of entrepreneurs, sharing his vast experience and strong opinions. Fortunately, Chuck also has enough humility that he doesn't always need to be right. This sets him apart from most people in the upper echelons of the startup world, many of whom love to hear themselves talk, and often need to get the last word in. (But not me, I'm super humble.)

Chuck agrees to meet me for breakfast.

If America has a single common thread, knitting together the length and breadth of our society, it is the greasy spoon diner. The Golden Pancake House in downtown Chicago has the exact same cracked vinyl booths, linoleum flooring, and friendly staff as its doppelgängers in Wyoming, Appalachia, or Portland. They will make your eggs any way you'd like them, your bacon crispy. The waitress, who's got a big heart, and too many kids, but wouldn't trade them for the world, will serve you bottomless vats of hot coffee and sticky pancake syrup, and will always tell you to pay at the counter, even though everyone already knows that.

"Congrats on winning the NVC," Chuck says.

The win has given GrubHub a lot of credibility. In turn, this allowed me to get someone like Chuck to agree to meet with me. I want him to be my mentor.

"Now that the NVC is over, and you don't need to spin the truth, why don't you tell me what the warts are on your business?" Chuck says as our breakfasts arrive.

This is a variation on the standard question that all investors ask, "What keeps you up at night?" which is itself a variation on the standard interview question, "What's your biggest flaw?" Everybody knows the best thing to do is to make up something that sounds negative, but which is actually a positive.

"Well, now that we're growing so fast, I need help, which means employees, which means office space. All of which takes so much time that I'm not really focused on growing the business." I pour the syrup.

"That's not what I'm asking," Chuck says, evenly. "I know growing a business is hard. What I'm asking is, what's fundamentally *wrong* with your business? What's the thing you would never tell the judges at a startup competition, or investors for that matter?"

"Expanding into San Francisco didn't work," I concede.

"In the competition, you said you had one hundred customers, and they were getting tons of orders." Chuck senses an opening.

"Yes, we have one hundred restaurants there," I say, "but we signed up almost triple that, and most of them canceled. It took well over a year to get to the one hundred point. The whole time the city has been draining cash. I'm worried we might not be able to get past just being a Chicago phenomenon."

Chuck is nodding along as I speak.

"That sounds familiar," he says. "We had the same problem at Open-Table. We expanded too quickly. If a restaurant didn't get at least twenty reservations a week, they'd cancel. We should have focused more on getting those early cities up to a point where they were self-sustaining. It turns out there's a tipping point where this happens. For us it was about thirty or forty restaurants, with enough diners showing up to fill at least two tables every night."

"How did you solve it?" I ask.

"We didn't know we had a problem until we were in a dozen cities. Then, a plane hit a building in New York, and the economy went nuts. We closed down everything but San Francisco, New York, and Las Vegas and started over with just them."

"So, did you quit them, or did you give up?"

"What's the difference?" Chuck seems confused.

"Giving up is something you do when things get too hard," I explain, "but quitting is something you do when your goal is no longer attainable, or when your goals have changed. Giving up is bad. But refusing to quit something after it's changed, or the business has changed, or I get new information, is even worse. Quitting is good, when done at the right time."

"Huh, I never thought of it that way." My koan causes Chuck to lean back in the booth. Then he says, "We quit them. Our original goal was to get big, to go national, but the reasons for that were terrible. It's what start-ups are supposed to do. Then we shifted to trying to build a real business. We couldn't make the shift while having twenty cities bleeding cash."

"So, it just came down to money and focus?"

"And time. A year isn't too long to launch a new city."

"In my case, that means I need more cash," I admit, "but investors create weird pressure. You said it yourself—you felt pressured to do the typical startup thing, instead of the smart thing. I've bootstrapped it to this point. I'm not sure I actually want investors."

(*Bootstrapping* is just fancy startup lingo for creating a profitable business before taking any investment—also known as running a normal business, like 99 percent of the country.)

"I don't think it's a cash issue," Chuck says, warily. "You need more expertise. Money is just the means to the end."

"Well, same difference to my eye," I shoot back. "I need to be able to pay real salaries to attract experienced employees."

"Yes, but you don't just need good sales and marketing people. You, personally, Mike Evans, need more expertise. And for that you need a good board of directors."

I just don't want to hear this.

"I quit my last job because I didn't want a boss," I say. "Why would I possibly want to have five bosses? No thanks."

Chuck exhales and begins listing out the benefits of a board, counting them out on his fingers.

"First, strategic thinking: A board helps you think about the big picture, the forest for the trees. Second, a board has domain expertise—you can't be good at everything. Investors don't run the business, but it's important that they are good at something specific likes sales, marketing, or product. Third, partnership introductions—actually, this might be less important for your business, since you sell directly to customers, so forget that. Fourth, employee networking—the people on the board will naturally have lots of connections to senior executives and can help you with hiring. Finally, you need a group that can see your blind spots, because, by definition, you can't see them yourself."

It feels like he's missing out the biggest benefit. "And cash, right?"

"It's less important than you think," Chuck says. "Everybody's money is the same color green."

This doesn't seem like the point. "I'm not convinced," I say. "Sure, I need the money. Beyond that, I guess I'm going to have to figure out how to limit the interference of a board."

Chuck has been pretty stoic in this meeting so far, but my answer clearly annoys him. He sets his jaw tightly.

"If you think that's the right approach," he says. "I'm just one data point."

The translation is, "What the hell, dude? You asked me for advice. If you're going to just ignore me, because you've got it all figured out, why am I wasting my time trying to help you?" That's not something I want to make a potential mentor feel.

During the NVC, I learned an important lesson: Interested parties argue with you, but the ones who are meekly agreeing are in fact just cooking up an escape strategy.

I've made a critical error—I haven't been "coachable." I need to signal that I'm open to his advice.

"I lost you. What did I get wrong?" I ask.

Chuck stops trying to find the waitress to settle the check and focuses back on me.

"You need a board," he says, a little more emphatically now, "because you've got a lot to learn. Sure, you can keep going as before, and you'll probably be moderately successful. You'll have what's called a lifestyle business—safe and comfortable. But, if you want to push yourself, you've got to be vulnerable to correction, and surround yourself with people who will challenge you. That's the reason to take venture capital. Not the money."

I realize I'm still closed off to this idea. It doesn't feel like a growth opportunity. It feels like losing control. Just a little bit, to be sure, but I suspect it's a slippery slope. I worry that I might find myself stuck in a job that I don't like with the VCs (venture capitalists) looking a lot like bosses I don't respect. I escaped that life when I quit my programming job, and I sure as hell don't want to walk right back into it.

Chuck doesn't let up.

"Investors are just people," he says. "And like any group of people, there are effective ones and terrible ones; principled, and immoral; short- and long-term thinkers. Look, I get it—not everybody can give up being in total control. Once you cede a piece of your company, no matter how small, it's not fully yours anymore. You're just one of many owners. You have a legal duty to run the company for everyone's benefit."

"How do I find the right investors, then?"

"Just make sure cash is the thing you care the least about."

With that, he abruptly pays for breakfast and leaves. I can't really tell what he made of our meeting, except that he only ate half his food and didn't touch his coffee.

Once Chuck leaves, I have another weak cup of coffee and a strong think. I'm not really sure that my perspective on investors was much more sophisticated than "Ew, gross." I do know that it's very hard to get money out of investors, even though that is their literal job. I always figured it was easier to just build something that makes money than it was to spend a bunch of time asking people to give it to me.

The NVC was ostensibly about preparing students to raise capital from investors, but I never really thought of it that way. I was way more interested in learning the concepts they were teaching to run my business better.

But then, here's Chuck, saying that investors contribute to the success of a company in ways that go beyond the cash. More to the point, he's telling me that they would contribute to my growth as an individual. And, if I'm honest with myself, I've stagnated a bit. The frenetic pace of starting something, figuring out how to sell it, and tinkering with it until it works, has slowed down. Sure, I still have challenges ahead of me: Figuring out how to make GrubHub work in other cities is no small task. But it feels like there's an inevitability to finding a solution for that.

I have no idea how to work with investors. I've never been in a board meeting, let alone run one. Wouldn't it be pretty cool to learn how to do those things?

Yeah. It would.

———

I've been here before with this startup. There's a thing I need to do, and I have no clue how to do it. It was true with restaurant sales, marketing, and a dozen other essential domains of the startup world. The path from total ignorance to job done follow a pattern: Just start, figure out the details along the way.

I need investment. Investments are doled out by investors—people whose entire job is to take money from some rich person's bank and deposit it in startups, hoping to see it grow. They *want* to give that money away. So, all I need to do is find them and give them the opportunity.

Oh, honey. Bless your heart.

The first investor we get to return our calls is Michael Polsky. We have a leg up in getting an introduction because we just won the startup competition at the Polsky Entrepreneurship Center at the University of Chicago. His name is literally on the front door. This should be a slam dunk. Michael doesn't quite take a meeting with us, but he at least schedules a call.

"I'm skeptical," he says to Matt and me over a conference line. "I'm not sure there's a lot of money in online ordering for delivery. It seems like a nice-to-have kind of a business, not a need-to-have one."

"Have you ever had the 'not-it' moment?" I ask.

"What's that?"

"You're hanging out with some friends, or another family, and someone says, 'Let's order a pizza.' But nobody wants to call the restaurant. Everyone basically says 'not it.'"

"Yeah, that happens. But it's just a minor frustration. Somebody always buckles up and calls."

"Do they, though? Sometimes, you just rummage for food, or someone decides to go out to get pickup, or maybe you all go out to a restaurant. The market for food delivery is actually much bigger than it appears. It's the friction in the ordering process that prevents people from doing it more often."

"Maybe."

The conversation goes on like this over a handful of calls and emails. He raises objections. I answer them. He remains skeptical. In the end, he decides to take a chance on us, simply because we won the NVC, even if he's not much of a believer himself.

"OK, I think you guys are scrappy," he says. "But I think there's a ton of risk in this business, and that's going to affect the price of the investment."

He sends over an offer. He's willing to invest one million dollars in the business. Woohoo! But not for nothing. He wants over two-thirds of the ownership of the company. The million dollars dangles like a shiny prize, but both Chuck and Professor Deutsch say that the terms are so bad they are insulting.

So, I pass.

Regret sinks in as a month passes before I finally get another investor to even talk to me. Matt solves that problem by working through anyone even vaguely related to the NVC, or the University of Chicago. He'll talk to anybody who will listen. This strategy works, after a fashion. We do get meetings. But most of them are not with serious investors. There's a collection of investors called Hyde Park Angels that's much more of a social club than an investor group. Nothing comes of seemingly endless coffee conversations. But, as vexing as this can be, it turns out to be a minor frustration compared to the venture firms that eventually give in to Matt's relentless wooing. One by one, they agree to talk.

And talk.

And talk some more.

"The hardest thing to get from investors is a 'no,'" Chuck says, as I express frustration to him over a beer. "There's no reason for them to miss out on a potential opportunity. It makes more sense for them to keep asking for more data. They can 'wait and see' for an eternity. Unlike you, who need to have enough cash in the bank to make payroll."

But, what else can I do? I keep having conversations with half a dozen different firms. They never say no. Month after month they look at our financial data and purse their lips thoughtfully. Month after month they tell me that they are almost convinced, but they would prefer to track our progress just a bit longer. And before I know it, half a year has passed since we won the NVC.

On the bright side, the NVC awarded a $50,000 prize. The money is enough to bring Matt on full time. The cash won't last forever, but maybe it will last until we can finally get an investor. Matt focuses on that and marketing, freeing up more of my time to work on the technology.

The company continues growing quickly, revenue jumping by thousands each month. I hire a graphic designer, Jack Kent. He's a friend of a friend of Matt's. Before this gig, he was scooping ice cream at the Häagen-Dazs at Navy Pier in Chicago. It is not difficult to offer someone a better job than that. He agreed to spend thirty hours a week scanning, cleaning up, and typing restaurant menus, as long as he got to spend the other ten hours making the website look better. (I asked him to make the website look "more Smurfy," which, apparently, is not legitimate direction to a professional designer.)

We keep on growing, and I hire Todd Clark to do sales. Todd is not a typical salesperson. His demeanor is solid as a mountain. One day, Todd will likely be struck by a beer truck, because he combines a refusal to be rushed with a fierce belief that cars should stop for pedestrians in crosswalks. Or maybe he'll be just fine because he somehow manages to bend the universe to his will through the expression of deliberate certainty. This trait makes him a great *saver*—restaurants have a really hard time cancel-ing on him. I move him from new sales to managing existing accounts. Cancellations decrease dramatically.

But that still leaves a gap in sales. For all my hard-earned expertise in signing up restaurants, I sure would like to leave it to someone else who *likes* that kind of thing. Fortunately, one of the judges from the NVC introduces us to Nick Kellermeyer, an eager salesman who has been sniff-ing around for a startup to join. He's got a similar laid-back SoCal vibe to Tyler—which, along with Todd, marks the third time that I've hired this archetype to sell restaurants. He's quick, though, signing up a restaurant every day, sometimes two. So, that side of our marketplace is keeping pace with the rapidly growing traffic on the website. Or it's causing the increase. Hard to tell which causes which, really. Chicken and the egg, again.

That makes five of us in Chicago plus Tyler in San Fran. There's too many of us to cram into my apartment's guest bedroom, so I hunt down some office space for us. I sign the lease on an office that's little more than a closet. It's on the top floor of a three-story building in the Lakeview neighborhood of Chicago. The space itself is a single room: four walls, a door on one side, a window opposite it. The walls are off-white, trending toward yellow-gray in places. The radiator is halfway on its journey from painted silver to rusted brown. A single panel of fluorescent bulbs casts the five of us in a jaundiced glow.

Another half a year passes while we slowly grow the diners and restau-rants. Matt courts investors the whole time, but to no effect. Then finally, Matt gets a firm called OCA headed toward an investment. There is no magical breakthrough. He doesn't figure out the perfect way to convince them. We are successful simply by virtue of Matt's persistence. It's not sexy, but it works.

OCA gives us a term sheet, which is just a fancy document that out-lines the terms of an investment and, importantly, is not binding in any way. With OCA leading the deal, we get two other investors to climb in the passenger seat: Origin Ventures and the Chicagoland Entrepreneurial Center. Finally, we've got cash on the way.

In the meantime, we have grown the business for another year. GrubHub is actually quite a bit bigger than it was at the end of the NVC.

San Francisco, if not yet profitable, isn't exactly hemorrhaging cash anymore—more of a slow drip. All told, we're bringing in about half a million dollars a year, and we're spending just a tad less than that. And I've never taken a dime of investment. Not too shabby.

So, of course, with the momentum building, OCA chooses the moment that Matt goes on vacation to dump us.

"I've got some bad news," I announce as I arrive at the office for the morning. "Last night, the investors at OCA took me out for drinks and told me they weren't going to be involved."

"What happened? I thought they were about to send the money," Todd says.

"One of the folks in the firm got cold feet and voted no," I say to groans. "I haven't even met the guy. They only invest with unanimous opinion. It's so frustrating to be so close and have the thing blow up. But the money isn't in the bank until it's actually in the bank."

"Can we change their minds?" asks Jack.

"OCA is done; no way back on that one. But we had a second venture firm, Origin Ventures. Maybe I can salvage that. They're on their way in today to meet with me. I haven't actually spent much time with them, but with Matt on vacation in France, I've got to try my best to convince them to take the lead."

"Could we just scrap the whole thing and start from scratch?" Todd suggests. "I thought you said it wasn't a good deal anyway."

"Well, the terms on the term sheet were bad, but the actual individuals at Origin are highly respected. Chuck keeps pushing me on this idea that the right investors are more important than the terms of the investment. I could probably do a ton better if I flew out to Silicon Valley and started from scratch. But how involved will they be from a four-hour plane ride away? Besides, that whole process might take another six months or longer. Speed matters. The faster we get the money, the faster we'll take this thing national."

I met Bruce Barron and Steve Miller, the founding partners of Origin, back at the NVC. Initially they were uninterested in what we were doing, but once Matt convinced OCA, Origin changed their minds.

Bruce is the tall, mild-mannered elder statesman of the Chicago startup world. He's the type of person who always pauses to exchange kind words with the receptionist at a business, regardless of how tight his time crunch might be. He's genuinely interested in what's going on in people's lives around him. His empathy makes him the most brutally effective negotiator I've ever encountered—he kills with kindness.

Steve is the wealthy scion of a highly successful entrepreneur. His father and uncle founded Quill, which pioneered mail-order office supplies. Decades ago, being given no special treatment, Steve worked his way up within Quill with maniacal intensity, proving that he could contribute, rather than just inherit. He launched Quill's online store in version 1.0 of the internet, and while companies like Webvan, Kozmo, and pets.com burned through hundreds of millions of dollars, Steve was busy building an effective, profitable business. The family eventually sold the business for a cool billion dollars.

Steve is nothing like Bruce. Bruce is kind, Steve is a smart-ass. Bruce chooses the lightly seared trout at dinner; Steve is a fan of cherry cola slushies from 7-Eleven. But Steve's self-deprecating, smart-ass, favored-son-of-privilege schtick is all a smoke screen—behind it is an incisive mind with a deep grasp of human behavior.

We shoehorn ourselves into our chairs around a card table, and before we're properly settled, Bruce dives in.

"We heard from OCA. It's unfortunate that they've decided not to do the deal. How are you doing?"

This is classic Bruce. He's concerned about the person first, and the business second. This is not a common trait among venture capitalists.

I shrug.

"Obviously it is disappointing," I admit, "but it's not the end of the world. We're not running out of cash anytime soon. The business is profitable and growing. Our last attempt to launch San Francisco didn't go great—we were too cheap about it. We're hoping to invest more heavily in the next city, getting launched much quicker. But this investment has never been about surviving. It's about accelerating."

"You're not mad at OCA?" Bruce asks.

"No, of course not. It's just business. From what I can tell, venture firms fail because they say yes to failures, rather than no to successes. Still, it's going to sting when they realize we were the one that got away."

"Do you know why they backed out?" Steve prods.

I take a deep breath.

"They don't believe we have 'exit opportunities.'" *Exit* is investor-speak for ultimately selling the business and cashing in the chips.

Bruce digs in on this idea.

"Do you think their concern about not finding a buyer is justified?"

"It's entirely too early in the business to be worried about this," I say. "Will Google buy us? Or Citysearch? Or AOL? Maybe. Maybe not. It's not helpful to speculate. The players change so fast that some of them might not even be around by the time we get big enough to sell. We're in no rush. Our plan is to build a big business. Selling is the furthest thing from my mind right now."

This isn't entirely true. I would *love* to sell the business quickly, and live debt-free. But serious investors don't want quick wins. As Daniel Burnham, the legendary architect who designed much of Chicago, once said, "Make no little plans; they have no magic to stir men's blood and probably themselves will not be realized. Make big plans; aim high in hope and work." Serious investors want the chance to buy into something that has the potential to be truly huge.

I gesture around to the office.

"I mean, look at this. There's five of us in this tiny office, and we're just getting started. All this talk of exits reeks of get-rich-quick schemes. If it works out that way, then fine, but we shouldn't be seeking it out. It seems to me like we need to focus on getting more customers, signing more restaurants, and serving both better."

Bruce and Steve make eye contact. Apparently, I passed some kind of test, because Bruce says, "We're not overly influenced by what OCA did. We're interested in leading this deal now that they've stepped out."

"That's great," I say, trying not to whoop and holler. "What would that look like?"

"There's no sense in starting from scratch, but we have a few additional items we'd like to add to the terms."

And boy howdy, do they.

"We really like the way you've bypassed a lot of problems working with the restaurants," Bruce goes on. "Using the fax machines as a way to send orders, instead of getting caught up in integrating with their point of sales systems, was genius."

Steve kicks in. "But we're concerned with the high rate of attrition. It's going to be increasingly difficult to grow the bigger you get. We have some concerns that this business may plateau before it gets big enough to justify the investment dollars."

"Therefore, we have added this term here," Bruce adds, good copping Steve's bad cop, or is it the other way round?

With a flourish, a term sheet appears on the table. The piece of paper is a summary of terms (the actual investment documents are hundreds of pages). I can see from a quick glance that it is loosely based on the previous term sheet from OCA but has a few additional items.

Bruce is pointing one out with a pencil.

"You can see that we've removed the cap on the participating preferred to compensate for the risk."

I have no idea what that means.

I nod and say uh-huh, trying to project competence and gravity. I'll figure all this stuff out later. The meeting goes on like this for some time, Bruce playing good cop, praising some aspect of the business, Steve playing bad cop, bringing up something that's troubling them, then one of them suggesting a solution to the problem by way of adjusting the terms of investment that we had been seeking.

Eventually, I see them on their way and start Googling all these terms. It doesn't help much. With the benefit of hindsight, I come to understand that the most egregious term Origin has added is that one about "uncapped participating preferred investment." This basically means that if I sell the company, Origin gets back their one million dollars first, and then what's left gets split up among the rest of the shareholders of the company. The catch is that during the split, Origin still gets their full percentage. For example, if I sell for ten million bucks, and Origin owns 50 percent of the company, they take their $1 million, and then get 50 percent of the remaining $9 million.

All of this is explained to me by my lawyer, who, it will turn out, isn't very good at what he does. He does confirm the details that I've sussed out from the internet are correct. But what he *doesn't* tell me is that less than 5 percent of all venture deals have a capped participating preferred. *None* are uncapped. In the decade since this meeting, I've seen several hundred term sheets—exactly zero of them had a term this bad. There are dozens of other items that are less impactful than this big one but taken together they add up to death by paper cuts. I learned the hard way, a mediocre lawyer will focus on all those little details, whereas a good one not only does just that, but gives forceful holistic advice on the bigger picture. The difference costs me millions of dollars, in the end.

What's shaping out is investment terms that are very bad, from an investor that is very good. But that's no moral failing of theirs. They are looking out for their own interests and those of *their* investors. The deal is presented at a time when venture investors in Chicago are lagging behind Silicon Valley with regard to being "founder friendly," as they say on the West Coast.

Oh, and one more important thing: Matt and I can't be co-CEOs.

I call Matt in France to talk about all this. By default, I should be the CEO. I started the business and ran it for years before I brought him on board. But Matt really wants the CEO title. He assures me that regardless of who is CEO, we will keep things equal, running the business as partners and receiving identical compensation.

But it's not Matt's assurances that convince me to give up the CEO title. I love the idea of learning and pushing myself as we grow, take this thing national, and maybe even go so far as to change the way people interact with food in the United States. But, on the flip side, I loathe the idea of stagnating at a company, managing managers of managers, and sitting through long meetings about HR policy. Blech.

I know myself well enough at this point to know that as soon as I feel trapped, or stagnant, I'll start chafing for something new. It's likely to happen: My goals will change as I grow and learn. And then it will be time to quit, to go be a dad, hike the Appalachian Trail, sail around the world, or something. I really *like* quitting things so I can go do other things.

So, Matt and I make a bargain.

Matt wants to be at the company for life. I'm fine with giving him the CEO title if I get something in return. And here's what I get: a firm understanding that if we sell the business, I get paid and leave. This is very atypical. Most executives are subject to an "earnout." An earnout is a common arrangement in acquisitions, where the senior leadership of the acquired company is required to continue working *before* they get paid their fair share. Sometimes this is referred to as "golden handcuffs."

The idea of an earnout terrifies me: to work for years to build something, dynamically adapting to the market and customer needs, to then sell to some giant corporation and sit on my hands, waiting to get paid the big money. The horror.

Giving up the CEO title seems like a small trade-off. It allows me to work hard without the specter of getting *stuck*. In fact, being CEO would work *against* that goal.

I was successful because I had a personal definition of success. The alternative would have been to accept someone else's definition of success. Society. Parents. Bosses. Churches. Government. Friends. Spouses. Any one of these will gladly spoon-feed you a goal. It's why many people hate their jobs—they are working toward someone else's vision, not toward their own. Don't get spoon-fed your definition of success.

Bruce and Steve offer us just over $1 million in cash. That sounds like a lot, but, in VC terms, it's pocket change. And they are getting a big chunk of the company for their million. After that initial investment, option pool, all the other terms, and splitting half in my partnership with Matt, I will own just 14 percent of the company, along with the expectation to double that by "vesting" over four years. Owning 14 percent of a company I started from scratch on entirely my own effort in my living room, and which is now generating nearly half a million dollars in revenue, is a truly terrible deal. The final version of the investment documents could be enshrined in a Silicon Valley museum as the worst investment deal ever signed.

I don't need hindsight to know this. I know it's a terrible deal before I sign it. But it's only terrible when judged by someone else's goals. It's perfect for what I want: the opportunity to grow, both the company and personally, with no "golden handcuffs" keeping me tied to the company.

I'm also aware that the deal is unfair in many ways. Giving up so much to my partner is unfair. Forgoing the CEO title is unfair. Needing to re-earn a big chunk of a company I already own is unfair. Selling so much of the company for such a low price compared to what I could get in the valley is unfair.

So, why sign it?

I sign it because fairness doesn't matter. My goal is not to go through life insisting on getting what I'm entitled to. Neither is it my goal to become very wealthy. I have been very clear with myself and with Christine about this point: I want to pay off our debts, put aside a little nest egg, and be *free*.

The *chance* of an exit matters a lot more than the *size* of an exit. The lowball offer means I'm unlikely to ever be crazy wealthy, and that's fine by me. The inclusion of Bruce and Steve in GrubHub's story will only increase the likelihood of an exit.

I take the deal.

Good thing too. It works brilliantly.

Relaunching San Francisco is easy. A year of Tyler selling restaurants combined with the slow simmer of customers makes it fertile ground to become a breakout success. Basically, I just throw a hundred thousand dollars at advertisements—mostly Google and transit ads. The orders skyrocket. Restaurants go from getting one order a month to several orders a day. Chicago benefits from the same treatment. In the months following the investment, the Chicago revenue more than doubles.

It's time to take this thing national.

Day 1. Mile 14.

I find my way into old town Norfolk. Staying away from the main road leads me down some parallel residential streets. Rows of old Victorian homes punctuate the tree-lined streets. The riverfront has little touristy shops and a bunch of museums. A few sailboats are tied up to the pier, their skippers just across the dock, getting coffee from a mobile vendor.

These docks, and this river, are the part of the Intracoastal Waterway (ICW)—a sort of highway for boats that heads south all the way to Florida.

That's another dream I had while in the throes of GrubHub: sailing down the ICW someday. I look longingly south, daydreaming about what it would be like to sail through here. Then I chide myself for daydreaming about an adventure, while I'm already on an adventure. Again, it speaks to my discontent. I'm going to need to figure out how to be present in the moment.

The pedestrian ferry arrives. Maneuvering the bike aboard is almost impossible—the corners are too tight. I take off the saddlebags and man-handle it over the railing. The weird bike, along with four heavy bags of clothes, camping gear, and cameras, is an obvious conversation starter.

"What's all that for?" the captain asks.

He is tall, lanky, and unreasonably young for his position—maybe twenty-one or twenty-two. For all his youth, his eyes seem older—they hold a striking and obvious sadness.

"I'm riding across the country. Just started this morning."

"Well, ain't that something?" he says. "You camping the whole way?"

"Yeah, most of it. Depends on what I find when I get too tired to keep going. State and national parks, mostly. But I imagine I'll hit a KOA, or motel, from time to time. There are also a few hostels along the Trans-America route..."

"Is that a bike trail?" I'm surprised he hasn't heard of it, given that we're not too far from its source.

"It's more like a bunch of designated roads," I explain. "A few hundred people do it every summer, as far as I can tell. Hopefully should mean that car drivers, restaurants, and motels are used to this kind of thing."

"Well, first time I've ever seen it," he admits. I put his ignorance down to his youth. Maybe he's new on this job.

"I'm not on the official route, yet," I say. "It begins up in Yorktown, but I wanted to start at the ocean proper, not Chesapeake Bay."

"Makes sense. That's what I'd do too. What are you going to do when you hit the Rockies?"

"Pedal over them," I say, perhaps a bit too confidently.

"Damn. That's amazing. I wish I could do something like that." He's wide-eyed, looking like he doesn't believe he ever could.

"You *can*."

"Nah. Too much to take care of here at home. I'd never be able to get away for that long."

The captain talks at length about his dreams and how he feels trapped. He says, "Here I am piloting a ferry on the ICW, and I see people every day who are headed south along it to the Caribbean and beyond. I've always wanted to do something like that."

I look more closely at him now. He's clearly very young, but, based on his job, he's got enough skill to pilot a commercial vessel. To be trapped in obligation and frustration at his age? His life is too new to be this hard, surely. But I don't know what his situation is. I feel for him. Who knows what people go through, what they face?

We putter across the Elizabeth River, and when we arrive on the far side, he eagerly helps me get the bike and bags off.

"Enjoy your trip," he says. "Don't take it for granted. You're lucky."

He's not wrong. I think back to those early days, a decade past, blindly feeling my way through my first few restaurant sales. Creating a product with gut instincts that always took me two steps sideways for every three steps forward. Staying healthy and never having financial or personal emergencies derail the effort of starting something from scratch. Being surrounded by a supportive extended family and incredibly understanding wife.

I was lucky. It's true. I've told people this before. Nobody ever believes me. People angrily tell me I made my own luck. They desperately want to believe that if I bottle up some key wisdom, some elusive truth, they can take a sip and they can make their own luck too. Sure, I figured some things out. And they can be shared and learned.

But that doesn't mean I wasn't lucky too.

I got through it, and at the end, there was some sliver of the same person left that went into the thing. But wealth and success change a person, and not for the better. More than a decade of stress certainly doesn't help, either. If I kept some ember of that kid that walked into J.B. Alberto's, that's lucky too. So, here I am, on this bike trip, with a goal to breathe some life back into that ember, and maybe make it a flame again. And that will also take a bit of luck.

PART TWO

It gets big.
Too big.

7

Bigger than Me

Over the last year everything has been going excellent for GrubHub and fantastic for me. Back in February, we took in $28,000 in revenue in a single month. It was the satisfying result of a long slog, creating something from nothing. But then things really started to take off. All the stuff I learned at the New Venture Challenge (NVC) helped. But the thing that has really recharged me is having a business partner firing on all cylinders. Matt's contributions have sped up restaurant sales and marketing, while at the same time freeing me from the responsibility of doing everything myself. The result can be seen in cold, hard cash. In October, the business pulled in $70,000. A few days into November, and we're pacing to break that record. With Matt holding things down back in the office, and a million dollars in the bank I just took in from Origin Ventures, I've got two things in abundance that I was missing when I launched San Francisco: time and money.

I take a trip to Boston. I lived in Boston for five years during college. Coming back feels like coming home. In the cab to my hotel, just near the MIT campus, I pass the Charles River to my right. The leaves have turned, and, mostly, dropped, filling me with nostalgia from my college days. I spent many an afternoon enjoying runs along the tree-lined esplanade that borders the river. I think about stopping in to sit in on a lecture—it'll be fun to remember how much I've forgotten. I've got time to linger. In addition to having help on the business, I'm in no rush to get back to my house in Chicago because my wife moved to India.

Before we got married, Christine had always cherished the idea of going into the peace corps. But *I* happened. We fell in love and got married crazy young. But even as we did that, I had promised her that if the opportunity arose to go work overseas, we'd figure out a way to make it happen. I didn't know at the time that I'd be tethered closer to home by a shiny new startup, so that threw a wrench in things. So, we decided to do our marriage long distance for a year—Christine has landed a coveted fellowship at International Justice Mission, an organization similar to Doctors Without Borders, but for lawyers. She'll be a lawyer version of a superhero, using her mad legal skills to combat human trafficking and bonded labor.

She left for Chennai, India, in the late summer, off to save the world, while I stayed home, doing my damnedest to make America 2 percent fatter.

With nobody at home, a growing staff back in Chicago, and money in the bank, I've got a window where I can focus all my efforts on a single task: expanding GrubHub to new cities. Boston, New York, Philly, and DC, all in the next six months.

Or, more exactly, I plan to *start* those cities. I learned something when I launched San Francisco, and, in retrospect, it was a reality that was true for Chicago too. The lesson was that the launch of a new service area isn't instant. No amount of effort can skip over the necessary time it takes for a new product to worm its way into the collective consciousness of a new group of customers. My plan is to use my hard-earned investment cash to buy time for the initial marketing to take hold, and, in the meantime, to cover the expenses of a salesperson or two while the flywheel starts turning.

This idea runs counter to widely held expectations in the startup world. In my meetings with venture capitalists, underlined by the discussions at the NVC competition, everyone starts from the assumption that money solves all ills. There's a lot of groupthink around the idea that spending boatloads of cash on marketing will have the effect of supercharging growth. But it wasn't true in either Chicago or San Francisco. A few years of experiments have shown time and time again: There are no silver bullets in marketing, and there are no easy shortcuts. Creating a consumer brand takes time as well as money, and one can't be substituted for the other.

In Boston, I'm going to echo the things that worked in the first two markets. I start with laying the basic groundwork—get all the basic menus live, sign a few restaurants, and bide my time. Then, about three months later, I will start advertising. Slowly, but inevitably, the orders on the website will tick up each month, the flywheel gaining momentum.

I suspect, at some point, my new investors will ask why I can't just spend more money to speed this process up. But, in my gut, and underlined by the last two cities, I just don't think it will work. Throwing more money at the problem will just burn extra cash with little result.

Which isn't to say there isn't a way to use cash to speed up the growth of GrubHub overall. Just not within a single city. To speed up the growth of the business, in aggregate, the answer is simple: launch multiple cities in parallel, letting each one grow at a deliberate pace. It's the cumulative impact of each individual city's contributions that total up to a very fast-growing business. The sum is greater than the parts. Mutual embiggening.

I have a name for this deliberately paced individual market growth, aggregated to a much bigger total with parallel launches. I call it the simmer strategy. Spoiler alert: It works incredibly well. Fast-forward a decade, and I've seen it succeed, not just at GrubHub, but at half a dozen other startups where I sat on boards and made investments. (Hell, it will even work on my second business, Fixer.com, but now I'm getting too far ahead of myself. Wait for the sequel.)

So, here I am, in Boston, launching GrubHub in city number three as a precursor to being in a dozen cities in the next year.

After checking into my hotel, I wander down Commonwealth Avenue, headed toward Ankara Cafe, one of my favorite spots for grub back in the day. It's a little hole in the wall, with just a dozen feet of storefront. The inside has a tiny dining area jammed with four tables. The rest of the space is dominated by enormous display freezers—the kind you'd find in an ice-cream shop.

"The usual?" Selim Gurel, the owner, asks. "Grape-Nuts. Reese's Pieces?" I'm amazed that he recalls me and my order—I haven't stepped foot in here in five years. Selim's forearms are even more gargantuan than I remember—maybe because he's been scooping frozen yogurt for thousands upon thousands of college students for decades.

Ankara Cafe (I knew it as Angora Café, but they seem to have changed the name, though not much) serves a dish like the Dairy Queen Blizzard—frozen yogurt with two or three other ingredients ground in. After a hundred or so experimental combinations, I settled on the base of Grape-Nuts cereal to pair a crunchy texture with the creamy ice-creamish yogurt. The Reese's Pieces added little shocks of übersweetness to the concoction.

The first mouthful brings me home even more than the Charles River did.

"You'll want pepperoni too," Selim says. (For the pizza, obviously, not the yogurt.) Apparently, I'm a creature of habit, and he has a photographic memory. He pulls a slice of pizza from the display case and slings it into the back of the brick-fired oven.

"Do you have a minute to talk about a business thing?" I ask as we both wait for the pizza to heat. "After college, I started a company in the restaurant industry, and you might find it interesting."

"Sure; let me get you the pizza and we can sit."

We head to a table, and I reach out a formal hand.

"I'm Mike Evans; nice to meet you properly after all these years! Anyway, my business is called GrubHub. We do online ordering for delivery restaurants."

"Like Foodler?" Selim asks, shaking my hand.

"Who?"

"Foodler. We use them to do our online ordering."

Hmm. That's not good. This isn't the first time I've encountered other online ordering platforms. There's maybe a half dozen that exist by this point, but generally, they are geared around enabling a restaurant's preexisting website to accept online orders. I only know about these because I search for them online. This is the first time I've heard a restaurant bring this up. His objection gives me an inkling of self-doubt. But now is not the time to worry about it.

(By the way, there's never a good time to worry about self-doubt. It's always there: before every sales meeting, at every investor pitch, firing employees, hiring employees. A little self-doubt is a reasonable thing to have when taking people's money, disrupting an industry, and messing with employee livelihoods. To the degree it enables me to pause, and take all of this very seriously, it's helpful. Beyond that, it's just crippling. All of us are struggling with imposter syndrome. I still haven't figured out a way to solve that problem. That voice in the head can't be silenced. Only ignored.)

"I hadn't heard about them," I say. "Anyway, the idea behind GrubHub is that we advertise your business, and send you orders via fax. We don't make a dime unless you make a dollar."

"A dime? You charge *ten* percent? That's more than Foodler. They only charge six percent."

This is definitely not good. I can't come in with a higher percentage because we haven't launched here yet and have no diner base—we haven't proven ourselves, so how can we even think about charging more? I experience the thing that every business faces eventually: Competition drives prices down.

"Well, we're just starting out, so we only charge five percent," I say, thinking on my feet.

"Including credit card fees?" This guy has clearly done his homework.

"No, that's *excluding*."

My answer thuds.

"No thanks," he says. "That's too expensive."

If I *included* credit card fees, that would be equal to about half of the already reduced 5 percent fee. Given the costs of advertising on top, I wouldn't be able to make a profit.

I decide to retreat and do some research on this Foodler thing. I thank Selim for his time and insight, finish my pizza, and head back to my hotel to work on the frozen yogurt.

It doesn't take me long to see the extent of the problem I'm facing. Foodler has about one hundred restaurants in Boston. Besides Foodler, I also discover a restaurant delivery service, Dining In—they do the deliveries themselves, rather than relying on the restaurants to provide the drivers. There's more competition in Boston than I thought.

In Chicago, the minimum rate for a restaurant is 10 percent to get online ordering, and it goes up from there if a restaurant wants the top listing. But 10 percent is way too high in Boston with an entrenched competitor that is charging less.

It's not a disaster, though, because I've designed the system so that it doesn't really matter what the minimum rate is—it's the *top* of the auction listing that really generates most of the cash for GrubHub. I tweak my sales approach. I slash the minimum price from 10 percent of the order to 5 percent. In fact, this fits way better into the simmer strategy. *Maybe* the lower introductory rate will keep restaurants on board while I'm waiting for the demand side of the business to pick up.

With the new discounted pricing, making sales is way easier. I spend a month in Boston. By the time I leave, I've signed up thirty restaurants, picked up a few hundred menus, and hired an eager new salesperson.

Boston is officially simmering.

New York is next. It's the big one. There's more money to be made in the big apple than the next five cities combined. But, five years of grinding away at this thing has taken a lot out of me. I'm beat, and I miss Christine. So I tell Matt to take a crack at it, and I take a vacation in India. Sort of.

————

Six city blocks in the pre-monsoon heat of Chennai, India, is enough to blot out all memory of a brisk fall week in Boston. Sweat rolls down my back, and the stink of the heavily polluted Cooum River has me longing for the air-conditioned desk that Christine's NGO has graciously provided for me while I'm here visiting.

I have been here for six weeks, working most of that time. But it's a weird kind of work. I've gone cold turkey on the thousand little things I do every week to keep the business going. Matt will be watching to see what breaks if I'm not around to Band-Aid every problem. This is the first time I've gone more than two days without checking email since I got an account at MIT back in 1995. It's *wonderful*.

My short sabbatical has me finishing up some long overdue software. Up until now, our cobbled together monitoring systems deliver their alerts via email. If a restaurant fails to confirm an online order via the automated phone system, these systems shoot off a message. If someone happens to be looking at the shared email inbox that gets these messages when that happens, we might call the restaurant.

If no one is looking, and something goes wrong, then the food doesn't show up. This, to say the least, is a major problem. There's no way to make up for this mistake. There's no discount, concession, or apology that suffices. Customers don't forgive a company that makes them go hungry. So, I need to create version one of our customer service software that will allow us to monitor the orders in real time.

I haven't seen Christine this morning. I wasn't awake when she left at six in the morning. Which was a mistake. Getting to work early is more about avoiding the heat than it is about work culture. Just up ahead is the office of International Justice Mission (IJM), where my wife has been working for the last six months. It is a jumble of half a dozen whitewashed buildings, each topped with corrugated iron, a beefy air-conditioning unit, and a dense nest of electrical wires. Cool air washes over me as I enter the building and make my way to the desk.

I pass by a glass conference room, packed wall to wall with Indian, English, and American legal tomes. Christine is teaching a class to several students. Even though she is only a few years out of law school, her knowledge is valuable here. Newly minted Indian attorneys rely heavily on the firms they join to complete their legal training. IJM, in turn relies on volunteer legal fellows, like Christine, to be a viable option to attract young Indian attorneys.

Given the importance and gravity of her work, I don't wave at her. But she sees me anyway and flashes a sincere smile that I return with a stupid big grin. Later today, one of her coworkers will tell me that we must be very much in love, based on that unguarded smile. She's not wrong.

In some ways, having a big coding project feels a lot more like the early days at GrubHub, when it was just me and my laptop. But there's an urgency to this work that I didn't feel back then. A thousand orders a night are going through the system now. Getting this software into the wild will have an immediate impact.

And not a moment too soon. Foodler spooked me. And they aren't the only one. Matt's worried about another competitor in New York, SeamlessWeb. Seamless is a company focused on online ordering for investment bankers and lawyers in Manhattan. But it's only a matter of time before they pivot into what we do. Whatever head start I had on competition is rapidly disappearing.

In startups, standing still is the same as getting left behind. Online ordering was innovative when I launched it, but it's quickly just becoming table stakes as other startups have taken note and started offering their own. We need an edge if we're going to stay ahead of the competition.

My solution to this problem is to increase the quality of the service. It's not enough to just provide a communication channel to the restaurant through online ordering. We need to start being proactive in making sure that people get their food.

What I'm coding from my desk in India is a command center. It's a bit of software that lets someone at GrubHub see the orders going through the system in a visual way: a bunch of green rectangles marching along as orders come in and are confirmed. The ones that don't get confirmed in ten minutes will turn yellow, then change to red after twenty. With this system, a customer service agent can intervene anytime an order goes awry, calling both the restaurant to get the whereabouts of the food, and the customer to let them know we're on top of it.

Morning gives way to afternoon as I pleasantly code away. I skip lunch, as I often do when I'm into my work. Not that I had much choice. There's no GrubHub here. In fact, there's not much of a culture of leaving work for lunch. Instead, everyone brings home-prepared meals in a tiffin. A tiffin consists of pie-size tin trays that stack together and clasp in place to keep a multicourse meal fresh for traveling. In fact, they're the main reason that I don't think GrubHub would work in India. A fresh tiffin delivered meal is never more than a neighbor, friend, or grandparent away for most Indians.

I don't have any such home-prepared meal, and I'm not about to brave the heat outside anyway to go search for an open restaurant. So, I keep coding, staying in flow state, and ignoring my growing hunger. By the time Christine eventually emerges from her work in late afternoon, she looks as happy as I feel, the result of doing a good day's work that *matters*.

"I'm starving," she says.

"Yeah, let's get food on the way to the station," I say.

For my final week in India, Christine has made a reservation at a hotel in "hill country" a few hundred kilometers inland from the coastal city of Chennai. We have train tickets to a pair of berths in a sleeper car tonight to get there. The train leaves at six. Should be plenty of time.

Outside the office, I'm blasted by the pre-monsoon furnace heat again, which has only grown more unbearable as the city bakes in the unrelenting sun. The traffic has, impossibly, gotten even more intense. Hundreds of autos, mopeds, and cars rush by. Christine snakes her way through an unofficial open-air market that has sprung up on the roadside during our time in the office, which includes, among other things, a vendor selling shoes spread out on a threadbare carpet, a barber cutting hair with a line of waiting customers five deep, and a man with smoking candles that are somehow used to remove earwax.

Christine holds her hand up, hoping an auto driver spots us. Within seconds, we're both sweating profusely. Within minutes, both of our arms are tired.

"This isn't working," I grumble.

"Do you have a better idea?"

"Let's try over there." I say, spotting a few passengers successfully grabbing a vacant ride on the other side of the road.

Christine shrugs and steps boldly into the road.

This seems like a suicidal move, with the dense traffic. But magically, a gap appears in the flow just as Christine takes the step. It closes in her wake. She continues walking, making it to the tiny brick median. I'm still waiting for an opening when Christine yells across the fourteen lanes of unorganized traffic.

She shouts, "Keep a steady pace, everyone will go around you. Don't stop! They won't expect that, and you'll get hit if you do."

I'm skeptical that I will survive this method, but I trust my wife. More to the point, I'm anxious, hungry, and hot, and just standing here is clearly not going to solve any of those problems. So, I gird myself to get smacked and take a blind step into moving traffic.

Horns blare and drivers shout, but I don't get hit. One step follows another, and true to Christine's prediction, I arrive at the median unharmed. She laughs, and I can't help but smile in return. This is kind of fun. The second half of the journey is equally uneventful, and within minutes, we're squeezing into the back of an auto.

We're moving, and the stifling still air has become a slightly less stifling hot breeze. The traffic is something fearsome to behold. The ride goes on forever, kilometer after kilometer, with constant beeping, weaving, and slamming on the brakes. Christine turns green from motion sickness by the time we unfold ourselves from the back and shuffle toward the platform at the best pace our creaking muscles can manage.

Using a combination of questions, gestures, and charades, we find the train with a couple of minutes to spare. Further questions and gestures have us back off the train and sprinting toward the rear to get to the correct car.

My hunger blots out all rational thought. I haven't had a real meal since dinner last night. Obviously, I know I should be hungry, but this is beyond anything I've ever experienced. I don't know this at the time, but I've also picked up what Christine's coworkers refer to as a "special friend." Which sounds cute but is actually a pretty serious parasite that will cost me fifteen pounds over the next two weeks.

The deep, gnawing emptiness in my gut brings the problem I'm trying to solve at GrubHub home in a literally visceral way. It's this feeling that people have in their belly when an order doesn't arrive. Again, there's no solution to this problem once it happens. Offering a five-dollar coupon in the face of this kind of physical discomfort is just fanning the flames.

Despairing, I step on the train, resigned to an overnight trip without any dinner. With seconds left before departure, there's no time to grab a bite from the plentiful vendors selling food across the platform. I can see food, just there. But it's beyond reach.

———

On my first day back at the office after seven weeks away, I brace for the onslaught of things that broke in my absence. The biggest one was a twelve-hour site crash. It turns out that my personal credit card was still being used to pay the company's server hosting invoices. It had been flagged for fraud when I used it in India. Blissfully unaware, I did not see the increasingly panicked emails as the site was down for twelve hours.

In addition to this big item, a bunch of little things went wrong, as well. Some vendors didn't get paid on time. Nobody ordered a computer for a new employee. Not a single happy hour was attended after work. But then, after stuff went wrong, the dozen employees we have around the office figured out fixes. And then, without any intervention on my part, they just assumed responsibility from that point on.

I'd been spending twenty hours a week propping up systems and doing manual jobs to keep the company running. But stepping away from the day-to-day has been revealing. Stuff broke, yes. But some stuff unbroke by itself. Some other things stayed broken, but there were few consequences.

This is an important startup lesson. The world doesn't end when the boss walks away. Before delegation comes prioritization. Part of figuring out what to prioritize is accepting the consequences of *not* doing some of the to-do items. Going forward, I decide to let things break more. There's always some kind of huge four-alarm fire going on at a startup. That's why it's important to just let the little fires burn.

So, what am I going to work on? There's a special and unique moment coming back from time away, where I can see the forest instead of the trees, and I want to take advantage of having some distance from the day-to-day issues at the company.

I decide to leave my computer idle and walk around the office. Grub-Hub's second office is closer to downtown in the River North neighborhood, and it's about ten times the size of the first one. Even so, we were bursting at the seams from just about the moment we moved in. There were fifteen of us in the office when I left for India. Six weeks later, we're pushing twenty.

It doesn't take long for me to realize that this is my job now. The customer service software was fun to write, but it's time to stop coding and start thinking about things like prioritization, goal setting, and motivating people. The thought fills me with a pang of nostalgia. I like coding. I'm good at it. But this stuff? I've never managed anyone before starting this thing. Of course, I've never cooked a pizza in my life either, but that didn't keep me from trying to change the entire industry. I have no choice but to just figure it out as I go along. Fortunately, I've got a board of directors and Chuck. When I asked Chuck about this he suggested, "Manage by walking around." Which sounds overly simplistic, but I try it.

The office is split into four main rooms, with two given over to customer service and sales, one for engineering, and the fourth for everyone else. I walk about, listening to conversations and talking with everyone about what's on their mind. I'm expecting a big topic to be the New York City launch, which Matt started the week I left.

I amble over to the customer service department, where Todd is urgently trying to soothe a rattled restaurant owner. As always, Todd is calm and collected, but there's a slight edge to his voice, and I can tell something is not right.

"Uh-huh. Uh-huh. Yes. I understand. Uh-huh. Can I get a word in, please? I hear you. It looks like we messed up. Can you give me fifteen minutes to look into this on our side and see what happened? Uh-huh. Yes. I understand. Yes. Thanks for your patience. I'll investigate. Thanks."

Todd hangs up.

"What was that about?" I ask.

"Restaurant in New York. They didn't know about phone orders. Freaked out when they got the bill."

"Who's the salesperson?"

"Damien."

"I don't think I know him."

"We hired him about six weeks ago, right when we started the New York launch. He's a handful."

"How so?"

"I worry he's been underhanded with the restaurants—not one of them knew about phone orders until I talked to them. Also, he won't follow directions—he batches sign-ups from restaurants and then sends them in the day before payroll. Then on top of that, he's been badgering the data entry team to get the restaurants live same day so he can collect his commission on them without waiting."

"How many restaurants?" I ask.

"Thirty-six last month," Todd says.

I whistle. The target is twelve. I think about all the stuff I learned about sales, including the line about "once they're sold, stop selling." I can see how someone would want to gloss over the phone orders once they get a signature on the dotted line. Overall, I'm not sure I see a problem here. After all, I have Todd, who is great at explaining stuff, after the fact.

I say, "So, he's a *good* salesperson, he wants his commissions, and what's more, he's a good *New York* salesperson, who doesn't have time for excuses."

"Maybe," Todd says, "though I'm not so sure. I didn't want to throw anyone under the bus, but we have a bigger problem."

Todd hands me a sign-up sheet. It looks normal. Then, he hands me another.

"The first one is from a month back—one of Damien's first sign-ups," Todd says. "This second one is a different restaurant, signed this week. Look closely at the signature."

"It looks about the same as the first," I say.

"Yeah. Same handwriting," Todd says.

"What am I looking at here? The restaurateur has two restaurants?"

Todd says, "It's the same signature, but I don't think it's two sign-ups from the same person."

"Oh. What *is* it then?"

"I think Damien forged the signatures. I don't think the restaurateur signed up."

Todd and I look at each other, realizing that this is not good, not good *at all*.

"I noticed because I got a call yesterday from the owner," Todd says. "He was confused about the orders he had received. He wasn't mad. In fact, he was pleasantly surprised about the increase in business, and he wants to continue the service. But he did point out that, well, it seems he had never actually signed up to GrubHub. Which is odd because you can see a signature right there."

Damien had taken it upon himself to sign up to GrubHub on this restaurant's behalf. Five minutes of investigation turned up yet another problem—it turns out that he had convinced numerous restaurants to sign up, get him his commission, quit GrubHub, and then sign up again a month later, thereby doubling his money.

It takes about ten minutes from leaving the conversation with Todd to fire my fraudulent salesman. Since Matt hired him while I was in India, it's a weird conversation: "Hi, I'm Mike, you don't know me. But you're fired." But that's not the end of it. I'm deeply concerned that this rot goes deeper than a single immoral individual.

I tell Matt about the situation later.

"I don't see the problem," he says. "In fact, it's brilliant."

"Really?"

"Yeah. Why not just sign up every restaurant for online ordering. Skip sales completely. We could make the minimum price zero percent, and just charge for the higher ranking on the site."

"Yeah, but…. but…it's unethical."

"Is it?"

"I mean. Yes. Obviously."

"It's not obvious to me. We could call it 'online ordering for all.' Project OOFA."

"Look, Matt. There are a lot of issues here. Even if it weren't wildly wrong to sign up restaurants without their knowledge, it's just a bad product. What if the restaurant doesn't send the food?"

"I'm sure we can work through the issues. Let's get everyone together…"

"No, Matt. This is a terrible idea. OOFA is a bear. Don't poke it."

"OK, OK," he relents. But I can tell this is not the end of this conversation.

Throughout the next week, I start seeing additional things inside Grub-Hub that are subtle and dangerous. I hear a software developer frustrated that users on the website can't see obvious buttons—as opposed to assuming the button needs to be more obvious. I hear an account manager (not Todd) refer to a restaurateur as "stupid" for not understanding the order confirmation system. I hear a customer service rep tell a customer that restaurants frequently mix up Thai iced coffee and Thai iced tea, and that there's nothing we can do about it because the restaurant is already closed.

The heady combination of crazy fast growth, money in the bank, and a rapidly increasing head count is driving us toward a get-rich-quick culture. This happens to a lot of startups—maybe all of them. As they get bigger, they change. Mark Zuckerberg famously said, "Move fast. Break things." (Which might be acceptable early in a company's life cycle but becomes a problem when your social platform is influencing elections and is the target of Russian hackers.) Or, in our case, when restaurant entrepreneurs and staff are increasingly depending on our platform for their livelihood.

By this point, it's clear that GrubHub is going to overshoot my original goal, which was to simply pay off my student debts and maybe get a nest egg. It's equally clear that we are increasingly obligated to perform ethically for our restaurants and diners. But what does that mean if each person in the company has their own interpretation of what's ethical?

I need to do more... and less. I've been writing software, ordering laptops, and setting up the office Wi-Fi network. These are all exactly the wrong things to do. I need to take a big step back and think about what kind of culture we want to have. What is it we're trying to accomplish? How are we going to go about doing it? What are our shared values?

This isn't the kind of thing that I can just dictate by fiat. If I really want everyone to buy in to a company culture, I need everyone to help me create it. With so many new faces around in Chicago, it's time we sit down face-to-face and decide who we *are* as a company.

I call an emergency all-company meeting for a whole day. We stop everything. We turn off customer service and bring everyone together.

"So, what is it we're trying to do?" I ask, opening up the conversation.

A few uncomfortable murmurs fill the silence, but nobody offers a serious answer.

"Get rich?" someone asks. I don't quite catch who.

This generates some more vaguely affirmative murmurs. But few people want to admit this out loud.

"OK. That's fair. We're all taking low salaries in the hopes of a big payday. It's riskier than corporate America, and we each hope we grabbed a lucky lotto ticket. But why food delivery? There's a ton of other startups out there. We picked this one for a reason. So, what are we trying to do *as a company*?"

"Bring ordering into the twenty-first century?" Jack asks, "I mean, the old way hasn't changed since Bell invented the telephone."

"Yes, that's good. But it's not enough. Technology, in and of itself, isn't good or bad. It's just a means to an end. What does it matter if people order on a website instead of a phone?"

"Ordering by phone is terrible," Nick says. "There's mistakes. You get put on hold. You have to read your credit card over the phone."

Matt chimes in, seeing where I'm going. "We make ordering more convenient, more accurate, and more secure."

"Yes, but why?"

"So, people order more," Matt says.

"Which does what?"

"Makes us money," Matt says. Everybody laughs.

"No. That's not right. We don't do things to make money. We create value for customers, and we get paid as a natural outcome of that. Ironic as it is, the best way to go out of business is to focus on making money as the primary goal. Successful businesses think about customers first. So, who is our customer? Is it diners or restaurants?"

"Diners," several people say.

"Restaurants," others retort.

"It's both," Matt says.

"Sure, it's both," I say. "But if there's a conflict between the two, who do we choose to help? The restaurant or the diner?"

A big debate rages over this question, with first the consensus leaning toward diners, and then swinging back toward restaurants. Back and forth it goes. I let it go on for about an hour. Nick hits on a key insight.

"We shouldn't do anything that hurts restaurants. Ever," he says.

"Let's flip that around, and say it as a positive statement," I say. "We only act in ways that help restaurants. The restaurant industry is hard. A quarter of all of them close their doors every year. What if we say that our mission is to make restaurants more likely to stay in business?"

"But that leaves out the diners," Matt challenges.

"You're right. We need to make delivery better for them too. Not just restaurants."

"That's it," Matt says.

"What?"

"We make delivery better," he says. "That's what we're trying to do."

"Yeah," I say, "that works for both restaurants and diners. And how do we know if it's working?"

Nick says, "if restaurants survive at a higher rate because they work with us, it's working."

Jack says, "And we know it's working for diners if they order more than they did before they discovered us."

We talk through these ideas for a bit. A few alternate suggestions come up, but we keep coming back to the phrase "making delivery better." Eventually, I move the conversation along, "So, that's the mission, making delivery better. That's *what* we do, but it still leaves the question, *how* we go about it. We already said that an important part of this is keeping restaurants in business. How do we translate that to a set of core values? What are our morals?"

Groans. Every single one of us has seen meaningless corporate drivel about company values, and the related cheesy inspirational posters that go along with them.

I push on, "Look, this stuff is important. There are three or four religions represented in this room. We all come from different backgrounds. Each of us will implicitly assume the others share our beliefs, but that couldn't be further from the truth. We need to state them explicitly. I'll start. We need a value related to honesty, or integrity, or transparency."

Over the course of that day, we have conversations about what we believe in as a group. What values do we each bring to the company? What values do we all share? How should those values be used in interactions with each other? With restaurants? With diners? How about hiring and firing decisions?

Religion comes up. Gender diversity. Racial equity. It becomes shockingly clear that I should have thought of these things much sooner, and that by relying on my network of friends to find early employees, I was leaning into my biases. By not addressing this issue from the start, I have, myself, contributed to furthering one of the biggest problems of the tech industry: The first six employees were all white men. We need to do better. *I* need to do better.

Coming out of that day, GrubHub creates a set of core values. On the top of the list are honesty and respect. We also plaster the mission statement "Make delivery better" on *everything.*

These new values and mission are displayed in every room, printed on every agenda, and talked about in the first five minutes of every meeting in the company for the next five years. Every potential employee is evaluated against the values and asked to respond to the mission statement. They become our North Star.

I shelve the goal of paying off my student loans; it no longer tracks. I still have the loans, but my income is higher now, and it's starting to look like I'll get a life-changing payout from GrubHub at some point in the future.

Quietly, I set a new personal goal: Build a company that helps restaurants.

8

Big Money

It's the fall of 2010, and high time to get a *big* investor.

GrubHub is in fourteen markets, and we're profitable. The simmer strategy has worked—we've got over one thousand restaurants signed up across fourteen cities, and they're all getting at least one order a day. We're done simmering. It's time to do what the venture capitalists (VCs) keep telling us to do: throw piles of cash into growth and see what happens.

Venture capital firms have their big meeting every Monday. Partners and associates come back from their far-flung adventures all over the globe working with promising companies to meet up and touch base. Usually, one or two startups are invited to pitch the partnership at one of these gatherings. Getting an invite is incredibly difficult—fewer than one in a hundred businesses secure venture capital investment. And not all venture firms are created equal. The top tier firms, the ones that funded Facebook, Google, and others, are even more exclusive, with less than one in twenty companies capturing their attention.

There's a longer-term seasonal trend to keep in mind with VCs too. Most investment firms shut down for vacations in January, then again in August. Startups that are in the middle of fundraising that get interrupted by these breaks can find their momentum completely stalled. Which is a problem because momentum is king in getting a deal done. A founder that fails to close a deal by December 20 will find their calls going to voice mail. By February, when the money starts flowing again, that founder is ancient history. This means that getting a VC meeting following Labor Day is the most coveted slot.

Getting a meeting is a big deal, and Matt managed to line up three: with Sequoia (Apple; Google; Oracle), Benchmark (OpenTable; Uber; Yelp), and Accel (Facebook; Kayak). This is an astonishing achievement. I give Matt a lot of crap for being absent in the beginning years at GrubHub, but by this point, the progress we're making as a team goes well beyond what either of us could have done alone. Getting the top three venture firms in the world to meet with us is little short of a miracle.

It all came together last minute. Twenty-four hours earlier, we had just one meeting with Accel at 11 a.m. Matt leaked the information about the meeting to an acquaintance, and within hours the news got back to the partner at Sequoia who Matt had been wooing, resulting in us getting an invitation to meet with them at 9:00 a.m. The same trick worked one more time with Benchmark, who actually moved up the start of *their* partner meeting to 7:30 a.m. to get us in before Sequoia. Matt has expertly wielded the most powerful force in the venture world: FOMO (fear of missing out).

We head toward Menlo Park, south out of San Francisco on the 280. Eventually, we pull off the interstate onto Sand Hill Road, the capitol of venture capital. A quick left brings us into Benchmark headquarters. I was expecting some sleek glass and steel architectural statement worthy of these titans of technological innovation.

It's not that.

Benchmark headquarters is a low-slung office building that wouldn't look out of place in a crappy strip mall. The ocher-colored walls look pulled right out of somebody's idea in the 1970s of what a fancy building in the 1980s would look like. To complete the effect, the outside of the building is textured similarly to the popcorn ceiling of my childhood bedroom. The windows are small; the entrance intercom is a decade out of date.

My momentary letdown is forgotten as Bill Gurley greets us. Bill is larger than life—literally: he's close to, oh, I don't know, nine feet tall? Behind the physical presence is the aura of his reputation—this guy has the Midas touch. Most companies he invests in go from small potatoes to over a billion dollars in value. This is not an exaggeration. His record is over 50 percent.

"Welcome guys," Bill says, hunching a bit to where the air is a little thicker. "We moved up the meeting to get you in, but some of the partners couldn't make it to the earlier time, so they'll be walking in while you're giving your pitch. Oh, and you've only got fifteen minutes—don't go over."

This is all delivered in three seconds, in a Texas drawl, sped up past real time, delivered at stadium volume, finished with an about-face and a rapid departing march into a conference room.

After about five minutes of standing around like morons in the hallway, the conference room door opens, and we're ushered in. Twenty or so guys (yes, all guys, yes, mostly white) have squeezed to the near side of a ten-person conference table. Otherwise, it's standing room only, with just a small stagelike kind of thing at one end. I push my way through the crowd, getting uncomfortably intimate with the gentlemen seated there, who make a half-hearted attempt to lean out of the way.

"Welcome guys!" Bill shouts. "We've got the active partners here, but also the former partners who came in just for this Labor Day meeting. We've also got a few portfolio company founders—most relevant of which, to your business at least, is Rich Barton, who founded Zillow and Glass-Door. He's familiar with marketplace businesses."

Matt and I have practiced our pitch ad nauseam. We worked on it after our failure to launch San Francisco, and we won the New Venture Challenge with it. But this is no classroom. This is the big leagues. That's fine— we have the track record to back it up.

"We connect hungry diners with local restaurants," Matt says. "The problem we're solving isn't technology—though, obviously, we're changing customer behavior with online ordering. No, what we're doing is creating a marketing platform that drives new diners to restaurants. It is so effective and so much better than calling on the phone that our diners— who, by the way, never leave us—order takeout far more frequently than they did before discovering us."

"Every diner we bring to the platform orders from multiple restaurants. Every restaurant we bring to the platform attracts more diners. The combination creates a virtuous cycle, that accelerates over time, creating a runaway train. It is outrageously hard to get this flywheel started, though, but we've done just that. We've been spinning it up over the last seven years and with only three million in capital we've created the nucleus of a national network in the largest fourteen cities in the US."

I jump in, playing up my role as MIT nerd. I employ a trick that Chuck Templeton told me he particularly likes: I deliver every statistic with two decimal points to convey precision.

"We acquire diners," I announce, "for a blended cost of $7.27. They earn just over ten times that for the company in their first year. On the restaurant side, it costs us $638.17 per acquisition, which the restaurants return in revenue to us over the course of about two hundred orders. In a new market, that means each restaurant breaks even in about four months. In our more mature cities, it's closer to two weeks. On average, our restaurants stay with us for two and a half years."

Matt and I perform our duet, riffing off each other's comments, Matt painting a big picture, and me grounding that picture with hard numbers. We pass the fifteen minutes of allotted time and just keep on trucking. We share information on our competition. We talk about the team's background. The heart of the show is about our traction, investor-speak for success-to-date. We show slides on the growth of our first four markets. The graphs go up and to the right. They say "money" in a language that investors understand.

The presentation has been carefully designed. We're not expecting a check at the end of our dog and pony show. Rather, the goal of the presentation is to intrigue, to excite, and to activate FOMO. To this end, we've left one key slide out on purpose: The one where we talk about how big the business can get. We know that if we don't mention it, someone will ask (provided they are interested, and aren't scanning for exits). This is critical because partners like to ask gotcha questions that make the question-asker look clever. By leaving the slide out, we're hoping to invite this question so we can do our big reveal.

The fish who takes the bait is Matt Cohler. He was a very early employee at Facebook. He is in the process of starting as a partner on the Benchmark team. This is his first Benchmark partner meeting. Sure enough, Cohler asks the million-dollar question—strike that. He asks the *billion-dollar* question.

"But how big can the business really get?" Cohler asks.

Gotcha.

I go full-on MIT data nerd.

"If you'll flip to the appendix of the presentation we sent, you can see from the bottom-up analysis here, across all the restaurants in our fourteen markets…" I go on for a few minutes about the fact that if you extrapolate our traction outward, we are showing a lot of untapped potential. This is called a bottom-up approach.

Then, I flip the script.

"And for a fifty-thousand-foot, top-down analysis, we can compare Domino's and similar chains to show how big just one cuisine can be." More analysis follows. I'm boring. I lean into the character of the math quant. There are nods—both of agreement and drowsiness.

As planned, Matt cuts me off with feigned boredom and plays the showman.

"We could go on for some time about our analysis here, but the point is this: How much money can GrubHub make? Crazy billions!" He's literally waving his hands in the air as he says it.

Then, out of nowhere, the sound of clapping. The Benchmark partnership is *clapping*. Bill laughs out loud. Our pitch had been scheduled for fifteen minutes. But we've been there for an hour.

We nailed it.

We leave the room, and Bill follows us out.

"That was great, guys. It's rare for anyone to get that amount of engagement from the team. Give me a few minutes to finish up, and let's talk about next steps."

"Thanks, Bill," I say, doing my best to look as harried as possible, "but we can't stick around right now. We've got another scheduled conversation with Sequoia in ten minutes, and we can't be late, because that will push our Accel pitch. Maybe we can meet up early evening?"

I could have just said, "Hey, Bill, would you like a FOMO sandwich?"

There's a chance I'm playing with fire, but I'm caught up in it now. Shouting our goodbyes, we run out the door and Matt drives like a maniac to Sequoia. Once again, the same conference room and the same cast of mostly white, all males.

Our host this time is Alfred Lin. Alfred, one of the founders of Zappos, is fresh to Sequoia after that company's sale to Amazon. We lean into the presentation—delivering our second flawless performance for the day. Except this time, before we're halfway through somebody shouts out the "Yeah, but how big can it get?" question. We pivot to the appendix and run out all the numbers. Matt gets to his "crazy billions" punchline.

Crickets. A solitary tumbleweed rolls into the room, in front of me and Matt, and then back out the conference room door.

Alfred Lin breaks the awkward silence.

"Let's dig in on the consumer acquisition numbers. I'm not quite sure I understand the repeat purchase dynamics."

Matt steps back to let me do my thing. Alfred and I go back and forth on the data. It's a good thing that the whole "quant" act isn't actually an act. I can math. Even so, Alfred catches me flat-footed with some detailed questions about cohort analysis, which is a highly technical way of measuring how groups of customers behave over time.

Another partner cuts in.

"It looks like you two should spend some time with Alfred going through a spreadsheet exercise."

We're ushered out of the room to an unassuming cubicle where for the next hour it takes all my faculties to keep up with Alfred as he constructs modeling spreadsheets on the fly. It's both intimidating and impressive just how quick he is with the numbers. There's a reason these firms are the best in the world—the partners are razor-sharp.

By the time we get out of there, my brain feels like a limp noodle.

"Nice work in there. He was trying to break you down, but you kept going at it," Matt says.

I'm wiped out, and we still have an 11:00 a.m. meeting with Accel on the books. It's 10:50 and their offices are twenty minutes down the road. Matt peels out of the Sequoia lot, hitting double the speed limit down Sand Hill. Getting into Palo Alto, it's pretty obvious that parking is going to be a disaster. Therefore, we don't—we simply get out of the car, leaving it on the street, and leave the hazards on, right on University Ave. This is a meeting for tens of millions of dollars. Whatever the ticket is, we'll happily pay it.

Accel's office is not like the others—instead of strip mall chic we find a sleek five-story glass and metal office building. Downtown Palo Alto is the epicenter of startupdom—ground zero for newfound wealth. All the early companies of the venture capital revolution started here. The elevator is shiny, the lobby glass and chrome.

The meeting isn't so slick—in fact, it doesn't happen at all. The partner is suddenly unavailable, so we're passed off to an entry-level research associate. He, in turn, wants us out of the office as quick as possible and we oblige him—in fact, we never even make it past the lobby. It's less than ten minutes from leaving the car to getting back to it.

The ticket is $200.

But Silicon Valley isn't done with us today. We've made a splash. We're the "it" deal, and everyone wants in. Other firms contact us out of the blue and ask us to come pitch. Matt and I take three more meetings. We are so exhausted that we barely know our names by the time we meet up with Bill Gurley from Benchmark in downtown San Francisco for drinks that evening.

The meeting lasts about six minutes, and it goes something like this:

Bill Gurley orders a plate of buffalo wings and a round of old-fashioned cocktails. The wings arriving blazingly fast and he tears into them. Matt and I, acutely aware of the difficulty of eating wings and maintaining a sense of business decorum, watch him eat. Before he's finished the first wing, he says—well, shouts: "We want to make you an offer. We think you've got something here and it could change the entire restaurant industry. You've done an amazing job getting this far on so little capital, and you're definitely the team to make this happen."

Bill throws down the bones of the first wing and starts in on the second. The wings look delicious. The spicy tangy smell makes my stomach clench and my mouth water. But there is no way in hell I'm going to grab one of those tasty critters and go to town while casually discussing investment valuations and terms. We know we're kinda like those wings—he's about to bite into us. We're just waiting for the "but," and sure enough...

"But," he says, sucking the gristle, "we don't want to end up in a horse race competing with another term sheet from Sequoia. I get what you're trying to do—maximizing your options and serving up a plate of FOMO. Good job—but it's time to stop the games and get down to business."

And here I am, thinking how smart we'd been. Second wing discarded, third already started.

"We're willing to offer eleven million for a third of the company," Bill Gurley announces, instantly changing my life, Matt's life, and so many others. "Also, all those crazy terms that your previous investors put in need to be wiped out. We'll start from scratch. Those investors can say yes or no, but we won't negotiate. If this is something you're interested in, and you can make a decision by Friday, let us know and we'll write up a term sheet and send it to you."

The third wing is defeated; the old-fashioned gulped; and then Bill Gurley is done.

"Have a great night, guys," he says, reassuming his, oh I don't know, nearly fifteen feet in height. "I gave the bar my credit card. Go crazy. We'll chat again tomorrow."

That was it. Six minutes, three wings, one old-fashioned, $11 million, and Gurley is gone.

"That guy is not kidding around," Matt says.

I'm still reeling from what I've just witnessed.

"We should take it," I say.

"No shit," Matt says, looking into the middle distance.

We sign the deal with Benchmark by the end of that week (we'd also gotten written offers from Sequoia and a group called Battery Ventures). A week after that, Bill introduces us to DAG, a firm that sometimes does "follow on" investments at a premium price. They toss in another twenty million dollars.

Thirty-one million dollars in two weeks.

Nothing would ever be the same again.

9

Getting Better

It's late at night, back in my Chicago apartment. Christine went to bed an hour ago. I also went to bed an hour ago, but my mind won't shut off. I lay tossing and turning, frustrated about a long boring day, followed by a short argumentative evening.

Christine and I don't have shouting matches. It's not our style. But for the lack of fireworks, we'd still just had one of the worst fights of our marriage. At the root of the issue is GrubHub's success, which has surpassed anything I could have expected, back when I was flailing about trying to figure out how to sell restaurants.

The surprising thing about success is, it has an obligation all its own. When I started GrubHub, it was a means to an end: I wanted to pay off my school debt, while avoiding the pesky reality of having a boss. But ironically, I'm now saddled with more obligation than when I started. I took money from investors, and I owe them a return. I'm now supporting one hundred employees, and their families, and they are working for less pay than they could in corporate America, hoping for a big stock payout. And, most importantly, a lot of the restaurants on the platform are increasingly dependent on us for their continued existence.

But I owe Christine also. And I'm coming up short on that obligation. Christine's career options in international human rights are severely limited because we're stuck in Chicago. It's not like I can move to Geneva or The Hague. If GrubHub's rise had been slower, I probably could have sold for a tidy sum a year or two ago and followed Christine as she pursued her passion around the world. She got a taste of it a couple years back in India, but since then, her career has been sluggish. Accordingly, this has created a simmering resentment toward GrubHub, and by extension, toward me.

I don't even remember what set off our fight earlier. Probably not doing the dishes or something. But, as is so often the case, our fight wasn't about the superficial thing that sparked it. It was about this: Christine is stuck and frustrated, and I'm not willing to bail out of this rocket ship I've created until it's taken us all the way to financial independence.

Aside from causing mounting tension in my marriage, the success at GrubHub has been good for me, personally. After seven years of fifteen-hour days, I'm finally making a salary beyond what I had been making as a software developer. Better yet, now that we have the resources to hire enough people to run the business, I don't need to burn the midnight oil anymore. Which sounds great, right?

Right?

Be careful what you wish for. You just might get it. My job is now a never-ending parade of eight hours straight of meetings. Honestly, it's pretty dull.

This particular morning, I began with the menu entry team, working through operations challenges. We recently began a project called "live by dinner." It's aimed at getting new customers their first order on the same day they sign up. I discover a whole community of people who have coalesced around a methodology on operations execution called lean operations. We buy some books, hire some consultants, and put the ideas to work, hoping to shorten the time frame from sale to live on the website from two weeks to two hours.

Then, I headed straight to a discussion of hiring and discipline processes with our new head of HR. We want to make sure our core values are being used to evaluate all job candidates, while at the same time ensuring that we don't hire carbon copies of the people already at the company. After reflecting on how homogenous we were, and then seeing that mirrored in the venture world, both Matt and I wanted to be more intentional about being inclusive in the company—especially with regard to representation in the hiring process and thoughtfulness about where we post our job openings. We started out on the wrong foot. It will take years to correct that mistake, and as important as it is, again, it seems to take an *awful* lot of meetings. Still, it's time well spent: Rooting out biases on gender, race, and age will be an unending effort, but I'm cautiously optimistic about the direction we're headed.

Then, it was meetings with our new financial controller. We're growing faster than we expected, and it's unlikely we're going to use all the investment cash. We need to ferret out places to put our excess money to work to grow *even faster*. Honestly, though, we're doubling every eight months. How much faster can we really go without the wheels coming off the bus?

All of this stuff is important work, but it's just so tedious. I never expected success to be boring.

Then just before the day ended, things took an interesting turn. Nick Kellermeyer, who's been heading up sales ever since I put him in charge of Tyler, in San Francisco, years ago, swung by my desk.

He said, "Hey Mike, we had an interesting thing happen today. A restaurant in San Francisco reached out to us to sign up."

"I thought that was happening pretty regularly nowadays."

"Yeah, we get a couple of inbound requests per day, but this one was different. They aren't all that interested in online ordering, or getting more customers," Nick said.

"That's weird. Then why did they want to sign up?" I ask.

"Their drivers threatened to quit unless the restaurant signed up with GrubHub."

"Really?"

"Apparently, GrubHub orders are getting bigger tips than their normal orders. My guess would be it's because the tips are on a credit card instead of cash."

"So, the restaurant is signing up because their drivers will get better tips. That's unexpected."

"Yeah. But I'll take it!" he said.

After my fight with Christine. I can't get back to sleep. I lie in bed for an hour stewing with frustration and guilt with the situation in my marriage, wondering what I'm going to do about it. But there's no easy solution to that problem, so I get up and head to my computer, to distract myself with some work until my mind settles down.

That little tidbit from Nick might be helpful in combating the emerging competition we're seeing in our industry. Which is becoming a major problem for us.

We had widely publicized the Benchmark/DAG investment deal. It was all over the place online, and I even had a brief interview on TV. Shouting the news from the virtual rooftops was a mistake—one that all startups make. It garnered us virtually no new customers, but it did kick off a flurry of investments in copycats.

Competition has increased dramatically. There is now Seamless, delivery.com, Foodler, Eat24Hours, OrderUp, Groupon, and LivingSocial. There are European companies sniffing around the US market too—Just Eat, Delivery Hero, and a few others. In the year since Bill Gurley joined our board, he's mentioned a few times that we're going to get caught flat-footed if we don't start thinking about our own driver team, rather than relying on the restaurants to do the deliveries. I don't realize this at the time, but Bill, who is a board member at Uber in addition to GrubHub, is hinting carefully and vaguely that another major competitor is about to enter the fray when Uber launches Uber Eats. With over one hundred million dollars flowing into competitors over the course of 2011, our head start won't last.

We need a new competitive edge. But how? We're just a connector.

Take, for example, this horrible statistic: Thirteen percent of all delivery orders have something wrong with them. The most common mistakes are late orders and missing or wrong items, but there's a hundred other little things that come up less frequently too. The prevailing logic among the company, and indeed, the bourgeoning industry, is that the high error rate isn't our fault or our problem: the restaurants make and deliver the food.

But drivers preferring GrubHub because we get them bigger tips disproves the theory that we're just a connector. We've become something more. If we have the ability to improve someone's livelihood in that way, what if we applied it more intentionally? Before leaving for the day, I casually asked one of our developers if we could adjust the suggested tips section of the website. The default choices are currently 5, 7.5, and 10 percent. "Let's go to ten percent, fifteen percent, and twenty percent," I said. With just this little tweak, we could neatly double the drivers' take-home pay at restaurants, which, in turn, would drive even faster sign-ups.

My request didn't go as I thought it would.

Mike Leiseca, our head developer, brusquely told to put this new idea on the feature list, replied that he would get to it when he was done releasing the iPhone app. It is true that I was the one who had previously insisted on prohibiting these kinds of "just this little tweak" requests, but I never expected the rule to be used against me! I'm the boss! It was infuriating that such a small and potentially meaningful change would take weeks or months to roll out.

Since I can't sleep, I decide to do it myself.

In a well-run company, software isn't done the way I've been doing it. For example, the founder doesn't just write a bunch of software while he's on vacation in India and release it into the wild. First, it goes to a testing environment, where it's subjected to a host of automated and manual assessments. I'm trying to make this the norm of how we do things. But maybe this is worth an exception. This seems like such an innocent change. No need to road test this one—takes two minutes; easy peasy. I log into the production servers and make the change. Then I go to bed.

I invented GrubHub. I can do this.

I am wrong.

The next morning, I arrive at the office sweaty from my bike ride down the lake path, but before I have a chance to freshen up and change, I find Mike blocking my way as I emerge from the bike room.

"You logged into production last night and changed the tip defaults," Mike announces, as if I don't already know that.

"Yup," I said. "I didn't want to wait."

"Did you ever consider that since you are no longer on call in the middle of the night to respond to outages, it's an asshole move to make changes to production at two in the morning?"

My employee just called me an asshole. Now, I've been pretty intentional about creating an egalitarian workplace, and I try pretty hard not to take myself too seriously, but even to me, this is obviously crossing the line.

"Did something happen?" I ask, trying to keep a semblance of calm.

"No, that's not the point," Mike says. "It's the *principle* of the thing. When was the last time you came to an architecture meeting, or joined us to talk about our code review and testing policies?" Again, these are changes I insisted on myself, but, like any human, I'm not a huge fan of being attacked, especially while wearing sweaty bike shorts.

"That stuff bores the crap out of me," I say, hoping that a bit of levity might signal to him that there's a tone issue here, and it's not an issue with *my* tone.

"I'm glad you think this is funny."

Well, that didn't work.

By this point, I'm starting to get angry. I've been trying to create a progressive organization, but it would be nice if I got a little credit, not to mention a dash of benefit of the doubt. Barring that, a touch of respect would do. I remind him just how we got here. "Eighty percent of the code base is still stuff I wrote. I know this code base like the back of my hand. I guarantee what I changed didn't cause a bug. It was the simplest change imaginable."

"Well, actually, I reverted the change from last night and I revoked your access and changed all the passwords to the production server."

I'm shocked by this, but before I can respond, he continues.

"You can still check in code to the source control" (gee, thanks!), "but I insist you follow our normal process and come to the team meetings if you're going to keep writing code. Obviously, it's your company, and you can reverse my decision, but if you do, I resign."

"OK, you bring up good points, but I don't love the confrontation and disrespect. I'm not going to react out of feeling attacked, so I'll spend the day thinking about whether I agree, or you're fired. Or maybe both."

Asshole.

Instead of going to my desk, I turn back around and head outside, intent on walking a few laps around the block before I fire his ass. On the first lap, I realize that firing him out of anger will probably involve several follow-up meetings with HR. They will be very tedious meetings. So that's a pretty strong disincentive.

By the second lap, I'm starting to see his point. It is true that the servers have crashed in the past, and it's also true that we have a whole process and schedule to make sure that doesn't happen when people are ordering food. I did, in fact, disregard all those processes.

By the third lap, I'm fuming at the interaction. I've never insisted on hierarchy, but his attitude is beyond the pale. I envision in my mind's eye marching in there, handing him a banker's box, and telling him he has ten minutes to vacate the premises.

By the fourth lap, I've relented. I'm the big boss now, and any action is amplified a thousand times. It's not possible for me to make little tweaks anymore. Everything I do hits with the force of a sledgehammer. Yes, my ego is bruised. Is that worth ruining someone's livelihood? Probably not. Is it worth the blowback from the other engineers? Definitely not.

By the fifth lap, I've shelved all of that. This isn't about reason and logic. I'm *pissed*. And I have a right to be. No, I shouldn't have made the change last night. But you know what's worse than a know-it-all who's wrong? A know-it-all who's right.

So, before I go back into the building, I take a moment to calm myself down. I take a deep breath. I stand there on the street, and speaking to nobody, I say my goal out loud.

"I'm running GrubHub so I can help independent restaurants. Mike helps with that goal. Having an ego doesn't. Let it go."

Then, I walk back inside and I keep my mouth shut—but it burns.

I guess I'm not a coder anymore.

This doesn't make me entirely unhappy. If I don't need to pull all-nighters, coding up telecom servers, do Google searches for the radius of the Earth to make a geocoder, or stumble upon accidental bugs in the phone system, causing it to call a restaurant a couple hundred times while I'm on a camping trip in Michigan, then I guess that's a good thing.

Right?

No more actually *doing*. My job, now, is to think and to talk a lot.

I didn't sign up for this. It sucks.

To cap it all off, later that week, Jessica, one of our brilliant engineers, refers to me as "post-technical." I think she means it as a compliment.

She can keep her compliments.

———

Eventually, once it's allowed to exist on the website I invented (grumble grumble), raising the tip suggestions works. People usually have no idea what to tip, so they tend to thread the needle between feeling either guilty or fleeced. Furthermore, no newspaper is ever going to print an article claiming our tip suggestions are too *high*. As a society, we have too much collective guilt to suggest such a thing. So, we can make the tips as high as we want, benefiting both the company and the drivers, and nobody will say boo about it. Accordingly, tip amounts go through the roof and the drivers are ecstatic.

It works like a charm. High-end restaurants—who are providing more expensive food, like sushi shops and French bistros—suddenly have a huge advantage when hiring drivers. Tip suggestions, which are based as a percentage instead of a flat fee, can be ten bucks for one of these high-end restaurants, instead of the more typical three or four for a pizza. This difference drives a greater availability of varied cuisines across the nation, shifting the mix away from pizza. And to be perfectly honest, since Grub-Hub takes a percentage of the order, these higher ticket cuisines are *great* for our bottom line.

Angry software developers aside, I'm on to something. The industry is changing because we changed it.

A while back we did some customer surveys and the results were confusing. Apparently, when the food tastes good, GrubHub gets the credit, but when it tastes bad, GrubHub gets the blame. There's no logic to this. I can understand us getting the blame if the food is late or cold, because we had some influence on the accuracy of delivery estimates, and setting expectations is a big part of beating them. But the flavor of the food itself? This stumps me.

So, if diners expect us to be responsible for the actual taste of the food, what if we leaned into that, even though we're not the ones cooking it? Because that's what waitresses do—they answer for the quality of the food, while the chef stays safely in the kitchen. Is GrubHub so different?

I wonder if an actual restaurateur can help us out.

The manager at Pompeii restaurant in Lakeview, David Morton, offers to give our team an education in service.

The Lakeview location has a dining room that can seat well over one hundred customers. The red vinyl booths are fresh and clean, with no cracks in the upholstery, no stuffing spilling out. The ambience is half American diner, half soda shop. It's the kind of place that is equally busy on a late Saturday night after the bars close as it is on a Sunday afternoon for kids' birthday parties.

Importantly for our purposes, their food isn't *great*. It's not bad, it's just not spectacular, at least not compared to legendary places in the city like Leona's or Giordano's. Given that other restaurants have arguably better food, it follows that Pompeii must be winning customers by being good at service. (I don't tell David that this is why I asked him to help us. I've got more tact than that. Though I guess he knows now.)

We arrive and settle into a bunch of booths.

"So, you're all here to learn how a restaurant does world-class service?" David asks. "It's pretty simple," he says. "It's not about being perfect. You don't need permanently happy employees or fancy consultants. Mission statements are great, but they don't really help change attitudes. No, what matters comes down to one simple rule."

David pauses for dramatic effect, then he lets us have it.

"When something goes wrong, you have to make the resolution more memorable than the problem."

We're hooked, now. We lean in.

"The nice thing about this concept is that it's easy to start," David says. "But there's no end to getting better at it. So, for example, let's say that a server trips, flinging a salad onto the lap of the father of a family of four, covering Dad in ranch dressing. That's a pretty big thing you need to fix. How do we make the resolution even more memorable than the ruined pants?"

"Apologize," Matt offers, "and pay for the meal and his dry cleaning?"

"That's a good start," David says, as though that's *always* the first answer to his question. "But it doesn't get us there."

"Pay for his next meal too," someone suggests.

"Keep going."

"Give him free food for life."

"Nope, not that. You're just throwing money at the problem. People hate that. They don't like being bought off."

We rattle off a few more suggestions, but each one is met with a "not enough" or a "too much." Eventually David realizes we're not going to get it.

"I'll give you all a great life secret," David says. "Apologies are a two-step process. The first is making the problem right, *instantly*. Every employee needs to be empowered to comp the meal and get poor Dad cleaned up. That might or might not include dry cleaning. In this case, probably yes. We leave that up to the server's discretion.

"But very few people understand the *second* step of the apology—the thing that really makes it real. You have to promise that it won't happen again and describe the specific steps you'll take to make that promise come true."

"Does that mean you promise to give your employees training on how to walk?" I ask.

I didn't ever claim I asked helpful questions.

"No, but thanks for the useless suggestion, Mike. Here's what we do: After comping the meal and solving the immediate problem, you say, 'Sir, we're also going to look into why the server tripped and make sure we find the source of the problem. It might be an uneven floor, or the wrong type of shoes, or oil spilled in the kitchen, who knows? We'll get to the bottom of it, and make sure it never happens again.'"

"Customers love this response," David continues. "It's humble and sincere—and it's also rare enough that it is memorable. Everybody experiences tons of frustrations every day. Most companies take a cover-their-ass approach. Some blame the customer; others will do a service recovery, making the problem right. But only a very few actually follow through to commit to fixing the root problems."

"Then you actually have to do it," I say, "the follow through, I mean."

"Yeah, of course," David says, as though he's talking to a small child. "But that really should go without saying. If you're comfortable promising things to customers and not following through on them, you've got bigger issues."

The monster calzone arrives, and my three booth mates help me destroy the thing.

———

We double down on customer service. What started out as a question—"Can we take responsibility for the quality of the food?"—naturally extends to, "We will own the diner experience." In other words, we will no longer pass the buck, even if the buck is passable.

As a first priority, we decide to stop sending customer service calls to the restaurants themselves. Telling diners to "call the restaurant" when a problem arises doesn't work. The restaurants that cause the most problems are the same ones that are terrible at handling these calls. This, in turn, causes a customer experience death spiral, making a bad problem worse and losing a GrubHub customer for life.

To get ahead of the problem, we poach the head of customer experience at Virgin Atlantic, Todd Provino. Virgin is an airline that has become a shining example of service in an industry that has a well-deserved reputation for terrible service (not to mention a propensity for passing the buck, blaming regulation and security). Todd gets to work immediately on two things: building out our customer service team with professionals, and starting conversations with the rest of us on how to reorient everything we do around service.

With Todd in place, I can focus on the next version of our customer service software (ideas, this time, not code) that gets to the first part of what David was talking about: solving a problem, *instantly*. We create a ticketing system that gathers information from inbound calls, chats, or texts, and which shows a customer service agent the customer's history, along with their current and previous orders. The system evolves to the point where we can answer the phone by saying, as just one example, "Hey, Bill, I can see you're calling about order number 123456—it looks like it's fifty-five minutes since you ordered. How about I get in touch with the restaurant and text you with the whereabouts of your food?" Customers love this—then we sweeten the pot by offering them a five-dollar-off coupon on their next order. The system pings the driver via app or text, and then automatically texts the customer the response. And just like that, a twenty-second phone call and a five-dollar-off coupon converts a hangry customer into a lifetime GrubHub advocate.

That's step one, but I keep in mind what David at Pompeii taught us— now we have to fix the underlying problem.

How? We don't cook the food. We never even touch it.

The answer lies in statistics.

By now, GrubHub is processing millions of orders a year, meaning we have access to droves of data—in fact, we're swimming in it. But data isn't *information*—turning data into information requires asking the correct question of the data. The question we come up with is, *"Which restaurants consistently deliver the best quality food?"* The question goes beyond who delivers the fastest, or who cooks the best. It's about who does both of those things well.

Let me regale you with the tale of two burritos.

The first burrito is the steak burrito from Garcia's in Lincoln Square in Chicago. This burrito has the highest rating of all the food on our platform. In other words, it's the burrito our diners say they love the most. Garcia's is set among a bunch of bars that don't have their own kitchens. The path from the interstate to Wrigley Field goes right past the place too—this is deep blue Cubby territory. People love Garcia's steak burrito—it's big and greasy, and filled with flavor. Our review system is filled with stories that start with a Cubs loss, move into a drunken evening to drown sorrows, and ends with a Garcia's steak burrito.

The other steak burrito is from Carbón, a Mexican restaurant in the Bridgeport neighborhood of Chicago. This is South Side—White Sox country. Carbón's steak burrito is the most frequently reordered food item *in the United States.* Carbón's burrito doesn't have a ton of customer ratings or reviews, but it clearly has a committed following, because to repeat, because it bears repeating: Carbón's steak burrito is the most frequently reordered food item *in the United States.* There are people who order this steak burrito every Sunday night for years on end.

So, which one is better? I hypothesize that customer *activity* is a much stronger indicator of quality than customer *opinion.* In other words, trust what the customers *do*, not what they *say.*

(This is why the question *"Would you refer a customer?"* on the ten-point "Net Promoter Score" surveys we are all subjected to these days is so useless. Instead, companies should just ask a customer to *actually* make a referral and then measure whether or not they *do*.)

So, I'm pretty sure I figured out the answer to the question, "Which restaurant has the better food?" It's Carbón. But that answer just drives deeper questions. What follows is a series of ever-deeper investigations.

How often do Carbón's orders trigger a customer service call? Very infre-quently. *How often do diners who order from Carbón order from other restaurants on GrubHub compared to the whole population of diners?*

The answer astounds me—about *five times* as frequently. And *not just from Carbón!* This is a huge revelation.

Statistics bear this concept out. This pattern repeats itself across tens of thousands of restaurants. Again and again, we see that the best restau-rants create loyalty for themselves, but in a much stronger sense, the best restaurants create loyalty for *GrubHub.* In other words, the best way to have customers keep coming back is to give them the best-quality prod-uct. This is not a novel or unexpected concept. But knowing it, deeply and personally, with rock-hard certainty, is a hard-won insight. One that GrubHub forgets in later years, substituting fabulous amounts of spending on marketing instead of service. It's a trade many businesses make, and it's a poor one.

It's one thing to know that quality matters. It's quite another to capi-talize on the concept.

GrubHub has always been based on an auction system, with those restaurants choosing to pay the highest percentage to us sorting to the top. But now we introduce the idea of the quality of the experience to the diner into the sorting algorithm.

Using the insight that the best restaurants cause increased loyalty and frequency of ordering among our diners, and that the worst restaurants cause diners to abandon using GrubHub, we label the top restaurants "golden children" and the worst restaurants "problem children." About 5 percent of the restaurants get the "golden" tag and about 2 percent get the "problem" tag. Then, we put quality modifiers in place on the restau-rant sorting—in our lingo, we "buff up" the quality restaurants and "nerf down" the problem ones. But, because our mission is to make delivery better, and my goal is to help independent restaurants, we don't stop there.

We do the hard work of having conversations with the golden children to get to the root of what they are doing right. Then we call up the prob-lem children and share best practices with them, so they at least have an opportunity to improve their service and quality of food for diners.

We change our sales strategy and commission structure. Specifically, we target the "golden" restaurants for upsells. If we can get them to pay more on the auction system, and then double down with giving them a boost to their sorting rank, tons more orders will be flowing through to the best restaurants. Diners will have a better experience, causing an increase in both the length of their loyalty to GrubHub and their frequency with which they use our service. Everyone wins: golden restaurants, diners, and GrubHub.

We put a lot of effort into identifying quality restaurants before we sell them, using information like the age of the business, their Yelp reviews, and a few other indicators. (I should hasten to point out that this is not so different from what Matt pointed out, way back at Moody's when he asked "Why not just sell the good restaurants?") We award bounties to salespeople for the top restaurants in a city, which we dub "neighborhood gems" (because "golden children" is way too problematic and paternalistic).

It takes almost a year to get all of these people, systems, and processes in place. We go through a lot of growing pains expanding the size of our customer service team and extending our hours to 24-7. And that's just step one: apologizing.

The second part is way harder: fixing the root problems. What starts as statistics and data mining becomes operations and technology. Instead of fixing things that went wrong, we focus our efforts on preventing the service problems before they even exist. We release a drivers' app and start tracking delivery times, preemptively offering coupons on late orders.

Does it work?

Boy howdy, it works!

Our customer loyalty numbers climb. More importantly, our customer *frequency* increases. Our *average* customer is now ordering more than once per week. Those customers are referring us to friends, meaning our customer acquisition costs drop. We're getting almost as many inbound calls from restaurants as we make outbound. We launch even more markets, growing to over fifty cities in the US. Our expansion plan evolves to have a strong focus on getting the neighborhood gems online first.

Those $31 million we had in the bank? We spend less than a third of it before we're profitable again and still doubling every ten months... doubling on much higher numbers. Three magical letters start getting whispered: IPO.

Which is why everybody—our restaurants, employees, diners, and investors—are all insanely happy with us. Um, actually, no, that's not what happens.

Greed.

Greed happens.

Day 2. Mile 138.

The slightest hint of blue filters through the fabric of the tent as the sky brightens outside. An unknown songbird somewhere sings its complex, trilling repetition. Frogs croak a deep basso nearby.

My tent may look flimsy but it's surprisingly strong. I ascribe to the ultralight camping philosophy, but not dogmatically. This is why I've got a super light tent, instead of a tarp. It was advertised as a freestanding tent, but it's not really. Unless I stake it down, the whole thing refuses to stay upright. But, when done correctly, it is a careful balance of competing tensions.

I suppose, then, the tent is a bit like me. I'm excited about finally getting into the meat of this trip. After twelve years of pouring my heart and soul into starting GrubHub, I have started my reset. And that's exciting. But there's grief here too. I miss it. Well, parts of it anyway: the challenges, the people. And, frankly, it was fun to be the leader of the winning team.

But here I am, out here trying something new and crazy (again). It was important to give myself a big challenge to avoid falling into a funk after leaving the company I started. It is also crucial to give myself some distance from the wealth that came with the success of the business, rather than letting that take over my life. At some point on this long ride, I need to make a decision about what company I want to start next. And when.

The tent is just over six feet long, and just over two feet wide, meaning there's a scant two inches between me and the tent wall, lying prone. The door opens into a vestibule, formed by the gap between the inner tent and outer rain cover, or as I think of it, my palatial dining room. The space is just big enough to hold my saddlebags, with enough spare room to balance my camp stove, and that's about it.

As I reach out the door for my bags, my hamstrings scream in protest. There's one spot in particular, just between the back of the leg and the bottom of my ass, that's burning. I wonder if this will be a problem. (Spoiler alert: It will.)

I trained hard for this trip. In the month since the IPO, I ran thirty miles every week, and rode a ton, including several centuries (a century is riding over one hundred miles in a single day). But all those miles were on a normal bike because the recumbent was late arriving from the factory. In fact, I rode it only once before dipping the wheel in the Atlantic.

Today's ride starts with a long bridge over the Chickahominy River. Pain in my newly discovered ass-thigh muscles wraps its way up my lower back as I climb. The bridge is steep. I take my time ascending as I survey the river below winding peacefully among the marshy forest. Fortunately, there's plenty of room for bike and car. The latter are patient and give a wide berth. I stop at the top and take in the river valley.

On the other side of the bridge, the road has been recently paved with broad shoulders. Grand stands of trees line the sides. Hours pass with nary a bridge, nor any traffic. Every few miles there's a black-and-white sign with the numbers 76—that's the Virginia designation for the TransAm Bike trail.

Eventually, an actual bike trail splits off from the road. Trees arc their branches overhead. Long-haul hikers, like those that hike the Appalachian Trail, call this "the green tunnel," but I hadn't expected to experience it on the TransAm. My world shrinks to the trail ahead and the branches above. After a hundred miles of strip malls and bridges, this is paradise.

The tunnel opens up, and I find myself riding alongside a field of tobacco. There are some grand homes in the distance, plantation-style places—I could stop and have a look, but I'm having too much fun just rolling along.

The path veers back into the trees—then, about one mile in, the trail suddenly comes to an end. I'm faced with a backhoe and beyond that: mud. There's a scar of brown through the green forest that is not yet paved, riddled with grapefruit-sized rocks and squelching clay.

I look left, then forward, then behind me. I make eye contact with a squirrel.

"Are you seeing this?" I ask it.

I tentatively step onto the surface, testing to see if I might be able to ride over it. My foot instantly sinks into the stinking mud. My shoe comes off as I try to work it free. The road is out of sight, off to the left, too far to get to through the woods.

Backtracking to a point where the road comes closer to the trail isn't all that far—less than a quarter mile—but the idyllic spell of the morning is broken. Every needless turn of the pedal makes me unreasonably frustrated.

Another hour of riding finds me on the outskirts of Richmond during the a.m. rush hour. The bike lane disappears; the woods have long since fallen away, replaced now by an uncountable number of mattress stores. Also, there are now hills, even as the strip malls start to dominate. I have not yet arrived at the foothills of the Appalachians, but neither am I on the coast any longer.

The traffic grows and close passes start to feel personal. Mathematically speaking, the best technique for cycling with traffic is to go fast— this naturally reduces the number of vehicles that pass, and for those that do, the speed differential is smaller, the faster I go. This, theoretically at least, reduces the chances of a collision. But hill after hill makes speed an impossibility.

Eventually, Richmond falls behind, giving way to the Eastern Virginia lowlands. Traffic dies down, and once again it's stunningly beautiful. But it's still difficult to find peace in the moment: My legs ache; my lower back is a twisted knot; my shoulders are somewhere above my ears from the tension of the cars shooting past all day.

Even as I leave Richmond behind, and the traffic fades, I'm starting to worry—the mountains are still ahead of me. It shouldn't be this hard—I'm not even two hundred miles into a four-thousand-mile trip. Fortunately, there's a bed waiting for me, just up ahead at the famously hospitable Mineral Fire Station.

The town of Mineral, Virginia, is everything that is right with America. There's a bike lane that starts exactly at the town limits, and what's more, it's wide and swept free of debris. There's a big sign that says welcome to all, and a smaller sign that specifically welcomes cyclists. The little homes dotting the road are well kept and pleasant. The dogs are leashed or inside fences. People leave their doors unlocked and their Wi-Fi unpassworded.

I roll to a stop near the amphitheater and little park near the center of town. From my vantage point I see two competing ice-cream shops, a resale store, a couple of boutiques, and a café. The vibrant and authentic downtown presents a stark contrast to the strip malls and sameness of Richmond, Norfolk, and Virginia Beach.

There's not a chain store in sight.

Reflecting on what I created at GrubHub, I experience a moment of pride: connecting seventy thousand independent restaurants to millions of hungry diners, without a single national chain on the platform. To think that I helped, in my small way, in resisting the same-ification of America, is something I hadn't really appreciated until I had to bike past six Applebee's in two days.

A banner over the main street announces the county fair is starting tonight. Woohoo! An ant hive of activity at the fire station and adjacent park confirms the imminent festivities.

The TransAm maps I'm following have sung glories of the Mineral Fire Station. They are a fixture on the route, known for their hospitality, allowing cyclists to bunk in the firehouse. But disaster: The county fair is in full swing, so the fire station is closed. I can't sleep there. The fireman I talk to is deeply sorry about the inconvenience, but he helpfully points out a spot that they have reserved on the far side of the park, away from the noise, for any arriving TransAm cyclists.

The fair doesn't start for a few hours, so I set up my tent and open my Kindle to a new book: Cheryl Strayed's memoir *Wild*, about her backpacking trek along the Pacific Coast Trail. I immediately feel a kinship with her, even though our lives are so vastly different. I wonder if I'll ever write my own memoir about my journey through GrubHub and eventually on the TransAm. (It may be exceedingly obvious, but, yes, that's exactly what I did.)

At some point, I nod off. At some other point, probably a few hours later, by the dimming of the light filtering through my tent, I hear somebody setting up shelter for the night. I peek my head out.

"John!" I shout.

"Mike!"

John has been planning his own TransAm adventure for months. We met online through the bike touring website, crazyguyonabike.com. Seven or eight of us spent much of the winter comparing gear, talking about training, and debating start days on that site. I had imagined a whole posse of us, meeting and leapfrogging each other as we went.

Most of these proto-friends had faded away before the promise of their companionship had become a real thing. Some were unable to tear away from work or unwilling to leave loved ones for a time; a few simply had delays. A week behind on the TransAm is a universe apart. The people that I'm likely to meet on this trip have already started.

John and I embrace like long-lost friends. As we catch up about our first days on the trail, a couple arrives. The woman is on a standard touring setup, panniers over both wheels, four saddlebags in total, but the man is on a recumbent. It looks nothing like mine, though—both wheels are the same size, forcing the rider into a deeply reclined position, almost lying flat on his back. He wobbles as he comes to a stop, and then is suddenly upright.

"John!" the man and woman call out.

"This is Reudi and Heida, from Switzerland," John says. "Reudi, Heida, this is Mike, from Chicago. We've been talking for months online."

"Is great to see recumbent," Reudi says. "How are your legs? Much pain, yes?"

"I thought it was just me," I say, relieved it isn't. "I didn't train on a recumbent, just a normal upright bike, so..."

"Not me," Reudi says. "I train. Very much. I experienced same pain in my leg, training in Der Schweiss. No pain now."

Heida interrupts.

"Ignore him," she says, with a glint in her eye. "He's also in a lot of pain. He just wants to look tough, like Arnold Schwarzenegger."

"I thought he was from Austria," I say.

"Oh," says Heida, embarrassed. "We did not think that Americans knew the difference."

"Of course we do—Switzerland is chocolate and cheese, not body-builders."

"Ja!" says Reudi, laughing. Then he turns serious. "This pain, in your legs. It is problem. What is the word? Excruciating? Yes? Upright bike is no good. You have big muscles in wrong places. Much pain. Better if you had not trained at all."

"Yes, he complained about it nonstop," Heida says. "At one point, he could not walk. Very painful. Very bad."

Oh yay, something to look forward to.

"How long did it take for you to adjust to the different bike?" I ask, putting the emphasis on *adjust* as a hopeful attempt at, well, hope.

"Two weeks," Reudi says. "Maybe, for you, less? Ten days maybe. Past Appalachians. Much pain."

"Well, I'll just need to push through it."

"Of course. No quitting. Keep pedaling. Of course, you must."

I wonder though, must I? I think back to that phone system, and the years of wasted effort getting GrubHub started in an unnecessarily difficult way. Is this the same thing? Should I scrap this recumbent bike, and just buy a normal one? I'm torn, just like my hamstring.

Seeing the apprehension on my face, Reudi changes the subject.

"Tell me, where can we find corn dog? I always want to eat this!"

The fair takes a while to get going, so we pregame with ice-cream cones from one of the stores. When the fair does open, we are the first ones in line. We spin on teacups, and ride on four-cart dragons. Reudi gets his corn dog. We watch as earnest young men shoot BB guns at targets to win plush animals for attentive young women. The pure innocence of the thing has my hard-bitten Chicago self a bit nauseated. But the Mike that I want to be thinks it's sweet.

Reudi's warnings (and the screaming pain in my legs) have increased the anxiety that settled in my gut back in Richmond. Before bed, I swing by the ice-cream shop to ask for a cardboard box (and a tasty mint choco-late ice-cream cone, just for research, you understand).

I rummage through my stuff, throwing things into the box. Two pairs of casual shorts; one pair of running shorts (what was I thinking?). Coffee mug. Two hundred business cards with blog address. Stuff sacks. Wallet. Winter sleeping bag. Two camera lenses. Another pair of pants. An extra inch of my toothbrush handle. I attack the hardware underneath the seat that holds two of the four saddlebags too. I throw the gear, two saddlebags, and all the other stuff in the box.

A scale in the bathroom shows nine pounds, eight ounces of stuff. This may be the first time in history that a visit to an ice-cream shop has resulted in losing weight. Having spent the last decade thinking about how to help restaurants succeed, putting a scale in an ice-cream shop never made it high on the list of effective strategies.

Tomorrow morning, I'll stop by the post office before leaving town and ship it all home.

With a lightened load and a lighter heart, I make my way back to my tent. I fall asleep to the sounds of good, honest, small-town fair fun echoing from the other side of town.

10

Greed

The waiter at the Tortoise Supper Club in Chicago is trendy AF. His neatly trimmed beard is perfectly complemented by a meticulously organized mustache. He has carefully curated his outfit too: His checkered shirt, skinny jeans, and suede leather work boots suggest that serving finely crafted cocktails is simply a side gig—what he really does for a living is ironic lumberjacking.

The restaurant, like its staff, is trendy AF. The walls are painted with a dark wine red that adds gravity to the already heavy wooden beams crisscrossing the ceiling. The tables are stained dark as midnight. There are shelves filled with color-coordinated, serious-looking books. There is a silver trophy sitting on a shelf next to a black-and-white photograph of a football team from a bygone era, the players bedecked in thick cotton jerseys and leather helmets. This could be a Princeton fraternity. There's a feeling of old wealth here that is a carefully crafted illusion for a restaurant only two years old.

The waiter is listening patiently to the newest member of GrubHub's board, Justin Caldbeck, who is establishing his credentials as a connoisseur of fine wine in hushed tones. Justin is delighted to discover that the cellar has a supply of bottles rare enough to be special, but common enough that he has enjoyed them all in the past. Predictably, this concludes with the waiter bowing deeply from the waist and saying, "Very good, sir."

Justin just ordered two bottles of wine that exceed five hundred dollars each. I'm trusting that he's fully aware that it is tradition for investors to pick up the bill at a board dinner. But why do I care? Justin's firm has just led a fifty-million-dollar investment in GrubHub.

Before I can even start enjoying the almond-crusted, fried goat cheese, with a side of locally sourced honey appetizer, Bill Gurley fires an opening salvo.

"We should start prepping for an IPO," he says.

The hubbub around the table dies down. This is a big deal. The concept has come up before, but never at this level, and never stated so cleanly. And certainly not by the investor with the most sway.

Justin isn't having it.

"No, we're a decade out from that," Justin says. "It makes much more sense to get growth capital and consolidate the industry, buying up all the competition."

These positions are not surprising. Justin just invested in the company at a valuation over $200 million, ten times the value when Bill invested two years earlier. If we were to IPO right away, Bill would be looking at getting a huge return, whereas Justin's would be paltry.

"Too many companies these days stay private too long," Bill says. "The public markets bring a lot of publicity and legitimacy to a company. Since a public company's stock value is readily apparent, determined by supply and demand, we'd also have a legitimate currency to make the consolidation happen—one which we can print more of by issuing stock. If we want to buy up competition, that's fine, but the public company has a huge advantage in this, because their value is set independently. Otherwise, negotiations just become dueling blowfish, with each side exaggerating how great they are."

"But public valuation is extremely dependent on growth with little regard to profitability," Justin says, warming to the fight. "This means that GrubHub won't get its proper pricing. The company is profitable. Something they have over every other tech company that has gone public in the last five years, and they'll get nothing out of it. It makes more sense to let the team do its thing without the pressure of quarterly targets that mean so much to Wall Street."

Bill disagrees; Justin fires back; the wine flows; discussion becomes argument. There's a lot of anger.

I haven't seen this before. Historically, our board dinners and meetings have been friendly. Some of that is the simple fact that it is easy to run a business when the revenue graphs are going up and to the right. But that doesn't mean we didn't have disagreements. Up until now, though, they've always been civil. This is heading in the opposite direction. The comments flying back and forth are barbed, and I'm getting uncomfortable. With each round, they seem to get a little more pointed, a little more personal. I'm wondering if having Justin on the board is going to be a mistake. I guess it's possible that Bill could be the one to fault, but something about Justin is making my skin crawl. It's hard to put a finger on it. I decide to stop partaking of the wine.

"We're not going to come to a conclusion during this dinner," I interrupt, trying to change the subject. "Before we get to the question of the IPO, we've got big questions to consider about branding..."

In addition to myself, Matt, Bill, and Justin, there are two other board members here: Bruce Barron, our original investor, and Chuck Templeton. Bruce responds to my comment about branding and offers some opinions on this. Our sidebar conversation sucks Justin in as well. The large group splinters into two conversations, with Matt talking to Bill, and me handling Justin. It feels a bit like we're between rounds at a boxing match, with Matt and I tending to our fighters.

Justin orders a third bottle of wine, then a fourth. The restaurant staff skips the usual tasting and just pours; Justin makes a face and says that a bottle is turned; the waiter, realizing that by skipping the taste and mixing the bottles in the glasses he might have created a $2,000 problem, retreats to get the manager. The manager does not agree that the wine is turned. Bill makes things worse by siding with the manager, which, of course, makes Justin dig in his heels and declare that not only won't he pay for the most recent bottle, but since it's mixed with prior bottles, he won't pay for those, either.

Matt calls a time-out. Justin heads to the restroom. The manager retreats. Matt pays the check in Justin's absence, hoping to avoid escalating the confrontation into all-out war. Eventually, the dinner breaks up, handshakes all around, if not smiles.

This dinner does not bode great things for the board meeting tomorrow.

———

Our bank account hasn't dropped below $20 million since Bill Gurley led our first big round of financing. In 2011, the year just past, we generated about $22 million in revenue, up from $14 the year before. That's big growth on a big number. Better yet, we expect to double that number this year, and then double it again in 2013. Our investment in customer service, and our early success with one of the first iPhone apps, has given us extremely loyal diners. Not just loyal—*frequent*. We're coming up on a million of them, and they're ordering, on average, at least once a month.

Better yet, our restaurants love us. *Love.* We've kept thousands of them in business over the course of the 2007–2008 housing crisis. We've never gouged prices, and their drivers get amazing tips. We even rolled out a product to create websites on their behalf, charging just enough to cover credit card costs on orders they get through their own marketing efforts.

We've managed to put independent restaurants on a level playing field with the big chains.

Logically, our best bet at this point would be to take our profits and start distributing them to investors while we continue to grow at a rapid clip. This is called a dividend. It's perfectly normal for big companies to do it. It's perfectly logical.

But venture capitalists are not logical.

Venture capital is a thing that people do with money that has all the appearance of intelligent investing but is actually only slightly less risky than going all in with a two five off suit at the final table of the World Series of Poker. The investors themselves recognize this, and they commonly talk about managing the risk by placing multiple bets. Their expectation is that about seven out of ten of their investments will either fail completely, or only return a portion of the cash they invested. They refer to these as "strike outs," or "singles." To counter the danger of these bets, they hope that two of the remaining three other investments are a double triple, yielding, as the names suggests, twice or three times their stake.

Out of the original ten investments, this leaves one—it's this one that makes all the money. To turn a profit on the whole portfolio, this last one *must* be a home run, yielding ten times multiple.

Occasionally, a company will surpass even a home run and be a grand slam. These unicorns return one hundred times the original investment or more. GrubHub has already passed home run status but isn't quite a grand slam...yet. Our early investors, the ones who put in a million bucks, are looking to get back about twenty-five million at this point. All of the other investments that fund has ever made, in aggregate, will only make a fraction of what our company accrues for them.

All of this success creates an unexpected (to me, at least) effect. Instead of being happy with our progress so far, these investors are gripped by a manic desire for it to be even bigger. The investors care far too much about our business, which leads to micromanagement. Every decision is up for discussion. Good news is never good *enough*. Everyone becomes an expert on diner and restaurant behavior.

And it's not just our investors who are pressuring us—other firms are putting on the hard court press to let them in on the action. They try to get at us from every angle possible: cold calls, meetings with our investors—hell, even some of our employees have been taken to lunch by a guy who's got big money and wants to invest.

Justin was particularly insistent and aggressive. To get him off our back, Matt made him an offer. If you can get Campusfood to sell to us, and provide the cash, we'll take your money.

We'd been interested in acquiring Campusfood for a while. We're in fifty of the largest cities in the US, and we've got a plan which will allow us to get deeper into middle America, but it will take a decade of the simmer strategy to make that happen. Campusfood, on the other hand, is already in three hundred college towns. We figure that with our technology, marketing, iPhone app, and customer service dominance, we can take their modest operation and supercharge it.

Unfortunately, in our initial conversations with Campusfood, Matt and I broke the first rule of mergers and acquisitions (and of life): Don't be an asshole. With the benefit of years of hindsight, I am embarrassed about my behavior during our first meeting.

As soon as I arrived at their midtown Manhattan offices, I scoffed aloud to Matt about what a dump they were. In our conversations with Mike Saunders, the founder of the company, I belittled the progress they had made, taunting that his company was less than a tenth the size of mine, and he had been working at it for years longer than I had. When comparing our future prospects, I disdained their ability to break into our markets, all of which were "primary," such as New York and Chicago, as opposed to his, which were "secondary," such as Ithaca and Ann Arbor. Then, to top it all off, I plastered GrubHub stickers around the office as we walked out.

Mike told me not to let the door smack me in the ass on the way out. Good on him.

Some small part of my behavior was understandable, if not excusable. Because if the first rule of mergers and acquisitions is "don't be an asshole," the second rule is "convince the other guy that your stuff is worth a lot more than their stuff." I fell trap to the temptation of "the dueling blowfish," as Bill Gurley calls it. This is what happens when two private companies are eyeing each other for a merger. Both try to exaggerate their own business's value and minimize the others'. It's a negotiation tactic. But, in my case, it went way over the line, from business to personal.

I'm not this guy. Or rather, I *wasn't* this guy. Yes, when I started Grub-Hub, I was moody and malcontent. But I wasn't an *asshole*. Eight years ago, I treated people with more respect. I didn't need to put anyone down to know my own worth. I wonder if I'm going to continue going down this path. I wonder if it might be time to cash in my chips, before I inevitably turn into a version of myself that I don't even realize I don't like.

Be careful. Running a business is dangerous business.

So, the Campusfood acquisition didn't move forward.

Then, a *deus ex Justina*—Justin Caldbeck manages to get Campusfood to be willing to sell to us. He did it selling the idea to Campusfood's investors directly, rather than the more customary, and frankly, more appropriate, route of convincing the CEO it was a good idea.

We buy Campusfood for $46 million. We raise the cash by selling a startlingly small portion of our company to Justin's firm, Lightspeed, along with a syndicate of investors. Overnight, GrubHub goes from serving fifty cities to three hundred.

This is the world I walk into the morning after the wine battle at the Tortoise Supper Club.

We are rapidly approaching "grand slam" territory.

Which, of course, means everyone wants us to grow even faster. Each success just brings more pressure. There's never a pause for celebration, just an insatiable appetite for more growth. Each year is driving a wedge between me and my wife. And since I hired all my friends, I can't totally relax, even when we grab a beer after work. Be careful what you ask for. Success can be a real drag.

———

The numbers I'm presenting at the board meeting this quarter are exciting. We killed it. "Conversion rate" measures the percentage of people who come to the site that eventually place an order, and ours is through the roof. It is hard to overstate how important this number is. Our company is paying for eyeballs—through TV, radio, outdoor, digital, print, and a dozen other channels. But all that spending—and it's in the millions at this point—doesn't matter if the customer "bounces" before placing an order.

So, what does "through the roof" look like? Twenty-eight percent—more than one quarter of visitors to our website place a transaction. This number is *astronomically* high. A typical website? Under 2 percent.

"Why is it so low?" asks Bruce.

I don't even know how to respond to the question. We've accomplished something incredible. The only other website I know of with higher conversion rates is booking.com, and they are the absolute masters of FOMO. If you've ever used them, you'll know that within thirty seconds of a search, you're being bombarded with messages that if you don't hit the "Book Now" button immediately, all the hotels in the area, and in the rest of the world, in perpetuity, will be sold out.

People want to find somewhere to sleep, but it's hard to create that level of FOMO with chicken wings. Twenty-eight percent is extraordinary. Still, Bruce's question did drive me to take yet another look at this number, and over the next six months we boost it to 33 percent. And they *still* weren't impressed.

Eventually, and with no small amount of grumpiness, I get everyone to move on from the supposedly abysmal conversion numbers (grumble

grumble) to other aspects of the business. Diner loyalty? Good, getting better. Customer acquisition costs? Low, getting lower. Restaurant retention? Great, getting greater.

Fortunately, I have more success getting agreement murmur that these numbers are good.

The love doesn't last long.

Our take rate—the amount we charge restaurants for our advertising—is averaging just under 17 percent.

"Why so low?" asks Justin.

We don't set this number—we simply measure it. Because the sorting on the website is an auction system with some quality modifiers, the restaurants *choose* what they want to pay. It's a question of supply and demand, but it's also a moral question.

Here's the issue: As more diners have found out about us, an ever-increasing percentage of our restaurants' business is originating from us. Some restaurants now get over 50 percent of their business from Grub-Hub. This kind of volume creates its own pressure, making it hard for a restaurant to forgo us. As more of them sign up, this creates increasing upward pressure on the bid prices in the auction system.

From a short-term perspective, GrubHub might decide to not care about that, but we're in it for the long haul. If the take rate is reasonable, we drive both revenue and profit for restaurants and don't kill them financially. But if the take rate is too high, their profit shrinks, risking their entire business. Traditionally, this kind of thing would be called a "prisoners' dilemma." It's terrible for their business, and not so great for ours, so we don't do it.

But more importantly, it's morally and ethically wrong. Our restaurant customers helped build our business—their trust in us has brought me success and wealth. My key goal for the last few years has been to help independent restaurants. Making delivery better is our mission—how does putting a restaurant out of business for short-term financial gain do that?

So that's what I tell the board.

"We have caps on the amount that a restaurant is able to bid," I say. "This dates back to the 'pizza wars' in which two bitter rival pizza restaurants got all the way up to the high forties, out of spite for each other. There's simply no way for a restaurant to survive such high rates. Therefore, we don't let them bid that high."

There is silence around the table. This is not what they thought I'd say. In fact, it's clear that some folks think I'm quite mad.

"Wait, we artificially limit the maximum rate that the restaurants can pay?" Justin asks, incredulously. "That's a *terrible* idea. We need to stop doing that immediately. If a restaurant goes out of business, that's just more orders for the restaurants that are run well. GrubHub isn't a charity."

Bill's having none of it.

"Having a take rate too high opens up the door for lower-priced competitors. Seventeen percent is a bit high already, actually—eBay is way down in the single digits, but Ticketmaster is up near forty. The only way to keep rates that high, without fear of competition, is through regulatory capture or monopoly pressure."

Justin (unsurprisingly) disagrees.

"Look, I don't know about all that. What I *do* know is that if a customer wants to pay you more money, you say 'yes.'"

"I don't think it's right to overcharge restaurants that rely on us," Chuck says.

Now, it's Bruce's turn.

"I agree with Chuck, Bill, and Mike," he says, calmly.

This surprises me a little bit. I've frequently been on the other side of the table from Bruce when negotiating. He's obscenely good at it. I'm conditioned to expecting him to squeeze for the last drop. But he doesn't do it out of a sense of dominance—he's incredibly empathetic.

Then, darn it, Matt speaks up.

"I think we should remove the limits on what we let restaurants spend."

I knew this was Matt's position. We've argued about it extensively. Generally, Matt and I do fine when we disagree—in fact, some of the best decisions in the company have come from the two of us working out a compromise position. But to my eye this is a pretty black-and-white moral issue, and we just don't agree on it.

Only now we're disagreeing about it in a board meeting, with investors lining up on either side.

Fortunately, we're not dumb enough to call a vote about it.

Matt opts for conciliation.

"Thanks for the feedback, everyone," he says. "Mike and I will discuss this more, and we'll take a deep dive into it at a later board meeting."

In hindsight, I wonder if this was a mistake. Should I have kicked up a fuss there and then, and created a paper trail that would have been part of the public record post-IPO? Would it have mattered? Maybe things had grown too far beyond my control at this point. Maybe removing limits on restaurant fees was an inevitability. Maybe I created a Frankenstein, and this was just a matter of time. Still, I wish I had applied my bourgeoning assholiness to digging in on this point.

If there's a thing I regret about my creation, it's this one number. A take rate of 17 percent still enables us to be a highly profitable business, and one that helps independent restaurants. A take rate of 40 percent, which is where GrubHub peaks, years after this meeting, is something else entirely.

There's no other word for it. It is exploitation.

And still to this day, I'm mad as hell about it.

Day 6. Mile 326.

It's time to climb a mountain.

Mountains are not a 'bent's best friend. The bike tips over easily at slow speeds and the gearing hasn't been designed for climbing, requiring me to keep the speed up, even as I can't shift down. My tortured hamstrings push hard against the mountain. The mountain pushes back. Each turn of the crank is a brutal battle between gravity and my sinews.

Taking advantage of the light traffic, I make broad S curves as I climb, weaving from shoulder to shoulder, creating my own switchbacks. At this rate, it will take all day to reach the top. That's fine, though—slow and steady. I do my best to not think about the implications this all holds for the much taller Rockies.

Eventually, I fall into a rhythm, grinding away. My legs pump steadily. I drink water; I eat snacks. Every twenty minutes or so, I pause to take in the view, husbanding my strength. One overlook has a little nature trail off it, and I hop off the bike and walk around a bit, stretching out my legs. My leg hurts, but by babying it, I'm no worse off than when I crawled out of my tent this morning.

Cold and damp with the morning's dew, nursing cramping legs and a sore back, I finally realize how Ryan felt, helping me pick up menus back in San Francisco. Unfortunately, it seems unlikely that there will be a warm Chinese restaurant with hot green tea as I crest the summit of the Appalachians.

After four hours, I'm up onto the Blue Ridge Parkway, which runs along the top of the Appalachians. I'm still headed up, but the grade is more forgiving, and the road is perfectly smooth. Cars are infrequent, sometimes ten, or even fifteen minutes apart. It is calm and peaceful and all the things that I've wanted out of the trip. The rolling hills of Appalachia are on either side of the ridge, occasionally peeking through breaks in the trees. Wreathes of mist clothe the peaks. The work is hard, but it is wonderful.

A mile or so from the top, an unwelcome obstacle blocks my path—flaggers with walkie-talkies have stopped traffic. The road has been torn up for repaving. What remains is a single grooved lane, scattered with gravel. I don't have a ton of stamina left to sprint through this, a line of cars behind me, impatient to get on with their day.

My concern is misplaced. The construction workers see me coming and stop the cars to wave me through. As I pass, the flagger smiles and calls me over.

"We'll hold traffic from the other direction until you're through," he says.

"How far is it?"

"About a mile," he says, as though that's nothing.

"That might take me almost fifteen minutes. I move slow on this thing," I say, waving at the 'bent underneath me.

"Take your time. This is a parkway. You've got as much right to be here as any car. No need to rush."

The final bit isn't as steep as the middle ascent, so I'm cruising along at a respectable clip just north of a light jogging speed. As I reach the end, there's a peloton of MAMILs (middle-aged men in Lycra) waiting for the all clear. (Waiting for me, therefore.) These guys are serious cyclists. You can tell that they are serious by the cost of their equipment and the tightness of their shorts.

As I pass them, they break into clapping and cheering. They have seen TransAm riders before, so they understand what I'm doing. And I've just climbed the eastern edge of the Appalachians on a loaded recumbent bike. They are impressed.

I'm proud. I *earned* this.

And that's pretty great.

You know what else is great? Riding a 'bent down a mountain.

The drop off the Blue Ridge Parkway to the town of Vesuvius appears on the American Cycling Association's elevation map as a vertical line. The 'bent's low profile makes me fast on downhills. The windshield makes me even faster. I hit thirty miles per hour.

Forty.

I pass fifty. This is fantastic.

But, despite the rush of speed, something in my mind also suggests that pushing fifty-five miles per hour on a curvy mountain road might be dangerous. I take it down a notch, slowing my descent; in fact, the rest of the way down, I hold the brakes slightly depressed. I have disk brakes—a pair of calipers clamping on to a metal disk—similar to those on a car.

Rolling to a stop, she—my 'bent is a she, recently dubbed *Persephone*—makes a loud popping sound. It's the noise that a car makes as it cools in the garage after hard driving on a hot day. My bike frame is titanium. Titanium does not pop…at least, not unless it gets *extraordinarily* hot.

I stop the bike and lean it against a tree, dragging it through the underbrush. A sapling brushes the back brakes. It curls and browns, sending up smoke.

Oh crap. That is *really* hot.

A squirt from my water bottle instantly boils off as steam. I laugh, pleased with myself: That steam was caused by the friction of overusing my brakes descending a mountain. The energy for this was created entirely by me, ascending the other side. This means I came close to melting titanium with my muscles.

No wonder my hamstring hurts.

Having triumphed over my first mountain range, I decide to depart from the official TransAm route for a few days, relishing my freedom and refusing to be bounded by the official maps. This is, perhaps, not the wisest choice of my life, as there's no cell service for me to pull up directions, but I figure as long as I pedal toward the sunset, I should hit the Pacific eventually.

Over the course of the first day off-trail, the rural Virginia road number conventions have begun to make sense. A road numbered in the 600s seems to signify, "Kind of a real road, but kind of just a path into the back country," as opposed to the 700s, which means, I think, "I guess some people call this a road." A few roads are numbered in the 1,000s, which clearly means, "For reals, not a road." The 1,000s mostly start out like any other road, only to gradually deteriorate into gravel, or a dirt track, or, once, a muddy strip between two horse pastures.

I twist and meander, sometimes climbing, sometimes falling. From time to time the pavement disappears. The 'bent doesn't handle gravel like a champ, so there's some pushing and dragging through a few sections. It doesn't bother me much. This is beautiful country, the kind of country that inspires bluegrass ballads.

Getting rolling from a stop is a bit tricky on gravel. I do a kind of jogging waddle, with a leg on either side of the lawn chair seat, and then just plop backward into it. There's about three seconds to get my feet up and pedaling before I lose momentum and fall over. The mud sticks to my cycling cleats, accenting the waddle, plop, pedal maneuver with a wet squish.

And then I see them: tens of horny, gun-toting, Confederate Mickey Mouses (Mice?).

It seems that a local artist has helped this community express their shared beliefs by creating brass and iron plates with Mickey Mouse depicted in bas-relief. Some of them are painted, but most just sport a patina of rust. There are various versions of this artwork, but they all have a few things in common: First, all the Mickeys are proudly hoisting a Confederate flag. Second, their eyes bug out at the ass of a naked lady, who adorns the other side of the brass plate. Variations on this theme have the buxom damsel holding a gun, waving her own Confederate flag, or firing a cannon, of all things.

The plates are everywhere, on mailboxes, fences, in display cases. At one point I find dozens of them perched atop an actual cannon, with a sign above that reads, "Covered in Glory."

What. The. Fuck.

Is this montage of seemingly unrelated themes a call to arms for the sons of the South? Is it a nostalgic remembrance of the growth from childhood to puberty, capturing both innocence and the discovery of sexuality? Is it something as simple as loving naked ladies, Mickey Mouse, and violence?

Still wondering at what I've just seen, I round a bend and come across a breathtakingly idyllic scene. There's a lone homestead, clearly hand-built, nestled amid a quaint garden. A few chickens peck at the ground. A thin stream of insubstantial smoke rises from the home, diffusing into the morning fog. A cute little pupper lifts its head and cocks it to the side.

Then, the dog attacks, its maw flinging foam into the heretofore tranquil fog.

It takes me a few precious seconds before I realize my life is in danger. Then, the signal hits my legs and I'm off like a rocket. Fortunately, dogs are not rocket scientists. It doesn't plot an intercept course, but instead comes right at me. I pass by it, just as it's losing steam. I continue on, smugly smarter than the canine.

I crest the top of the next hill... where another dog awaits.

What follows is hour upon hour of dodging vicious beasts. Over the next hundred miles I'm chased by 134 dogs. Studiously compiling the data, I have composed the following classification system.

Level One is the basic "Harrumphing Disapprover." Fido is pretty laid back, too old, or too mild to chase me. Don't be fooled: The dog still hates me. It would gladly clamp its jaws around my throat, but it would prefer me to come over and gently place my neck in its mouth, with its blackened gums and blacker heart. It may take a solid two days to gnaw through my jugular. It likes to savor a kill.

Level Two is the "Terrified Guardian." Fluffy hates me. But it doesn't know what to do about it. It always gives chase, but we both know it's a token effort. It's important to show willingness, even when it is clear it has no chance to catch me.

Level Three is a "Downhill Chaser." Buster decides to go for it. "Kill the bicycle beast," it thinks. Buster makes a lot of noise, really hams up the part and looks truly deranged. The "downhill" here refers to the bike's orientation, not the dog. I'm racing at full speed before the little mutt's murderous rage comes fully online. Basically, as long as I'm going downhill, everything is fine. With moderate effort and a nice downhill slope, I can outrun even the most determined pooch.

Level Four is the "Uphill Chaser." We're starting to get serious now. Princess noticed me just as I was passing. I've got a head start. That's key. Most uphill chasers are no big deal. They see how far I am out ahead, and once I kick in the high speed, they give it up pretty quick. But about one out of three thinks "challenge accepted!" and pours on the speed. Outrunning Princess isn't about speed, it's about endurance. Adrenaline is the enemy here—the situation calls for just enough velocity to make it hard for the dog and then for me to hold that pace for as long as I can. Twice, Princess almost gets me, requiring me to modify my technique by adding a maneuver I have titled the puppy overtaking outsmarting protocol, or POOP. This is essentially about embracing panic—it entails swerving wildly just as the doggy pulls even with my back wheel. Startled, it falls back, giving up with whatever the canine version of a harrumph sounds like.

Level Five is the "Uphill Interceptor." This is officially not good. Angel saw me coming and got a full head of steam before I was even close. The way to avoid this dog is to stick to the middle of the road, and just before the intercept, and its attendant mauling and maiming, I POOP. But that's not enough for Angel. I need something more. I layer in a whistle blast, upgrading the maneuver into a POOP! And not just any blow of any whistle—no, I have to explosively squeeze every possible bit of air out of my lungs explosively in an attempt to deafen myself, the dog, and even horny Mickey. This scares the ever-loving crap out of the pooch. If I do it right, this downgrades the Uphill Interceptor to an Uphill Chaser—proceed as per Level Four. But the element of surprise is key. POOP! only works once per dog. This is important: Don't POOP! until just pre-maul.

Then, there's Level Six. You never want a Level Six.

This day, I'm on county road 600-something before it gives way to road number 1,000-something. The pavement turns to gravel and bends skyward, gently at first and then more steeply.

Level Six: Uphill Gravel Road Bulldog Interceptor with Attitude.

POOP! POOP! POOP! poop. POOP! POOP! POOP! POOP!

Yes, the little poop is exactly what you think it is.

Butch catches me. I try to yank my leg out of the way of its gaping maw, but my cycling shoes are clipped into the pedals, and they don't come free. The bike goes out of balance, and I tip over, skidding painfully along the gravel, leaving a significant portion of my calf on the road. I instantly roll into a ball, hands up to protect myself before the killer canine gets at my fleshy neck bits.

Nothing happens. I look up to find Butch is right there, inches from my face.

And then he licks my eyeball.

His stubby gray tail is wagging happily. This is the best game of chase he's had in weeks! He flips on his back and presents his belly for rubbing. I scratch his belly, fingers trembling. I'm not sure if I should piss myself, laugh, or cry. I try a bit of each. The dog licks my road rash. It's sweet but hurts like hell.

How many of the 134 dogs I have encountered could have been belly rubbed? I'd like to believe that this encounter ending in belly scratches is the norm. But it only takes one misjudgment to get seriously hurt.

Probably better to just assume they are all vicious.

This is not one of the lessons I was hoping to learn on this trip.

11

Ducks in a Row

GrubHub's shiny new headquarters is smack-dab in the loop—downtown Chicago. Ironically, it's situated exactly two blocks away from the office where I quit my first programming job, nine years back. We've got the top floor of the building, which houses a glass and chrome boardroom with wraparound views. Outside those gleaming windows is a wide balcony with a half dozen shrubs that makes a killer lunch spot. It's fancy—not Silicon Valley fancy—but for a Midwest startup, founded by a kid from rural Georgia, it does the trick.

Today is gonna be fun. It's the official start of the IPO process, and the investment bankers are inbound.

Turns out, bankers travel like ducks.

The biggest, most important mallard leads the way, marching into the conference room with unimpeachable solemnity. He's dressed in a Boggi Milano suit, accented with a Patek Philippe wristwatch. His bespoke shoes gleam brightly from this morning's polish, so shiny, in fact, that I catch a glimpse of my own outfit in their reflection. I'm wearing jeans and a hoodie; the banker isn't the only stereotype here.

Behind the prime bird is another banker who sports salt-and-pepper hair. He's slightly junior to the top mallard, but he's still in the upper echelons of Goldman Sachs's IPO team. He's also in an expensive Italian suit, but he hasn't earned the pinstripes yet.

Next in line is a trio of middle management ducklings. No salt-and-pepper hair, and the watches have downgraded from Swiss to German. To finish out the line of bankers is a hassled pair of newborn chicks who are recent MBA grads, by the look of them. Their suits are also bespoke, and their watches are also fine, but there's a frayed edge to these two. The penultimate duckling looks to be creaking under the strain of endless work and the final one seems just happy to be here. He is the only one smiling, at least.

Today, Goldman Sachs is going to pitch GrubHub on why we should choose them to bring our company public. This is the first pitch of what is known as the "bake-off," which is the first official task of an IPO. The point of the bake-off is to pick an investment bank; the chosen bank, also known as the lead underwriter, manages the entire process. They coordinate the creation of the legal doc, called the S-1. They manage the lawyers, accountants, and other bankers, working to get them all to agree on key points. It's this lead bank's sales team that sells most of the initial shares and gets the biggest commission.

I'm as anxious as I am excited. As a first timer, I have little understanding of an IPO relative to the bankers, lawyers, and investors that have gone through it many times before. All these new terms—S-1, underwriters, bake-offs—they're Greek to me. This is dangerous, because all the parties are looking out for their own interests.

Figuring it out is harder than I would have expected. The process itself is very opaque to those outside it, and this is, in itself, my first lesson: The secrecy is inherent to the structure of the process. By convention (and SEC rules), the process is covered by a "quiet period," which lasts from the filing of the initial registration statement with the SEC all the way to the first public trade. So, mum's the word from this point out. Which is a shame, because I'm getting an inkling I want to write a book about this someday.

This meeting with the bankers is the mirrored opposite of the investment pitch that Matt and I delivered to a half dozen venture capital firms in the valley, some five years prior. Three of the five big Wall Street banks—Goldman, Citi, and Morgan Stanley—will be pitching us this week. The stakes for the meeting are high because this single transaction could net whichever investment bank we choose an eight-digit fee.

The lead Goldman banker begins, "Trusting your company's future to Goldman is the obvious choice. Nobody else has the reputation, sales teams, market reach, or expertise that we have. Pension funds line up to buy stocks from our IPO offerings. Ultrahigh net worth individuals employ our firm to preserve wealth, but also to grow it, and we frequently have long lists of billionaires aggressively seeking allocations. Why risk the stigma of a poor IPO with a lesser firm, when we have a track record of our companies doubling or more on the day of the IPO."

I'm a bit confused by this, so I ask a question, interrupting what's shaping up to be a heavy going self-congratulatory monologue.

"Why would we want the price to double on the first day? Wouldn't we rather get that higher price for the shares that we sell ourselves? Why give all of appreciation up to the purchasers in the IPO?"

The banker pauses and looks at me, and then to Matt and Bill, as if to ask, "Who let the toddler in the room?" But he deigns to answer my question, "Companies that don't have a 'pop' after the initial trade carry a stigma with them for decades. They're seen as a bad stock."

I'm trying not to be cynical, but I don't buy it. The reality is that this strategy is going to directly benefit Goldman's clients. These are pension funds, wealthy individuals, and sovereign wealth funds that buy the IPO offerings at a depressed price, and then sell them an hour later after this "pop."

The banker continues his presentation, putting up slides that show a selection of Goldman's last dozen IPO offerings. He shows the relationships between these companies' revenue, and how much the public markets valued them at on the day of the IPO. He relates similar data for other non-Goldman IPOs, and makes the case that we'll all be *individually* richer if we choose Goldman.

There are more slides. They talk about their sales capabilities. They talk about their private wealth management expertise. They brag about their ability to turn Matt and me into polished versions of ourselves, able to charm even the most conservative pension fund manager, convincing them to buy our stocks. What they don't talk about is GrubHub.

In all, I sit through three hours of anecdotes about Goldman's amazingness before the seats are pushed back and they file out of the room. They are tedious and long-winded, and they are suffused with the unassailable presumption that we'd choose them. In all that time, they don't mention GrubHub once. Only themselves.

I want to say, "Get the fuck out."

I don't say that. I have *some* tact.

They line up in their precise pecking order to leave. The final hand-shakes are like the end of a little league baseball game, with both lines of teams passing by each other shaking hands and saying, "Good game."

I head to the bathroom to shimmy into my spandex and shoehorn myself into my bike shoes for my ride home. When I emerge, fifteen minutes later, I'm surprised that the bankers are still here, chatting to Bill Gurley. Because Bill is on the board of Uber as well as GrubHub, they are clearly homing in on their real target. The ducklings have gotten the smell of their favorite treat. Money.

Eventually, everyone shakes hands one more time and the bankers head to the elevator. I try to slink back into the boardroom, but one of the smaller mallards spots me and holds open the elevator doors.

Welp, this is awkward. Have you ever worn spandex bike shorts in a too small elevator with seven impeccably dressed Goldman Sachs investment bankers? It's actually not as uncomfortable as you might think. Give credit where credit is due—they are good at schmoozing. Number two chats me up about bike brands. He's a big fan of Bianchi, apparently.

———

The next morning, I'm up early. Too early. I'm anxious and worried after that disaster of a meeting yesterday. Making use of my time, I fry up some bacon and eggs, and a few thick slices of sourdough bread. The smell of bacon lures Christine from the bedroom, as I knew it would.

"Can't sleep?" Christine asks.

"Yeah, I'm worried about what GrubHub is going to become after we go public."

"Why do you care?"

"Until yesterday, I had never really realized the difference between private investors and public investors. Venture capitalists always asked the question, 'How are you going to sell a product to lots of customers to make me a ton of money?' But after Goldman's presentation, I worry that public investors ask merely, 'How are you going to make me a ton of money?'"

"You're not usually that cynical."

"You wouldn't have believed those bankers. I've never seen a group of people so laser focused on wealth. I got the sense they'd do anything for money. Anything. It made my skin crawl. What if they're all like that?"

"Maybe they are. But I'll ask again. Why are you anxious?"

"What do you mean?"

"Aren't you leaving? It's not going to be your company anymore. Wouldn't it be healthier to let it go?"

"I guess so. I don't know."

"Well, at any rate, we'll have more time together. Heck, maybe we can actually start the adoption process we've been talking about."

"Yeah. That's true."

"Remember back when you took that first investment from Origin. What did Chuck say? 'It's not your company anymore.' Once you sell the first part of it, you need to start letting go. This is just the final step."

"You're right. It will be nice to not put GrubHub first in all our decision-making. I know your career has been hard because of it. Once I leave, you can just be my sugar mama, and I'll just hang around the house like a bum."

"Yeah, right. You'll have five new hobbies the first week of retirement." She says it with a smile. She wants this for me, as much as she wants it for herself.

We linger over coffee for a bit, before I start layering on my gear and head out. Lake Michigan is calm today, the royal blue water as still as glass. Christine is right. It's time to let go and get on with my life. And though she didn't say it, it's time to stop making my wife second fiddle to my business. Before turning away from the lake and biking in toward the city proper I pause briefly to watch the sunrise. The sun strikes the glass sky-scrapers downtown, igniting them a brilliant orange.

On the elevator up, once again, I find myself standing next to a man dressed in an impeccable suit and sporting a fine wristwatch while I'm in spandex. He introduces himself.

"I'm Zaheed Kajani with Citi."

"Mike Evans," I reply.

He offers his hand, which I shake, then he pauses, taking a beat to make eye contact and flash a genuine smile. I head off to change. Next to the conference room is a little-used bathroom with a few lockers in it. I freshen up, drying off the little bit of sweat I worked up on a cold morning ride. Today, I put on a suit, which is decidedly not bespoke. Neither are the shoes I bought on Zappos. GrubHub is now getting an order every second, and I still own just under 10 percent of the company, so I *could* afford to dress like the bankers. But I'm not quite sure how I feel about that yet.

When I make it to the conference room, Zaheed is already in there. I'm a bit confused by the lack of minions—and it would be minions because this man is clearly in his forties, so there's no way he's an associate. It's up or out at the investment banks, and anyone who makes it to middle age without having a heart attack is upper management, simply by attrition.

Zaheed is dashing around the room, placing bound presentations in front of each seat. This whirlwind of activity confirms what I've heard about him—I'd already been told that he is the hardest working invest-ment banker around; folks use words like *ferocious* and *relentless* to describe him. And notably, Zaheed hasn't sent a first-year associate here to prep the room, he came to do it himself.

"You started this whole thing in your apartment, huh?" Zaheed says, continuing to whip around the room. "I can't believe you made it into fourteen markets with just three million in investment—that's astonish-ing. It's a classic rags-to-riches American story, isn't it? Your restaurants really love your business, by the way—a few of them even mentioned *you* by name. They remember you coming in to sell them on the business, ask-ing them to take a chance on you. What you've built here is truly unique."

To say that I'm impressed is an understatement. He clearly did his homework enough to understand not just the *company* story, but my story. I wonder if he did this level of research with Matt, or some of the other executives. He goes on like this for another ten minutes, barely taking a breath.

A few minutes later his colleagues arrive, six of them. Like Goldman's they're all wearing suits, but there's a range of styles, and one of them brought bagels—good bagels: super stinky garlic and onion everything bagels. There's smoked salmon too—also stinky. On the spectrum of inof-fensive meeting food, bagels are pretty far on the wrong end, up toward chicken wings. But I'm incapable of resisting an everything bagel with lox.

Zaheed digs into the food like I do. He's entirely unselfconscious about his stuffed face as he shakes the hands of the other GrubHub team members as they arrive.

I like this guy. I wonder what Matt will think of him. For that matter, I wonder what he thought of Goldman yesterday. We haven't gotten a chance to connect since that presentation. The board will follow Matt's and my lead, so really it just comes down to us agreeing on a bank.

Once we're all settled, Zaheed says, "Before we begin, I'd like to show a little video we put together." He dims the lights and fires up the projector. The scene opens with a restaurateur talking about what GrubHub means to him.

"GrubHub kept my business open during the housing crisis," the guy says. His eyes are glistening. "I would have had to fire all of my family members and close shop. But the orders just kept coming. Not only did we survive, we were busy, every night. Night after night. Hundreds of orders."

Seeing this testimonial from a restaurateur I've never met fills me with pride. For me, this has always been the real impact of the business—helping other entrepreneurs. Sure, there's been value to diners too. We provide convenience and access, which can make a big impact in everyone from a new mom short on sleep, to someone recovering from surgery, to those with allergy sensitivities. Those are important, but my heart will always be for the restaurateurs. The presentation goes through further testimonials. Restaurants are raving about us from all over the country and I get a little choked up seeing the parade of customers that love us. This is a testament to what I've been trying to accomplish for years.

When the video ends, Zaheed says, "We started out our research by trying to understand what GrubHub's customers think of the company. We do this before we contemplate taking on any new client for an IPO. In part, this is so we can understand the company better and have the right information for our sales team to represent you to our investor relationships. But it's also a part of our due diligence. We find that the best way to determine the legitimacy of a company is to talk to its *customers*. And, let me just say, your customers *love* you. I don't think I've ever seen such consistent and positive praise of a tech startup."

The contrast between this approach and that of Goldman Sachs could not be more pronounced. *This* presentation is about *GrubHub*, not the bank. Ultimately, we're hiring a bank to represent us, so this is a critically important distinction. They already know more about us than Goldman ever will, simply because they bothered to find out.

Remember back in Borders when I read *Selling for Dummies*? There are three steps for sales. One: Understand your clients' needs. Two: Explain how you can meet those needs. Three: Ask for the money. Goldman started at step two. Citi started at step one. Even the pros don't always get this right.

Zaheed and Citi nail it so well in this first meeting that they'll get the nod. I can't imagine the final presentation, by Morgan Stanley, will hold a candle to this one. Of course, there's lots of other meetings and decisions in the coming weeks. In addition to the primary bank, there are smaller niche investment banks that tag along on the deal. We need to figure out who will be our lawyer, and there's a million other little things. But, with Citi's presentation knocking it out of the park, it's starting to look like this thing is actually going to happen.

It's been four years since that first time I said, "Just one more year," to Christine back when she was offered a job in India. My unwillingness to make that promise a reality has intruded on a lot of our conversations about our future. Most notably, the possibility of kids. If I've been unwilling to quit my company, the default assumption would be that she is responsible for child-rearing.

Still, she wants to believe me when I say that *this* time, I'm almost done. And once it's over, I'm going to stay at home with some kids, and that home can be anywhere in the world that her career takes her. She wants so much to believe in this oft broken, but recently repeated promise that we've actually started the process of adoption.

Over dinner, I share my enthusiasm about Citi.

"Do you really think this is it? We'll be free to go live internationally? London, or The Hague, or Geneva?" she asks.

I say, "I don't see why not. I know you've been incredibly patient, putting your career on hold. But, this is it. The whole process is supposed to take about four or five months from the bake-off."

"Should I start applying for jobs?"

"I would. Or...maybe we can do a few months of backpacking in

Europe. Or spend a year in New Zealand. Maybe we'll sail around the world."

She's annoyed by this comment.

"What's wrong."

"I've passed up a dozen international jobs because we're rooted here in Chicago. Now that we have the freedom to be anywhere, we're not going on some kind of extended vacation, globetrotting around the world. It's my turn."

I hold up my hands in surrender. "Yes. Absolutely. I owe you."

"What happens if the IPO drags on or gets canceled?"

"I promise, if this thing is still dragging out a year from now, I'll just quit," I say. "I promise."

"I appreciate that," Christine says. Then, in all honestly, she also says, "I'm skeptical."

————

A month passes. Two pass.

Six pass.

There's lots of *activity*, but precious little *progress*.

Every Monday, Matt and I have an updated call with Zaheed on the IPO process. We do the conference call in his dedicated conference room, which is just across the hall from my dedicated conference room.

Over the last ten years, GrubHub has had four offices as we've grown. The first three were nothing to write home about, but this one is really quite nice. The first eight years of that ten, we were on very tight budgets for everything from salaries to office furnishings. But Matt has decided to flex a bit with our growing income, and has outfitted his conference room with what I think of as "grown-up furniture."

The two of us are seated along the far wall from the door in a pair of Eames lounge chairs flanked by live plants that we pay a service to keep alive. Above the set is a life-size half-naked photo of Iggy Pop screaming into a microphone. Matt and I spend a lot of time in these chairs talking through our strategy and tactics for the business.

The whisky bar is not for show. Matt, in particular, is starting to enjoy our newfound affluence. He's introduced me to thirty-year scotch. I still think of myself as that kid, raised by a single mother, who got piles of financial aid to go to college, but there are new cracks in that identity now, that allow for a dram of Blue Label. Honestly, it feels *good* to have nice things.

We've done a big pile of IPO-related stuff in the last six months. We finished the bake-off and picked the banks to help us. We created our filing document, and pored over details with lawyers—both ours and the banks—for months, racking up over a million bucks in legal fees (which, later this year, will earn me an invite to their annual ski trip, the boondogglest thing I've ever done). We passed our audit. Matt and I renegotiated our employment contracts. All necessary stuff, but so very time consuming.

Zaheed calls in.

"Hey guys. No news today."

This is the fifth week in a row that he's delivered this message.

Now we're in the part of the process called the "comment period." The entity making the comments is the Securities and Exchange Commission. And they are slow. Glacially slow. We submitted our public filing six weeks back, and they have yet to respond.

"Anything we can do to speed it up?" I ask.

Zaheed says, "You don't tell the SEC to speed up, Mike. You wait. Patiently."

I could scream with the frustration of it. From what I know of the next steps after this, we're running out of time to get this done in 2012. To make the cutoff, we need to get the final approval before Thanksgiving. Should be plenty of time, since it's currently just past Labor Day.

The next week finds Matt and me in the same office.

"The comments came in last night," Zaheed says. "Bad news. There's forty. This is going to take months to resolve."

True to his prediction, September and October pass by. Then, on Halloween, we find out that the SEC has cleared us for filing. I'm ecstatic. The finish line is in sight.

This means that next week, Matt and I will start the road show. The road show is an eight-day window in the IPO process, where Matt and I will be zipping around the country on a private jet, provided by Citi, pitching investors on the company. My bags are already packed. (In fact, they are packed with bespoke suits. After the spandex in the elevator episode, I decided it was time to upgrade my wardrobe.)

A few days later, Zaheed schedules an emergency conference call.

The connection is scratchy, Zaheed's voice goes in and out. It sounds like he's driving.

"We need to postpone the IPO," Zaheed says. I presume because of the bad line we've heard him wrong.

"We need to postpone the IPO," he repeats. We have not heard him wrong. "There's a bunch of private school holidays in New York City between now and the end of the year, all on different schedules," Zaheed says. "School breaks mean vacations. Any set of meetings is only going to get a portion of the investors. Since about half the money going into IPOs comes from investors in Manhattan, we need to wait until they aren't distracted. That means January, at the earliest."

"Are you kidding me?" I say, my heart sinking. The hard weeks of work, and never-ending delays, combined with the pressure to make good on my promises to Christine, all come bubbling out. "You're telling me that capital structure of the United States stock markets is heavily influenced by the teacher in-service days at some overpriced preschool on the Upper West Side?"

Before Zaheed can answer, we hear a huge bang.

"Guys," Zaheed croaks through the speakerphone. "Erm, sorry, but, erm, I need to call you back. I just got in an accident. I'm hurt."

The phone goes dead. We hope Zaheed isn't.

"Did that just happen?" I ask.

"Apparently," Matt says, looking as stunned as I feel.

"Let's call one of his teammates and let them know he got in a car wreck. We need to make sure he's OK. We can talk about the IPO some other time."

A few hours later Zaheed calls to tell us he's OK, but the IPO isn't. It is definitely stalled.

That same day, Seamless reaches out to ask if we will consider a merger.

In GrubHub's office culture, things moved smoothly, or friction-free, or efficiently—but nothing is ever *seamless*. The very word is excised from our company vocabulary. Sometimes a fresh new face would utter the taboo word and there would be a shocked hush around the office.

They are the enemy, and besides, GrubHub *won*. We launched every major market in the United States. In every market that Seamless has tried to compete with us, we have utterly crushed them. They can't get a foothold. We even wrested control of the Brooklyn, New York, market, right in their backyard.

But there is one big problem (apart from their name, which is horrible): Seamless gets more orders in Manhattan than GrubHub does in the rest of the country *combined*.

It's true that we have succeeded in blocking them from the ultimate startup goal: the IPO. For as much success as they've had in Manhattan, they are still a one-trick pony. But it's also possible that they have hurt our prospects at being a successful public company. What would it mean to go public with Seamless dominating Manhattan?

Part of me thinks no big deal—we're growing so much faster than Seamless that we'll overwhelm them in another two years. But I also know that Manhattan matters a lot. That's where all the investment bankers live, after all, with their kids in those too expensive private schools that just sidelined our IPO.

So, instead of flying on private jets to talk to investors, Matt and I fly to San Francisco as a neutral territory to meet with the New York–based Seamless leadership. I hate everything about this. I don't want to go. Matt insists we're just going to talk. But I know that once the possibility of a merger gets raised, it will have a life all its own, and I won't have much power to stop it.

The meeting is small. Myself, Matt, and Bill Gurley represent Grub-Hub. Jonathan Zabusky, the CEO at Seamless, brings a board member with him as well. No lawyers are present.

And you know what really sucks? Jonathan knows the first rule of mergers. Don't be an asshole. He reaches out and takes my hand in a firm shake.

"You've done amazing things with GrubHub," he says. "Every other company that's tried online ordering has ended up selling, like Seamless did to Aramark, or getting left as roadkill on the side of the road. The two of us are the only ones left standing, and you did it without any corporation support."

"Um, thanks," I mumble. Trying to reciprocate the compliment, I say, "And you all have managed to build a huge business, despite the worst name in the history of branding." I'm not *trying* to tank this deal. But clearly, this is not my best work.

And you know what? Jonathan smiles.

"Yeah, SeamlessWeb. It really is terrible, isn't it!"

We all laugh.

Jonathan is *likable*.

Crap. This thing might actually happen.

After all the greetings, we get down to business. Matt opens.

"Look, the reality is, a merger of our two companies would be looked on very favorably by the public markets. Reducing the number of competitors will demand a much higher value in the public markets than the sum of either company individually listing."

Jonathan says, "I agree. And the combined company would be far more efficient, if we were disciplined and generous about eliminating redundant departments. The result would be a far more profitable company."

Crap. This sucks. They are right of course. Mutual embiggening. I don't want this. I just want to have the IPO and ride off into the sunset.

And so begins phase two of merger conversations, the dueling blowfish.

Jonathan says, "Seamless generates nearly twice the revenue that GrubHub does, and so we think that it makes sense to have a two-thirds to one-third allocation of stock in a new company.

Matt counters, "Yes, but GrubHub has effectively blocked Seamless's ability to go public, by preventing your firm's ability to build a national presence."

Jonathan says, "But Seamless's dominance in Manhattan will severely hurt your pricing, since that's where most IPO investors and investment bankers live, and they are more familiar with our brand."

We get into hard numbers, sharing revenue, expenses, and a host of other data. It's all on a screen. Nobody is yet willing to send a file over email to the other side. But we're starting to get a picture of the two companies.

Matt says, "It seems clear that the operations, technology, customer service, and brand that Mike have built are all far superior to what Seamless has. We are massively more profitable than you, which counters any argument for Seamless getting more than fifty percent of the combined company by revenue alone."

Jonathan says, "Well, we wouldn't entertain a deal like that."

I finally chime in. "So, sounds like we don't have a deal. There's no world in which I'll give my required unanimous vote to this merger where it's anything other than fifty-fifty. Honestly, I don't want to do this merger. We're going to IPO in a few weeks, I'll be richer than I have any right to be, and I'll have made my investors huge amounts of cash. Good enough for me."

Bill Gurley says, "Willing Buyer, Willing Seller."

This is a very confusing thing to say. But, I've heard him explain it before. What he means is that, after all the spreadsheets, formulas, and arguments, the price of a company is determined by what someone is willing to sell it for, and what someone else is willing to buy it for.

My stance is that we've got a better offer than anything Seamless can bring us, if they insist on a pure financial formula. I can take the money and run, and that's just what I want to do. It's a hell of a negotiating tactic. Especially since it's not a tactic. Time to move on.

The meeting breaks up with no agreement. We fly home. I'm relieved.

But the calls continue. Inevitably, the bankers get involved. They argue that food delivery is a "winner takes most" industry, meaning that being the biggest is its own competitive differentiator. Everybody takes this perspective as the gospel truth.

Problem is, this idea is bullshit. Companies are not immune to competition simply because they are first and biggest. Not unless they are so big that they are a monopoly. A combined GrubHub and Seamless would still represent less than 2 percent of all take-out orders placed in the nation. We're nowhere close to that large.

All I know is that a combined company will be less agile and innovative than GrubHub has been. A merger will take a year or more, during which other competitors will be able to catch up to our head start. Uber

Eats is already ramping up, and there's a lot of noise about a new kid on the block: DoorDash.

And yet... if we do the merger with Seamless, and then subsequently do the IPO, Citi estimates our return will be *four* times as much.

What does it matter? How does anyone even spend all that money? What's the difference between $5 million in the bank versus $20 million? Is it a bigger jet, a vacation home in Vail, an even more expensive private school? Who the hell cares? Who would want all that headache?

Of course, there's the argument that even if I'm not enamored with the toys that come along with personal wealth, I could do a lot of *good* with that money. In fact, it's precisely because I don't have expensive tastes that this argument resonates with me. I could do a *lot* of good.

But what's the cost? Another two years? What will that two years in Chicago mean for Christine's career? Will it derail our adoption plans, given that we'd agreed I'm going to be the stay-at-home parent? And besides all that, what about my sanity? I'm just on the edge of burnout, and the finish line is weeks away. Do I have it in me to work at this another two years?

But it's not just about me.

A fourfold increase matters a ton for employees. If we do the IPO in a few weeks, some of our long-term customer service agents—who are now earning just under $50,000 a year—will get payouts of over $20,000 to $30,000. But if we do the merger, odds are, that number will be over $100,000. And for the early employees the numbers are even bigger. It's the difference between three early employees becoming millionaires versus *twenty* of them becoming millionaires. Ultimately, the merger would be the best thing for the employees.

Success means different things for different constituencies. An IPO now is good for some of them: myself and restaurants (assuming our mission statement stays the same through a GrubHub-only IPO). An IPO later is better for employees and investors. But, with Seamless's private equity and corporate owners, I worry that profits will take precedence over customers.

So, do I stick to my goal—helping independent restaurants—and cost my employees significant money and opportunity, or do I choose the "greater" good (at least as my employees might see it) and merge?

In my heart, the choice is clear: I want GrubHub to do its own IPO, with no merger. Two of the other board members agree with my logic, and they tell me so, privately. That means I've got three of six board votes. That's enough to block a merger.

But in my head, I just can't ignore the fact that my employees will get a massive cash payout if we do the merger. All of these people that I've spent the last decade working shoulder to shoulder with. I want to do right by them. In the end, it's this argument that swings me.

Dang it!

I throw up the white flag and say I won't resist a merger.

We scrap the IPO, and merge with Seamless.

Well, almost. There are a few shit shows to navigate first.

Day 8. Mile 464.

I reach the town of Draper, Virginia, early in the morning of my eighth day on the trail. The main drag features a quaint little gathering of shops, B&Bs, and eateries nestled right up against the river. Everything here is fresh and well-maintained, a sharp contrast to the dilapidated feel of the last few places I blew through. But as ever, I've only got a few minutes to decide if it's worth stopping for a look around before it, too, like so many other towns, will be behind me.

I'm starting to recognize a pattern. More than half the towns I ride through have a sameness to them. The same strip malls. The same Walmart. The same Chili's and Dollar General. There's not much to distinguish Virginia Beach from Mechanicsville from Richmond. The sameness leeches the vibrancy of these towns. Sure, they're prosperous enough, but, to my eyes at least, they feel like America in grayscale. The magenta ink has all run out.

But then, a few of them are different. I'm not sure why. But the downtown is saturated with color. Mineral was like that. As Draper unfolds around me, I get the sense this place is the same way. There will be a craft fair or parade, or a fun run every weekend of the summer.

What's the difference? Is it geography? Close proximity to a national park? Sufficient distance from an interstate? Is it the local Rotary Club, or a single proud individual? I can't tell yet, but I'm keenly interested in observing this over the next few months. It's a subject that's near and dear to my heart: the independent restaurants on GrubHub have always been the flavor, the spice. Taco Bell? Not so much, on the flavor.

I'm leaning toward stopping for a spell, but before my decision is made, a driver flags me down, leaning out of his beaten-up pickup truck. So far, encounters between me on a bike and a driver leaning out of a pickup truck have not been entirely positive. More times than you'd imagine, there's something thrown at me followed by raucous laughter. But before I can get too worked up, I need to remind myself that I'm trying to leave these snap judgments behind.

"You riding the TransAm?" the guy asks.

"I sure am."

So far so good.

"That's a sweet ride," using the kind of praise guys save for a tricked-out Harley.

"I'm Thomas," he says.

"Hi, Thomas, I'm Mike."

I already like this guy; a tiny lesson learned.

"I rode the TransAm a couple years ago," Thomas says. "Changed my life."

"Does it get any easier?"

"It does. Nice work getting this far, you're about an eighth of the way through."

This raises my spirits. With all my worrying about my hamstring and woolgathering about the Walmartification of America, I hadn't paused to reflect on what I've accomplished. I've already ridden from the coast past the highest point in the Appalachians, 408 miles, according to my odometer. Pride and joy bubble up in me, lighting up my face with a silly grin.

"I loved my ride so much that I opened up a bike shop on the other end of town, right on the route," Thomas proudly announces. "Come on down, I'll check out your bike for you, free of charge."

The Junction Bike Shop in Draper is half decked out in old-timey antiques, and half dedicated to serious bike equipment. Out front there are a couple of Adirondack rockers perched on a wide porch. Since this is a small town, off the beaten path, Thomas sells a half dozen brands of unrelated things, hoping to appeal to anybody who happens to be driving through: "Life is Good" T-shirts, Melissa and Doug toys, fishing rods and bait, bags of ice.

I waddle in, a bit bowlegged after days in the saddle.

"You winced as you were getting off the bike there," Thomas says, concerned. "You OK? Want some Advil?"

"Thanks. Hamstring is bothering me. I hoped it would get better by now."

"You had a rest day, yet?"

"I took an easy day in Christiansburg, back on the east side of the ridge," I say, remembering the relief of stopping early, and the dread of starting the next day.

"Christiansburg is *hilly*. Did you plan the rest day, or did you collapse?" This is a damn good question—perhaps I should be more strategic about this whole thing.

"Collapse, actually. How the heck did you know that? Christiansburg was a disaster. I walked four hills that day, eventually tapping out at a diner, well short of noon, and then walking my bike over to a motel. That was only day five. I thought I would be in better shape by now."

"You haven't had a rest day," Thomas says, clearly from hard-earned experience. "A low mileage day doesn't count. Calling it quits early because you're exhausted doesn't count. You need a *pre-planned* zero day—absolutely no miles. I know what I'm talking about. I was ten days in when I had my collapse, and it almost ended my ride. Most TransAmers who come through here are chasing miles. Wrong way to do it—you need to take it easy, especially in the beginning. Every fifth day should be a zero day, until you get to the Plains."

I think he's hit on something here. I've been chasing miles, like he said, trying to get to the next town before I stop each evening. Stretching out the distance between breaks. Why? It's not like I've got a tight deadline or anything. I'm unemployed, after all. But I'm not totally convinced. It isn't easy to just change because someone tells me I should.

"Sure, maybe I should take it a little easier," I allow. "But I think slow and steady wins the race, right? This zero-day concept seems a bit extreme."

"You're tired. Bone tired. You're not making good decisions, and if you don't take a zero day then you're going to end up quitting the trail. I bet some of the folks you met on crazyguyonabike have already quit, right?"

"Yeah. Two of them actually." I probably know he's right; I just don't *want* him to be. I like being an overachiever. It's my jam.

"If you're not careful, you'll be next. Especially with an injury. Zero day means no walking, either. Pick a boring town. Watch TV all day. Don't even leave the hotel room. Order food if you can. There is this cool app you can use called GrubHub. It's great. You can order without calling."

"You don't say," I say.

Thomas narrows his eyes at me for an uncomfortably long time before deciding that he's said his peace. Smartly, he changes the subject, looking down at the bike.

"I've never seen a titanium 'bent," he coos. "This thing is *amazing*. I can't believe how light it is."

On this, Thomas and I wholeheartedly agree.

Thomas proceeds to clean and oil the enormously long chain. He checks the head tube for play, and nods, satisfied. He adjusts the front fender and windshield, after diagnosing that they are rubbing slightly. Finally, he peers at the rear wheel and checks the brakes.

Nothing good comes after a mechanic either whistles or takes a sharp intake of breath. Thomas goes with a whistle.

I'm protective of my steed. I don't like that whistle.

"You've chewed through all the pads," he says. "It's nearly down to metal on metal. Lemme guess—you rode the brakes all the way down from the Blue Ridge to Vesuvius. Man, you've got to *pump* the brakes, not ride them. They get too hot if you ride them."

Thomas points out to a part.

"See that?"

I nod. The nod is a lie. I have no idea what he's pointing at. He can tell

I'm lying, so he grabs a pencil and points to something. Even I can see that it doesn't look quite right.

"You melted part of the caliper housing," he says. "Right here. I've never seen this. This is steel. How hot did it get?"

"Pretty hot, apparently." I don't know whether to be proud or embarrassed, so I'm both.

"Well, it's misshapen, but I think it can be salvaged. Let me file it down for you. Otherwise, you won't be able to adjust it as the pads wear over the next few thousand miles."

Thomas gets me a coffee before getting back to work. He tells me to sit down. He won't take no for an answer.

It does feel pretty good to sit down.

An hour later I leave Thomas's shop happy and refreshed. The 'bent is refreshed, too, so I'm feeling more confident. I make my way out of the river valley and begin the ascent into the town of Wytheville, Virginia, just shy of halfway between Roanoke and the Cumberland Gap, where Tennessee, Virginia, and Kentucky come together.

The ride up into town almost kills me.

By 10:00 a.m., the temperature has passed 90 degrees and it's still climbing. My legs feel like jelly. My cotton shirt is completely soaked through, and I'm wondering if the MAMILs might have been on to something with all their Lycra and spandex. I stop repeatedly, trying to regain some strength. But soon the stops get longer, the pedaling shorter. I walk my bike up insignificant hills. I stop for breakfast. Nothing helps.

It takes six hours to make the twenty-one miles from Draper to Wytheville.

Six. Hours.

I'm a blown horse as I walk into town. The idea of setting up a tent sounds like too much effort, so I head for the Comfort Inn. But even getting into the lobby is pure torture—by now, the back of my leg is in grinding, tearing agony. I pause short of the front door, hand on the wall, gasping in pain.

I need to get to a bed and rest. I straighten my back, slowly and deliberately. The pain shoots up and down my spine, from my knee to my neck.

Slowly, I shuffle toward the front desk.

"Hi, I'd like a room. Nonsmoking. Something on the ground floor, so I can roll my bike in without trying to fit it in the elevator, if you have it, please."

"How long will you be staying?"

I think about tomorrow's ride. My plan is for eighty miles. I doubt I can do twenty; I'm not sure I can do two. Then, after tomorrow, more miles. Thousands of them.

I can't do it.

It hits me like a brick. I'm lonely, tired, and injured. I'm not any more patient, peaceful, or Zen than when I started. I'm just tired. I am not a big deal. I'm just done.

I. Am. Done.

"Just one night," I say.

Tomorrow, I'll book a flight home. I just need to figure out if a cab can get me from wherever the hell I am to wherever I can fly from. I'll just leave the bike outside. Maybe I'll call Thomas and tell him he can drive up here and grab it. Hell, maybe I'll just toss it in the dumpster. Whatever. I'm rich now, anyway.

This bike trip was a terrible mistake.

————

Collapsed on the bed in the hotel room, I call Christine back in Chicago.

"I quit. I'm coming home," I whisper.

"You should give it another day," Christine says.

"I'm just so tired; I can't make it. I only rode twenty-five miles, and it took the whole day."

"But you haven't taken a rest day," she says.

"That's what the guy at the bike shop said." I tell her about Thomas and my conversation with him. I can almost hear her nodding along through the phone.

"Well, it doesn't make much of a difference if you come home tomorrow or the next day," she says, making perfect sense. "Why not do what he says and see how you feel?"

"Because I miss you, and I'm exhausted." I choke on my words, shame, loneliness, and frustration overwhelming me.

"Aw, that's sweet. I miss you too. But you'll be a nightmare if you come home early. You're so hard on yourself, and you'd regret giving up for years," she says.

"Thanks?" I say, seeing myself in a way that Christine always makes clear. Sometimes uncomfortably so.

"Look, you made it over the hardest part east of the Rockies, right? It's only a few weeks until you get to Wichita, and then we'll meet up. At least get to the halfway point—you can always quit there if you like. Then, if you ever want to do the second half, it's an obvious place to pick up the trail. You're always talking about the difference between quitting and giving up, and how quitting is good. What do you think this is?"

Thinking about the thousands of miles on the other side of a rest day, it hurts to admit she's right.

I say, "Giving up. You're right. This is giving up. I still want to accomplish the thing I set out to do. My goal hasn't changed. I'm just tired and moody."

We talk for another hour. Christine leads me like a skittish horse back to the idea of just taking an extra day off. I know she's right—if I quit this trip, I'll regret it for a long time.

I make a final whine, just to keep up appearances.

"I really don't want to."

"Suck it up, buttercup," Christine says, deftly combining mocking with encouragement, as she damn well knows will work on me. "You can quit in two days. Not now."

"Whatever. You're the worst."

She's the worst. She's not, but she is.

"I love you too," she says, smartly ignoring the little tired boy in me. "Talk to you tomorrow."

If I'm going to do this, I should wholly commit to this zero-day concept, I guess. That means no walking, which was a bit of a shame, as I got the sense on my miserable ride into Wytheville that it was quite a nice town and had a lot to offer. But I turn my back on it, spending the whole next day in bed, binge watching *Entourage* on HBO on my Mac Air.

Entourage stands for everything that I strive not to be. It's shallow, sexist, and materialistic, so it was the perfect thing to watch to remind myself who I don't want to be. Other than learning *that*, I accomplish nothing all day. I don't check email. I call no one; I don't read. Even visits to the bathroom are postponed for as long as my bladder will allow.

I order Domino's. Domino's! This is not so different from Bill Gates using a Mac.

But hey, it's pretty good!

This day off turned out to be profound. Shockingly. I wasn't looking for an epiphany. I wasn't seeking some fundamental change to my character. I wasn't seeking some learning or lesson.

But never before had I so perfectly accomplished nothing, and never since have I been so perfectly idle. I find stillness to be basically impossible. Even on vacation, I have an unshakable need to do something each day—a hike, a swim, a round of golf. As an avid reader, and enthusiastic introvert, Christine can't fathom this at all—she's forever shooing me out the door just so she can get some peace. In fact, this three-month bike trip is, from her perspective, an extended opportunity to read a good book or ten.

I just took a day off—from the TransAm, yes, but also from my life. In many ways, the TransAm and my life is split into before the zero day, and after. I can't say that I went so far as to live in the present and exist in a state of mindfulness. (I was, after all, watching *Entourage*, and that would be a big stretch.) But I do think that this perfectly idle day set me up nicely for being open to stillness. It's subtle and it slips through my fingers, both at the time and looking back at it. But doing nothing is important, sometimes. The more nothing, the more important.

Just shy of forty-eight hours from checking in, I awake refreshed. My quads feel like solid tree trunks. My energy is a deep well of untapped potential. My hamstring doesn't feel the slightest twinge of discomfort—all the tightness in my back has released too. I'm happy and excited to get pedaling. If the weather matches my mood, it will be the most perfect spring day outside.

And with that, in Wytheville, Virginia, I unquit the bike ride.

I now have a new rule for the rest of the trip, and maybe for the rest of my life: Don't give up the trip at the end of a hard day. If I'm going to quit, it needs to be when I'm rested, well-fed, and thinking clearly. If I still want to bail first thing in the morning, after a couple days' long rest, then so be it.

This rule is important. It has a razor's edge, cutting cleanly between the difference of reacting to something being difficult versus an intentional choice. There are a few others that have been swimming past my brain as I've ridden all these miles.

Mike's Rules for Hard Things:

One: Hard things are hard.

Two: Hard things have consequences.

Three: Hard things have big rewards.

Four: Don't give up hard things at the end of a long day. Wait until morning.

Five: Hard things become easier with a vision, or goal.

Number five is the main thing I learned through starting GrubHub, growing it to be truly gargantuan, losing control of it, and then doing the bike ride. But all this philosophizing won't make a recumbent bicycle move through time and space. That requires pedaling.

Outside the hotel, of course it's true that the weather does not even remotely match my internal sunshine. The sky is heavy and leaden, filled with a coming massive storm. The forecast includes phrases like "heavy rain, thunderstorms, and flash flood watch." I briefly wonder what happens when a bike gets hit by a flash flood, then I put it out of my mind. I consider hiding out in the hotel for another day, but I'm just bursting with too much energy.

I ride into the storm.

A few miles out, it's as if Zeus *himself* declares war upon my journey. The sky is rent asunder with peals of lightning and drenching sheets of rain. It rains cats and dogs. I am catted. I am dogged. The deluge makes a mockery of my REI jacket's taped seams. The padded seat, which to date has been such a source of comfort, becomes little more than a sponge. Things chafe. Things that ought not to chafe. No matter. I pedal onward. Rain or shine, the crank doesn't turn itself.

12

Odd Couple

We've announced the merger publicly. But the red tape is endless. Every night, I grind my teeth in frustration at delays in starting the merger. I'm filled with impotent rage. There's simply nothing I can do to speed things along.

The New York Attorney General (AG) has objected to the merger. From the government's perspective, Seamless creates unfair contracts, which limit restaurants from working with multiple order providers, and to their eyes, this has created an unfair competitive environment. The worst part is—I agree with them. Seamless's contracts are not just unfair, they are bad business. Why limit a restaurant's options with an impossible to enforce contract, instead of earning their loyalty by performing? But even though the combined company is perfectly willing to scrap the contracts, it's not that easy. The merger is a great moment for the AG to be seen to be doing something. In other words, they're grandstanding.

The AG's activity has, in turn, nabbed the attention of two other antitrust agencies—the Federal Trade Commission (FTC) and the Justice Department. Apparently, a twelve-year-old company with less than 1 percent market share can still be held up for antitrust approval.

The Seamless and GrubHub lawyers suggest that one of the ways to make this go away is to hire a recent, very high-level, employee at the FTC, in the hopes that he'll be able to tell his former subordinates to back down. Apparently, this is all totally normal—the man is, in fact, an employee at a law firm that has him on staff to be available *for this exact purpose*. This seems shady as shit to me, but the only other person who seems bothered by this is Jonathan, the CEO at Seamless. Our lawyers say this happens all the time, and our objections are patronizingly shunted aside. But they don't actually tell me the *name* of the person involved, so clearly, they had some hang-ups about this approach too. It's a moot point in the end because it fails spectacularly. The FTC tells their former colleague to go suck a lemon.

Accordingly, it takes *half a year* to get through antitrust approval. The thing that finally gets us a nod has nothing to do with the millions we spend on law firms either—Yelp ends up buying a minor competitor of ours, Eat24Hours. The Yelp/Eat24Hours company will have less than 5 percent of our orders—to put it in perspective, Domino's, Pizza Hut, and Jimmy John's combined have over twenty times our orders. From an antitrust perspective, the whole thing is just ridiculous.

It only gets worse.

The antitrust process is required by law to make a ruling by a certain date after the application, otherwise the merger is approved by default. The regulators admit that they intend to approve the merger, but not before the deadline. Therefore, since they won't be ready in time, they are going to deny the application unless we withdraw our intent to merge and refile, thereby paying the hundreds of thousands in filing fees and attorney fees all over again and resetting the clock.

They do this regularly, to maximize fees, so I'm told.

I tell our lawyers to call their bluff; our lawyers, in turn, call my bluff, choosing instead to listen to the Justice Department. Ugh. Lawyers.

Eventually, after months of delay and millions in expenses, we get the nod and the merger of the two companies is a go.

Now, we actually need to combine the two separate entities into a single functioning unit, before starting up the IPO process a second time. Because I want this done yesterday, I volunteer to run the merger.

———

I'm in charge of the merger. And I'm *excited*.

Why am *I* running this merger? Is it my boundless experience in this kind of thing? Nope. I've never led a merger. I've never even been in a company where a merger has happened. I don't have a business degree, and I've never sat through a class that addressed the topic even tangentially.

Over the course of six months of delay, I have spent a lot of time thinking about mergers. I read articles and books. I have talked to people who have run successful mergers. I've also talked to people who have run unsuccessful mergers.

Here's what I learned: The best way to mess up a merger is by *not* making decisions. The success of this activity will have little to do with being correct, but everything to do with *decisiveness*. Change like this is uncomfortable. We're messing with people's livelihoods, and, in most cases, they won't get much say about that change. This is especially true when it comes to employees whose positions are redundant in the combined company. The reality is there's just no need for two vice presidents (VPs) of business development, for example. It's better to be decisive and clear about this reality rather than muddle through in a misguided attempt to spare somebody's feelings.

The problem with this approach is that the person driving it is guaranteed to be hated. Which is why I'm perfect for the job. I'm going to leave after this merger, and then the subsequent IPO. I don't care who hates me if it means I can make this process go faster. So, I volunteer to run the merger, and both Matt and the Seamless leadership quickly step aside, perfectly happy to let me be the scapegoat for wildly unpopular decisions.

This is going to be fun.

The law firm of Kirkland and Ellis have granted me the use of their executive board room, free of charge, to kick off the merger. (Free, that is, if you ignore the $4 million in fees they rack up between the merger approval, reorganization, and two preparations for going public.)

Every department in GrubHub has its mirror at Seamless. We have two marketing departments, two sales groups, two service teams. In every case, those two groups need to become one. Sitting on top of each department is a leader, usually with a VP title. We don't need two VPs of marketing. So, out of forty executives, twenty are getting either demoted or canned. Ouch.

In preparation for this meeting, I've had each executive submit a one-page document describing their plans to merge the teams. All of those were collected into a booklet and sent out to the entire group. Using these documents, Matt, Jonathan, and I have decided who is going to lead each group. This homework assignment is a wonderfully efficient way to get everyone to dislike me from the word *go*. This strategy is not so different from a scene from the movie *Office Space*, wherein two outside consultants swagger in and make every employee reinterview for their job.

Making tough decisions isn't just for everyone else. Matt, Jonathan, and I did among ourselves too. Matt will be CEO; Jonathan, the former CEO of Seamless, will be president. That doesn't leave a lot of room for me, but everyone knows that after the IPO, I'll be gone. I take the chief operating officer title, hoping that I'm the COO of a public company for something short of a week before I peace out.

———

Since I'm the bad cop in this scenario, I communicated all the bad news yesterday, so it wouldn't be a surprise coming into this first combined meeting. The demoted employees have been invited to the meeting. The terminated ones have not.

I have arrived early to mentally prepare. The only other person in the room is a server setting up coffee service and pastries. I choose to take an everything bagel with barely enough garlic and salt to earn the name. It's delicious. (It may be apparent, at this point, that I truly love a good everything bagel. But what's less clear is that I also love a *bad* everything bagel. As long as a circular piece of bread is boiled, salted, and garlicked, even half-heartedly, it's fine by me.) I chew slowly on this mediocre bagel, waiting for my merger kickoff to start. I'm impatient to begin. Hell, I'm impatient to be done. I'm prepared to be merciless in making this thing happen *fast*.

The room fills by 9:00 a.m., and once everyone settles down, the GrubHubbers—who are familiar with the "put your thoughts on a single piece of paper and read at the start of the meeting" thing I do—open binders and begin reading. Seeing their new colleagues dive in with no instruction, about half the Seamlessians follow suit.

"I'm not sure this is the best way to start out the conversation," James Hwang, the head of customer care for Seamless, says. "Maybe we should make introductions."

"We've had nine months of delicate conversations," I say, "all the while under a legal restriction prohibiting us from getting into the meat of our plans while we waited for regulators to give us the green light on the merger. It's been the corporate equivalent of almost a year of small talk. Most of us are ready to get into the real planning, so I've decided to skip the icebreakers and introductions for this meeting and get right to it."

Fair to say that didn't exactly go how James hoped—he looks to Jonathan, his former CEO, for support, but Jonathan is already reading, scribbling notes as he goes. With that, the insurrection over before it even begins, everyone gets down to reading. It feels a bit like high school study hall. The quiet stretches for about half an hour before whispered conversations over muffins escalate to the point of distraction.

I say, "OK, thanks everyone for taking the time to write these and read them. Let's jump in with marketing. Mandy?"

Mandy Pekin, GrubHub's head of marketing, starts.

"As you can see in my straw man plan, we're going to keep all the brands: GrubHub, Seamless, Campusfood, menupages.com, and allmenus.com. But we're only going to spend brand advertising dollars against the Grub-Hub brand. In Manhattan, we'll do performance marketing against the Seamless website, but we won't be spending to increase brand equity."

This is marketing-speak for, "We're going to kill the Seamless brand eventually, but use it until we do so."

"But what about the upcoming campaigns we're already planning on?" a concerned Seamless employee asks.

"We're going to start from the assumption that everything is canceled," Mandy says, "and then go through each initiative on a case-by-case basis."

And just like that, the first real decisions are being made. This is the first step in building momentum to overcome the status quo. This is a new company and needs to be run with that in mind.

From marketing, we move on to customer service.

"Customer service will report to me," I announce. "Over the next few months, I'll be transitioning the Seamless departments to report to the GrubHub team. I expect this will create some redundancies in the Seamless structure. We're planning on offering significant severance packages."

The meeting goes on in this vein for about six hours. Various leaders present their plans. Other leaders voice anxiety. Mostly, tough decisions get made. In a few cases, we can't avoid kicking the can down the road, even with me pushing for decisions. The back and forth becomes routine, and eventually, I stop doing the pushing, as others take up the theme. By the end of the day, I'm dying of boredom. Which, when I think about it, is the best possible outcome.

———

Jonathan finds a chain Tex-Mex restaurant on the outskirts of Salt Lake City (SLC) for us all to have some downtime after a long day of meetings at the Seamless customer service offices nearby. Of the twenty local managers and executives we invited, exactly zero have shown up, leaving just the teams that traveled here from New York and Chicago to sip on margaritas and get to know each other. I sit across from Jonathan and start chatting.

"Should I be worried that nobody else showed up?" I ask.

"No, this is pretty normal. Almost all the employees here are strict Mormons and have a deep commitment to family time. They never do any activities after work hours. Though, whenever we do weekend picnics with families, almost everyone attends."

"Oh. How do you think today went?"

"Pretty good. Obviously, everyone is worried about change. There's a lot of skepticism about GrubHub's customer service software. The people here seem to appreciate your directness, but I don't think you'll ever be close friends with any of them."

"Yeah, I get the sense there's a much stronger sense of hierarchy here than I'm used to."

"How about you, how do you think today went?" he asks me.

"Honestly, it was brutal. Eight hours of meetings. My brain is fried. Back when I started GrubHub, and first started having employees, I'd always be annoyed at meetings because they got in the way of work. But then, slowly, without me noticing, meetings went from being an interruption of work to being the *actual* work that I do. I'm not cut out to be a bigwig executive. I just can't sit still that long."

"I'm surprised. You seem like you were in your element today."

"Oh, don't get me wrong. I'm *good* at meetings. In fact, it's because I hate them. I'm always trying to keep them short, because I want to *leave*."

"Is that why you're so ready to move on from the company? Boredom?"

"I mean, it's not usually boring these days. Things are moving quickly with the merger. I get to fly out here. I'm sticking around for the weekend to go skiing. And now we're talking over drinks, which is great. But, yes, around two o'clock today, I was seriously daydreaming about quitting."

"Well, please don't," he says, "there's a lot of hard work left."

I hesitate before bringing up a sensitive topic. But then I remember my rule not to sugarcoat anything. No time like the present.

I say, "Jonathan, we need to make a tough decision. GrubHub's software is just so much more efficient. We get less than a tenth of the phone calls that Seamless does for customer service issues, since we handle so much with text messages. And most of those are automated. We probably don't need more than fifty of the two hundred fifty employees here. And honestly, we could make up that gap in the Chicago office pretty easily. We need to shut down this office."

He nods, looking at his drink.

He says, "Yeah, you're not wrong. But it sucks. We already told these people their jobs are safe."

"And we thought they were, when we said it. But the more I learn, the harder it is to justify keeping the office open. And nothing I saw today changed my mind."

"Yeah, I can see that. But it sucks."

I can see that he's really upset by this. I'm upset by it too. Back when I wanted to get a pizza and started coding up a delivery guide, I had no idea that it would set me on a path where I'd end up firing hundreds of people. The very idea of it is nauseating.

"Look, I think we can soften the blow."

Jonathan says, "Big severance packages, and accelerate the stock options so they can still benefit from the IPO."

"Yeah, that's exactly what I was going to say. The board won't like it, but if we present a united front, they'll approve it."

"Yeah, I'm good with that."

"Also, I put out some feelers. You know Thumbtack?"

"Isn't that a website that does leads for handymen and yoga and stuff?"

"Yeah. Bill heard through the grapevine that they are looking to expand with a new customer service location. He put me in touch with their founder. I asked them if they'd be interested in hiring our customer service team and taking over our office lease here. It looks like they might be."

"That's amazing. So, we wouldn't have to fire anyone here."

"Well, no. It's not like we can just sell their employment. We'd still need to fire everyone, but it will be a much easier message to say we also found them all new jobs if they are interested."

Our sidebar conversation is interrupted as other colleagues show up. Todd Provino, GrubHub's head of customer service, slides into the booth. Karen Miller, Seamless's head of HR, arrives as well. Surprisingly, a few of the customer service managers from the SLC office show up too. Which is a bit awkward, given the conversation I just had with Jonathan.

Jonathan brings everyone into the conversation with an icebreaker.

"So, Mike, do you have any kids?"

"Not yet. Christine and I have been hoping to adopt. Been waiting for just under a year now."

"How about you?"

"Yeah…" he says, and shares about his family. The rest of the team joins in, talking about their kids. There's no more work talk. The margaritas are tangy, and the queso dip is spicy.

Later, in the parking lot, Jonathan approaches me.

"I'm so sorry about that, Mike. I shouldn't have put you on the spot like that for such a sensitive topic."

I laugh. "Don't sweat it. I wasn't even aware it was a sensitive topic. No big deal."

"You sure?" he asks.

"Yeah, seriously, I don't mind talking about adoption or the process at all. It didn't bother me."

As I drive away, I reflect on how much I like Jonathan. He's genuine, caring, and thoughtful. And for that matter, I like the whole Seamless team. One of the things that really strikes me about them is that they've been solving the exact same problems I've been trying to solve for the last decade. We have tons in common. It's true that we've always been closer to being friends than enemies, as we had assumed.

Which is another good reason why the first rule of mergers is "Don't be an asshole."

I stop early today, rolling into the charming little town of Paducah, nestled at the junction of the Tennessee and Ohio rivers, which then flow downstream to join the Mississippi. This town is a gateway, sitting as it does at the intersection of the Midwest, South, and West. River transport, railroads, and interstates make it the biggest transportation hub that nobody has heard of. In early United States history, it represented the extreme western end of the country, sitting halfway up the mighty river between New Orleans and Chicago.

The sun approaches high noon, and the heat starts climbing. The motel I pick out isn't ready for me yet, so I decide to walk around, too itchy with energy to sit still. After a haircut, and a visit to the National Quilt Museum, it's still pretty early in the day.

Really, only one thing for it. Time to start day drinking.

I make my way to the local microbrewery, Shandies. Turns out they specialize in making shandies (shandeii?). If you haven't golfed in the Midwest, you might not be familiar with shandy. A shandy is half beer, half lemonade. The typical recipe includes too sweet lemonade mixed with too bland beer. It should taste terrible, but through some mysterious alchemy, the end result is far better than the sum of its parts. This microbrew is selling novel variations. All-natural ingredients. Various brew styles. Different types of juice. Pomegranate mango with an imperial stout? Yes, please! I order a juicy burger as well.

The drink appears. Inhaling the aromas reveals strong stout beer notes underpinned by a hint of sweet citrus. The first sip is bold and refreshing. Delightful. I foresee more of these in my near future.

I pull out the Adventure Cycling Association TransAm maps to look at what the days ahead will bring, now that I'm rejoining the official route. Since I'm not in a hurry, I read the flavor text too.

In 1976, a group of enthusiasts of the newly popular concept of bikepacking organized a ride across America to celebrate the 200th anniversary of the Declaration of Independence. They dubbed it the Bikecentennial. It took years of fundraising, getting the word out, route planning, and most importantly, convincing farmers, churches, and VFWs to let thousands of cyclists stay on their land to make the ride a reality.

By the time the ride started, forty full-time staff were on board, working on that inaugural ride for four thousand riders. It was a tremendous feat of passion, logistics, and fundraising. Since they seemed to have a good thing going, the group organized into the Adventure Cycling Association (ACA). Along its sponsored routes, the ACA advocates for safe roads: broad shoulders free of rumble strips and cleaned of debris. They also promote lodging, services, and try to discourage heavy industry along the route, especially the opening of new quarries and mines, with their attendant killer dump trucks. Their maps do a great job of promoting local eateries, campsites, B&Bs, hostels, churches, and bike shops.

In addition to maps for the self-supported rider, they provide guides for organized rides. These appeal to hundreds of riders each year who would prefer to ride in a group, or simply would rather rely on experts for navigation and logistics. The consistency of these guided tours goes a long way to convincing churches, barns, schools, and farms to keep their spaces open and available for long-haul cyclists. Even though I'm forging my own path, I've benefited greatly from these guided groups.

There are also tours that recognize the reality of different ability levels, often shorter than a coast-to-coast trip, with support vans and accommodations for people of all physical abilities. When I tell strangers that they, too, can do a big touring ride, much of my confidence comes from this work the ACA does.

Since their founding, the ACA has created about twenty routes, but there are four that come up most often among tourers: three east-west routes, and one north-south. The Northern Tier is an east-west route tracking through the Pacific Northwest, around the Great Lakes, and into New England. The Southern Tier meanders through the Deep South, Texas, and the Southwest deserts. The Great Divide Mountain Bike Route is a bit of insanity starting in the Canadian Rockies and heading all the way south to the Mexican border along unpaved roads and single track.

The gem of the ACA's network is the TransAm. The TransAm goes straight across the middle of the country until it hits the Rockies, then zigzags up toward Canada, eventually swerving over to the coast through Oregon.

It's hard to say how many people complete the trip every year. (I asked the ACA—frankly, they shrugged.) From what I can tell from blogs, crazyguyonabike.com, guest books at diners, and chatter between cyclists, I estimate that about three to four hundred of us do this every year. About two-thirds of us go east to west, and one-third the opposite. That equates to about one cyclist per day going through any given town, leading to a not unfair supposition that TransAm cyclists should rarely meet. This might be true if the rides happened across the span of one full year—the reality is, the time frame for starting is compressed, with a window for leaving Virginia on the east-west jaunt somewhere between mid-May and mid-June. Any earlier, and you can hit snows in the Rockies; any later, and it becomes a slog through brutal heat, humidity, and mosquito bites. This tight starting window condenses the numbers and means that the daily tally of riders I tend to bump into is closer to five.

After the third shandy, my reading about the TransAm becomes more labored. I decide to embrace a guilty pleasure by ordering a second burger to go, getting a couple more canned shandies, and stumbling back to the motel to pass out watching more *Entourage*. This works out exactly as one would expect: I pass out early, and wake up with a nasty headache.

On the way out of town, I stop in at the gas station to grab a couple of Gatorades. A woman is standing by the stacked firewood. She's smoking a cigarette and drinking Mountain Dew. She nods and starts in.

"Nice ride," she says. "That some kind of Harley?"

"Nope. Just a bicycle. A little weirdly shaped."

"Where you headed?"

"Pacific Ocean."

"No kidding."

She takes a determined drag of a cigarette and says, "I wish I could do something like that."

"You can," I say.

"No, you see, I got my son to care for..."

Her son has developmental challenges. Her boyfriend is a creep. Her boss? Always on her case. She wanted to be an astronaut, then she tells me about her new hopes—they've been stamped, shrunk, and squished into little things until they're much smaller than astronaut dreams, but they are still dreams. Each one holds a teaspoon of hope.

And I do something I'd never done before zero day. I do nothing. I don't have an agenda. I don't have a place to be. I sit, listen, and hear her for as long as she needs to talk. It goes on for about an hour. I don't interrupt. She cries a couple times.

My evangelical upbringing makes me want to pray for her, so I do, silently. If prayer works, then it works in quiet stillness just as well as in flashy, flowing words. I pray that her new dreams can un-squish a little. Maybe they can overflow the teaspoon—maybe one day they could even fill a tablespoon, a cup, or an otherwise empty swimming pool.

I hope that happens. Because if her hopes keep getting compressed, they will disappear, obliterated by the pressures of living.

The woman asks for a hug, and I give her one. But I've got no place to be, so I just hold on until she's ready to let go. It gets uncomfortable; then it gets comfortable. Then she's done, and she's on her way and I'm biking west.

Since zero day, something fundamental changed in me. No longer addicted to the big mileage, I go as far as I feel like, and I don't push it. And what happens when I do that is I meet more people, people who are lonely to make a human connection, no matter how transient. Like all people.

I've got time.

Piles of time. A Scrooge McDuck bank of the stuff.

Time to listen.

So, at gas stations, diners, and campsites I talk. For hours.

This time, it's a young police officer that waves me down.

"Hey there," he says, amiably. "You doing OK? You lost?"

The sun passed noon hours ago, it hangs heavy and smoldering in the sky to the west.

"Nope," I say, slowing to a halt. "Sun's right there. Riding toward that."

"No kidding. How far?"

"To the end. The Pacific."

The cop looks at me incredulously, and whistles through his teeth.

"Wow, I wish I could do that."

"You can."

I've decided to say this to everyone on the hope that someday, someone will take me up on it.

"But I really can't..." he says, and then sets into talking. He's on duty and he's got places to be, so the officer doesn't talk as long as the woman at the gas station. But he unburdens just as honestly as she did. He tells me about his troubled marriage and trying to be a good person. He genuinely wants to help people, but all too often he's viewed with suspicion and fear. He's vulnerable. He laments that sometimes people have good reason to be fearful of a police officer, but still.

I don't solve any of his problems, but I don't need to. I'm just here to listen.

And then I'm on my way again, ever westward through all these towns, all these lives.

A bit later, I meet yet another version of the woman at the gas station and the police officer. This time, it's a thirteen-year-old boy in overalls, a checkered blue shirt, and suspenders, who is himself pedaling down the long lane leading up to what I presume is the farmhouse where he lives. He pulls in beside me, matching my speed.

"Howdy, mister!" he says, as easy as all that.

"How's your day going?" I say.

"Pretty swell," the boy says, with feeling. "Got to go feed the pigs."

"Pigs, huh?"

"Yeah, our farm is on both sides of the road here, and I like to get 'em fed right after lunch, or I get too sleepy," he says, riding alongside me as though we've known each other forever.

We ride silently for another quarter mile. I'm in listening mode, waiting for whatever he has to say. He's comfortable with silence, so it's just the familiar sound of bike cranks turning for a spell.

"That's a lot of gear you got stowed there," the boy says, eventually. "Where ya headed?"

"Pacific Ocean."

"No kidding! Golly, that's far!" he says, as though he's straight out of the *Wizard of Oz*.

"About three thousand miles. That way." I point ahead.

Like the cop before him, the boy whistles.

"Wish I could do that," he says, a refrain I'll hear so many times on this trip.

"You can," I say.

What would it be like for an Amish boy, just on the cusp of manhood, to contemplate riding all the way to the Pacific Ocean on that bike he's already sitting on? Is it tempting? So many people I've met and will meet on this trip love the idea, but they have responsibilities and commitments, or physical challenges, or a million other barriers.

It's easy to say, "you can." But I also realize how lucky I am.

On we chat, me and this Amish boy. He rides with me a mile. Then two. This kid has far more concerns about domesticated animals than anyone I've ever met, and eventually he yawns and says, "Well, pigs ain't gonna feed themselves!"

And with that, he turned his bike around and rides away. I never even asked his name. He is both the most innocent and oldest soul I have ever met. I hope that one day he rolls out of that farm and doesn't stop until his wheels are wet with the Pacific. I have faith he'll find someone to feed the pigs if he does.

Day after day passes like this. A week. Then two. I have become a kind of rolling confessor. People perceive that I've got nowhere to be and I'm not in a hurry to get there. They see my ridiculous bike, hear about my ridiculous trip, and decide I'm safe to talk to. I must look pretty vulnerable. Some ask me if I'm carrying a gun to protect myself and a few of those get unexpectedly angry when I say no.

What I hear through these dozens of conversations is that so many people are hurting. Sometimes it comes out as fear, anger, or occasionally even a brittle overconfident bravado. But under all of it are missed dreams, lost hopes, and a heart-wrenching loneliness. So many people are hurting.

But for all my listening to their problems, I come to understand that I am the one who's starting to heal. After all the years of high-stakes decisions, intense working relationships, fights, money, issues, emails, and meetings—after everything, I needed to get my wounds bandaged.

That's what all these strangers did for me.

Further down the TransAm, these conversations wane. At the time, I wondered if people were just different out west, but in retrospect I don't think that was it. It was that I was lonely and hurting too, and people saw that.

Just short of Wichita, the halfway mark of my cross-country ride, I find myself in a fully stocked grocery store. (Which is rarer than I expected—grocery stores tend to be near the strip malls and Jiffy Lubes, Burger Kings, and the ACA trail avoids the main roads.) It isn't open yet, so I just sit on the curb and wait, daydreaming of fresh fruit. I don't look at my phone or fidget. I just relax. Once the store opens, I head straight for the produce section. Oranges and berries and mangoes and lettuce and peppers and cucumbers and avocados. I grab an orange and smell it. The citrus tang hooks into my brain, just behind my eyeballs.

Then I start bawling. Big, embarrassing sobs.

Somehow, I kept my stuff together while acting the part of acciden-tal itinerant preacher. I listened to the deep and personal stories of total strangers. I hugged them. For long stretches. No waterworks then, not a drip.

But for some reason, this orange makes me lose my shit.

People are hurting. People just like me.

13

Compromised

It is Monday, 9:14 a.m. Exactly one hour ago, it was 9:12 a.m. Minutes take hours at the new GrubHub/Seamless. I already know that this is going to be a long day in a long week in what will be a short life. That's a lot of damn work to end up right back where I started at homefinder.com, bored with my job, and scanning for the exits.

Today, I have three meetings on my schedule. At 11:00, I'll be in the big company update meeting, where each of the departments shares its plans for the week. At 2:00, I'm going to be reviewing designs for plastic holders we're ordering for our new in-restaurant tablets. At 4:00, I'm catching up with the other five people on the executive team. The only thing I'm dreading more than each of these meetings is the long spaces of nothing in between.

It's my own damn fault, and I know it. During the tail end of running the merger, I engineered myself out of a job, knowing that I'd be leaving at the IPO. Be careful what you ask for, you just might get it. A couple years back, I was frustrated that my work had devolved into days of long meetings. Who would have thought that I'd miss those times?

With nothing better to do, I decide to walk around and talk to people.

The floor below me houses our customer service team. I head down there to see how things are going. I amble over to Peter Hammer's cubicle, one of our best customer service agents. Our friendship predates his work at GrubHub—I've known Peter almost fifteen years. Peter is just sitting down, still slightly sweaty from his own ride into work this morning.

Rather than wearing biker shorts, he's impeccably dressed, because I let him in on the secret of the lockers in the penthouse conference room.

"Hey, how are things going?" I ask.

"Pretty good. Just getting settled in." He looks at his screen. "Looks like chat is off."

That's frustrating. The online chat for the mobile app is the primary way for customers to get in touch with us. However, when we're under-staffed, the management team turns it off. I've tried a dozen times to get them to default to disabling inbound phone calls instead, sending them to voice mail. But most of the managers have come from traditional call centers and turning off the phones feels like a cardinal sin to them, even though chat is so much more efficient.

And there's exactly nothing I can do about it. They aren't my department anymore.

"Good ride this morning?"

"What?" He's already checked out of the conversation, focused on get-ting through the phone queue, so we can turn chat back on. "Oh. Yeah. Windy, though. Why is the wind always in your face on the lake path?"

"I've often wondered myself." Now, just a minute into this conversa-tion, I'm itching to leave. I feel out of place, like a stranger in the company I created. If I can't change anything, then I'm just being a pest.

I wander over toward the executive area. Todd, the head of the group, isn't in until later, but Tim Thornton, his chief lieutenant, is here.

"Hey Tim. Phones down?"

"Yeah. Since we shut down the Salt Lake City office, we just get drowned with phone calls from the Seamless orders. None of their websites or apps direct people toward chat, so we're working through the breakfast rush from New York."

Now this is something I might be able to change. I've still got a lot of pull with the software developers, not because I'm in charge of them any-more, but because I've retained some respect for having written all of the software in the first place.

However, what I can't do is go write software myself. This goes beyond the restrictions that the engineering team put on me a few years back.

Now, it's the company's auditors that prevent me from opening the hood and tinkering. The logic goes that if an executive can make changes to the software, they can easily embezzle from the company, rounding up pennies and siphoning them off to their personal bank account or some such. If I were to touch the code base, it would trigger a full technical audit of all of the code, costing weeks of productivity and a million bucks.

Technology is on the same floor as customer service, just over on the other side. It takes a few minutes to walk over there because the building occupies an entire city block. I'm still a bit surprised how big we've become. We've rented three whole floors of this building—this is a far cry from the spare bedroom in my apartment.

"Hey Jake," I say. Jake Battle was the head of GrubHub's technology group, before the merger. He has worked at GrubHub almost as long as me, as one of the first dozen employees. Nowadays he reports to his former counterpart at Seamless. He didn't love the demotion, but like every other employee in his situation, the promise of the IPO dollars is too attractive to pass up, so he has buckled down to do the work. The fact that he's a good friend makes me feel more than a little guilty about forcing the trade-off on him.

"Hey, customer service has turned the phones off. Turns out they are getting flooded with calls from Seamless customers. Is there any way we can prioritize getting the chat features more prominent on those websites?"

Jake throws up his hands in obvious frustration. "Good grief. If only you knew how hard I have been trying. I was in three meetings about this yesterday. Turns out that we can't change anything on the Seamless websites in less than six months."

"Why not? Is the technology stack all that different?"

"It's different, but that's not the problem. It's Goldman Sachs."

"What? How?"

"Back when SeamlessWeb launched, most of their customers were law firms and investment banks. Seamless was a perk—a way for all of their analysts' food. Goldman put a term in the contract that said Seamless can't change their user interface more than once every six months."

"That's crazy!"

"It gets worse. To get around it, they split their software into two versions, one for Goldman, and one for everyone else. It's so complicated that any changes to the system need to go through a specific set of software developers."

"Oh no. Don't tell me..."

"Yeah, it's the ones in Salt Lake City, who are currently without an office, since Thumbtack took over our old lease."

"So, it's going to be at least a couple of weeks until they get settled again."

"At least."

I say my goodbyes and head back up to my office. It's only been half an hour since I set out. I return frustrated and defeated. I simply can't accomplish anything useful anymore. I'm the lamest of ducks. I boot up my laptop and start up a video game, intent on burning the rest of the day.

———

Matt swings by my office sometime after 3:00. I hastily shut my laptop so he doesn't see me deeply immersed in a round of *Civilization 5*. Not that he'd care, or that I should, but it's probably best that I maintain some amount of professionalism here.

Matt is excited. He says, "I think I'm going to be able to get an exclusive contract with Yum!" Yum! Brands owns Taco Bell, KFC, and Pizza Hut.

"Wow, that's big. What terms?"

"Well, they'd get an exclusive, and in return they'd get the top listing."

"For how much?"

"Probably eight percent, maybe more."

"Matt, that's a *terrible* deal for us. Why on Earth would we sort Pizza Hut to the top, on top of all the independent restaurants, and then take *less* money from the chain than we do from the mom and pops? All the work we've done getting seventy thousand restaurants on board, and they'll drop like flies from the unfairness of it."

"People don't hate Pizza Hut, Mike."

"I don't think people hate Pizza Hut. I think that the owner of Pete's Pizza hates Pizza Hut."

"But our diners want it. And besides, Pizza Hut and Taco Bell are all over America. We're limited to the big cities and college towns. This gives us a foothold across the entire nation."

"Yes, you've got a point. Getting a base layer of restaurants across the whole country would be powerful. But this is the point I've been making for a while. We should offer our service for free. Zero percent to any restaurant that wants to sign up. Then, rely on the auction system as we add restaurants in each area. That would get us into another hundred thousand restaurants. But because of the auction system, we'd still maintain almost exactly the same revenue. If you screw with the auction system, giving chains a boost, you'll wreck the entire thing."

"But that would take years."

"Which is a feature, not a bug! If it takes us years, it will take a competitor years. I don't believe the idea that once we IPO, we'll be too big for anyone to catch up. Uber Eats and DoorDash are going to overtake us with marketing spend unless we stay unique in some way. Independent restaurants are the way to do that."

"You just hate chains."

"Of *course* I hate chains! Their food isn't as good, and they've got no character!"

"Mike, you've always had a blind spot here. People love chains because they are consistent and they're good. Pizza Hut is *comfortable*. Not everyone is a pizza snob, like you."

"It's true. I'm a pizza snob. And so are a few million of our diners. The foodies are the ones we can keep loyal, but only if we offer the best food and treat their beloved restaurants as the gems that they are. Chains dilute all of that."

"Why do you care?"

"What?"

"You're leaving. Why do you care?"

Honestly, it's a good question. It gives me pause.

"Because I think what we do makes a difference."

"Then stay. Be the chief operating officer. We'll be a better company if you do. Take a few months off. Do your bike trip. But then come back."

"Honestly, Matt. It's tempting. But I'm burnt out on this. I'm not sure I can constantly be the lone voice arguing for independent restaurants in the face of pressure for showing quarterly earnings. And the new board increasingly ignores me."

"That's bullshit and you know it," he says. "Sure, you won't win every argument. But you'll win a lot more of them if you're in the room than if you leave."

He heads out, on to his next meeting. He's not wrong. And I'm more than a little touched that he wants me to stay, even though we argue all the time. I think, in some ways, this is one of the things I'm going to miss most about GrubHub. Matt and I bicker, argue, and fight. But we also compromise. The decisions we work out together are just about always better than what either of us believes on our own.

But hard things are hard. And without a vision, they are too hard. I don't have a vision for GrubHub anymore. Without a vision for what I want the company to accomplish, I simply don't have the stamina to keep up with the constant demands of running the thing.

So, let's get this IPO done, shall we?

The lawyers are entirely caught up in the details of the corporate structure and tax implications of the IPO. One meeting in particular sticks in my mind: There were eight law firms involved—one each for Seamless, GrubHub, Aramark, venture investors, private equity investors, Seamless executives, GrubHub executives, and Citi. I total up the billable rate of all of the lawyers in the meeting and it comes to over $20,000 *per hour*.

No wonder they are dragging their feet.

A year after our aborted initial IPO, I'm not the only one getting restless. Matt's getting impatient; the Seamless team, too, is showing signs of stress; even Origin, our first investor, is getting antsy. There are at least two or three emails every day, from these various people, all asking for timing updates.

In particular, I'm becoming a bit of a pest. In board meetings and with the lawyers—I'm agitating constantly, obnoxious about it. It's not making me any friends on the newly combined board. It doesn't make the IPO process go any faster, but it does shake something loose.

Since most of the IPO shares go to big institutional investors that represent retirement and pension funds, Matt suggests, why not just sell a chunk to one of them pre-IPO? This gets everyone some cash now, without all the waiting and drama of the actual IPO. After shopping around a bit, T. Rowe Price offers to buy at $8.53 per share. It's a win-win. They get a discount from the $10 or maybe even $11 and I'll no longer have all my eggs in one basket.

I sell 400,000 shares and get a check for $3.4 million.

Fuck yeah.

I pay off all my school loans; I pay off Christine's school loans; our mortgage goes to zero; I send a check to my mom's various credit cards, her mortgage bank, and a couple payday loan sharks, wiping out all of her debt.

Heck, I even start shopping online for a sailboat on yachtworld.com. And, get this—I put a *minimum* in the search field but leave the *maximum* field empty. I do the same thing on Zillow, browsing for a ski condo. All the while I have a smile on my face, and I look around to the nonexistent audience in my office wanting to say, "Are you guys seeing this shit?" If all of this sounds fun, it's because it *is*.

And then there's the tax bill. It's not small. But I don't mind. Much.

Now, to be clear, I don't love paying taxes—who does? But—on the other hand, I couldn't have built GrubHub without all of the things that taxes pay for. Taxes pay for the workers who built the roads that delivery drivers use, taxes paid for twelve years of schools that educated all the professionals that built our software, and taxes paid the salaries of public health department workers that ensure restaurants are safe. Also, taxes made internet version 1.0. So, paying taxes seems fair to me.

But that feeling is not widely held among tech titans. Which is understandable, if unacceptable. An entrepreneur's journey begins with the unassailable belief that the world is broken in some way, and that it can be fixed. Not just that it can be fixed, but that said entrepreneur is uniquely qualified to fix it in some way that they alone have divined. Most entrepreneurs are shockingly wrong about this, and the vast majority of startups fail spectacularly. But there's a survival bias here. For the ones that *do* succeed, the founders have their exceptionalism confirmed. So, most entrepreneurs ascribe to the idea that they are self-made. There's a strong assumption that "*I did this*." That assumption gets subjected to a lot of confirmation bias as a business succeeds. It starts to feel like fact. And our popular culture celebrates and supports the idea. The American dream wants to believe in the possibility that work ethic and a clever idea can lead from rags to riches. That dream gets diluted if it depends on things like luck, or coworkers or, worst of all, *government.* Gasp!

But the self-made man (or woman) idea is bullshit. Each of us is standing on the shoulders of the giants that came before us. And it does take a village. And peace. And rule of law. And coworkers. And customers taking a chance on you. And, yes, a bit of luck.

The sum total of all of this is that I'm *theoretically* OK with paying taxes. But in *reality,* it's still uncomfortable to write a check for a million bucks to the IRS. Which is what I do. I've since learned it is atypical to drop a personal check with two commas in a blue mailbox. But Uncle Sam cashes it, all the same.

While all the internet window browsing for a vacation home and a boat were fun, I'm still close enough to the kid I was, growing up in Georgia, that it all feels a bit uncomfortable to me. I also have read enough books to know that the things we own end up owning us. So, I'm hesitant to change my lifestyle too rapidly.

Becoming suddenly wealthy is fun. Everyone should do it. But it's also scary and uncomfortable. But for all of the lack of instruction, it seems like people have a whole lot of expectations. It turns out there's not a guidebook for this. Which is why the best idea is to just shut up about it. (Which, of course, means that writing about it in a book could be a *spectacularly* bad idea.)

One thing I do know is that I want to do some good in the world, so I also create a foundation. I do this over the strong objections of the bankers at J.P. Morgan, where the deposit of several million dollars has earned me some attention. They suggest that rather than create a foundation, I should use a donor-advised fund—basically, this involves giving the bank all the money, and then politely asking them to donate it to the causes that I like, which they might just choose to do, or might not. Hard pass.

But the foundation stuff won't really go live for another year, at best. So, for now, I'm stuck sitting in my office, playing *Civilization*, feeling bored, rich, and useless.

I achieved my first goal, the one that I started with, back in the dark ages of the internet: pay off my student loans. Overshot by a bit, actually. With the loans gone, and benefiting restaurants no longer a priority for the company, I find myself asking a question: Why am I still here?

I don't need the cash. I can't steer the company, anymore. Holding out for the IPO seems like an exercise in vanity.

Honestly, I can't think of a good reason.

Fuck it.

I quit.

————

I'm in my living room, thoroughly enjoying an episode of *Survivor*, nursing a pint of Revolution Anti-Hero beer and working my way through an enormous portion of deliciously crunchy pad see ew, from Indie Café on Broadway, when Bruce Barron, from Origin Ventures, calls me about the resignation email I just sent to the board.

"Mike," he says, "I just got your email. I'm very concerned about this."

"We weren't planning on having my name on any of the IPO filings," I say, "and I wasn't going to do the road show, so I don't think it will matter. This won't have a significant impact on the IPO, or Origin's returns…"

"That's not why I called," Bruce interrupts. "I'm worried about you. What's going on? Where did this come from? Did something happen that the board should know about?"

This is a kindness, to make the call. The least I can do is be candid.

"The company is headed down a path I don't agree with," I explain. "All the talk at the board about removing all caps on our fees and creating a gig economy driver team seem like terrible ideas to me. Short-term gains, long-term losses. It's going to open up the company to competition from Uber Eats and DoorDash. And instead of doubling down on independent restaurants, Matt and the board are pushing hard on a strategy of signing up huge chains. I just can't get that excited about getting Pizza Hut another half million orders. What's the point?"

"Wouldn't you rather stay and influence it otherwise, then?" Bruce asks.

"I'm not sure it would work," I say. "The company removed Chuck from the board and replaced him with the CEO of an online payday loan company who's unlikely to throw up a red flag over the issue of exploiting restaurants."

"You agreed to that change."

"I know. And it kills me. I was wrong," I admit. "I'm not saying I'm blameless. I just made too many decisions to go back now. It's pretty clear that GrubHub is going to be one hundred percent about getting shareholder returns on a quarterly basis. There is just no appetite for doing the hard work and making long-term decisions."

"But you're walking away from almost a million dollars in options!"

"Meh," I say, and mean it. "The trade-off isn't worth it."

"What trade-off? What are you talking about?"

"The trade-off is simple: Time. Let's say I live another fifty years. One year of my life is two percent of what I've got left. If I stay for the options, will my life be two percent better? No way. It's a bad deal. I'd rather have the year."

"Mike, don't be an idiot."

I didn't realize I was being an idiot, but now I'm all ears.

"It's not about the money," Bruce continues. "How many people have founded a company and led it all the way through the IPO? You can name them: Jobs, Zuckerberg, Musk, maybe a dozen more. That's it."

"The whole reason I'm not CEO is because I wanted to leave *under* the radar," I say. "A decision you forced, by the way."

Bruce kindly ignores the jab.

"It's not about the fame," he says, "it's about how *rare* it is. It's a once in a lifetime opportunity. I've spent my whole career at Origin investing in entrepreneurs who have ideas and helping them succeed. You're *the only one* that's made it to this point. You can't just walk away!"

"Bruce, you know just how much I've put my life and marriage on hold over the last ten years. It's not like Christine and I decided not to have kids, so much as we just accidentally missed the dinner date where we were supposed to talk about it because I was too busy. I've given this company enough. It's time that I stop."

Bruce is empathetic in his response.

"If you're quitting because of your marriage, don't. Because if that's the reason you leave, it will be a problem *in your marriage* for the rest of your life. When you see Matt and the rest of them on TV, ringing the bell for the IPO, you'll be consumed by envy. You'll end up just being resentful and it will end up hurting your marriage more than helping it."

"I'm not leaving because of my marriage, it's just one factor. And I'm not leaving because I disagree with where the company is headed. In fact, I don't feel like the reasons to *leave* actually total up to a decision. The real issue is that there's no reason to *stay*. What's the point? Money? Don't need any more. Helping restaurants? The company has moved on from that goal. Fame? Vanity? The reasons get pretty thin, pretty quick."

Bruce doesn't let it go. The *Survivor* episode forgotten, I pace back and forth in my dining room, for *two hours* as, with kindness and empathy, he reasons, argues, heck he even *begs*, which is really pretty remarkable because he's not doing any of this for himself. This is purely out of concern for a friend, which makes it impossible to ignore. As he talks, my phone rings incessantly, as other board members are calling me, repeatedly. Eventually, I hang up with Bruce, to answer a call from Bill Gurley.

Bill gets to the point quicker, but his message is basically the same.

"I get it," Bill says, "you're burned out, and your life is on hold. This ain't my first rodeo. I've seen other founders do this too. All of them regret it. You should hang on for the IPO. You deserve it." He hangs up in less time than it would take to eat a single chicken wing.

Then it's Chuck Templeton's turn.

"I just heard through the grapevine that you're leaving before the IPO. I think it's a bad idea..."

It means a lot to me that Bruce, Bill, and Chuck react so strongly. The whole reason I got them involved in the first place (aside from their cash, obviously) was because I, like everybody else, have blind spots. I wanted to surround myself with people who can tell me when I'm making a bone-headed mistake.

What happens next goes against everything I preach about being intentional and goal-oriented: I change my mind. I call Matt and unquit (which I'm not entirely sure I can do) and I retract my statement to the board (again, not sure if this is a doable thing). I imagine they rolled their collective eyes, but they don't say no (which I was pretty sure they would).

The whole thing is supremely embarrassing, but it's not even close to the worst part. I'm dreading telling Christine that this thing is going to drag on for another year. I'm worried about what it's going to mean for her career. But she's been listening to me on the phone for the last three hours, so when I hang up with Chuck she says, graciously, "If you have to do it, I support you."

Day 34. Mile 1,776.

I make it to Wichita, approaching the halfway mark across the country, where I plan to meet up with Christine for a weekend.

We head to Riverfest, the big annual summer music festival in town. I try to win her a huge plush stuffed animal, throwing a ball at stacked tin cans. We tire of the fun, and head to a hotel where we have lots of giggly, newlywedish sex. Then she's gone, too, and I've got twenty-five hundred more miles to ride.

Seeing her, and mulling on what happened at GrubHub, something clarifies: Real relationships and total freedom are mutually exclusive. You simply can't have both. Not completely. To get a bit of either, the other needs to make room. So, I've got a decision to make. Do I keep doing my solo cycling thing, or do I join up with some other riders? What do I want out of the rest of this trip? Self-discovery or meaningful friendships? It has been easy to focus on the former, but the novelty of riding the bike is over and maybe I want something different out of the second half of this trip. Maybe I want some real friendships. Or maybe it isn't all that highfalutin—maybe I'm just lonesome.

But there's a problem. My recent detour off route, down into the connubial bliss that was Wichita, has dropped me almost two hundred miles behind the group of six riders I already know. Worse yet, five days behind me is the ACA's TransAm tour group of thirty people. They have their own gravity that pulls cyclists into their orbit and leaves the trail vacant for days ahead and behind.

I've got a choice to make. Either I slow down, a lot, or I sprint ahead. I've made some progress on patience, but not so much that I can stall for the better part of a week. So, slowing down is a nonstarter. Therefore, I'm going to be solo again unless I can catch up to the group in front. It's possible, technically, but since they aren't staying put, I need to cover four hundred miles in the next three days. Fortunately, Mike's rules for hard things, number five, comes into play here: Hard work gets easier when you've got a goal. Also, it helps that the wind is blowing from behind, turning my windshield into a sail, giving me a boost. So. A goal and a bit of luck. Again.

As I rush along to catch up to them, I bring to mind some of the things I learned from what happened at GrubHub and what it meant for what I wanted for this ride. I wanted to learn patience out here on my 'bent; I wanted to find a path of thoughtfulness and intention, rather than just playing the clichéd role of dot-com almost billionaire. But what I wanted from this trip is changing too. I relearn something: Startups and life are the same thing because once you attain a difficult goal, you're forever changed, and that new person finds themselves back at the start, once again urgently needing to establish a new vision. It's the cyclical nature of the hero's journey, of all human journeys. But, unlike a novel, it doesn't finish at the end. It starts anew.

Quitting, too, isn't that big a deal, as it turns out. It can happen for all sorts of reasons: A goal is attained, or it became unattainable. Or the individual behind the vision changed, and cares about different things than when they started—*because*, in fact, they started.

Actually, quitting might be the inevitable result of embracing hard things that force change. What's far worse than quitting, or even giving up, is simply failing to start—whether that be from a lack of vision, or even worse, having it, and not taking the first step (or pedal stroke, as the case may be).

So, I quit my original vision for the trip and embrace this new one.

No big deal.

The next morning, I'm at the Sunshine Café in Nickerson, Kansas, enjoying some well-earned pie, after sprinting through seventy miles since breaking camp at 5 a.m. The café's claim to fame is its farmhouse fresh pies. I have two: apple and peach. (Two *pies*, not two pieces.) As I'm filling in the corners with the final crumbs, I notice a guest ledger near the host stand. I see two names: Paul Dunt and Terry Wooler. The date next to the names is today.

Paul and Terry started the same day as me at the same spot in Virginia Beach, but they remained like phantoms to me. For two thousand miles, people—other cyclists, waitresses, hotel clerks—would ask me if I'd met "the Brits." But I was always up too early, or they stopped one town short, or one beyond me—or I was in a motel, and they were camped behind it. Then, finally, two days before Wichita, I met them, and we hit it off immediately before I turned off the trail to meet Christine.

By now, the Brits should be a couple hundred miles ahead. Something must have happened for them to have been here so recently. I'm off in hot pursuit, pushing Persephone as hard as she will go, creeping close to thirty miles per hour on the flats, powered by a combination of my quarry at hand, and a tailwind behind (and two pies worth of sugar, that we riders refer to as a "pie-bomb"). The straight-as-an-arrow roads of Kansas allow me to spot a pair of bikes far in the distance—it takes about a half hour to close the gap.

Paul Dunt is a few years older than me, over six feet tall, a TV producer for the BBC. Terry Wooler is pushing seventy, skinny as a beanpole, and a stronger cyclist than anyone else on the TransAm by a country mile. They invite me to join them, and just like that we're spending 24-7 together.

There's a strong possibility that this was not something they desired to be the case. But—and I cannot stress this enough—they are *very* English. Stereotypically so. They possess the language, but lack the capacity, to tell people to bugger off. This is a nagging concern for several thousand miles. But I get over it, and we ride together.

Over the coming days, I find out that Paul is a serious talker. He's also got a keen sense of observation honed by a couple decades making documentaries. We pedal along at ten miles per hour, chatting amicably through endless miles of thinning corn and hay as the landscape grows ever more arid. We get a treat when we enter the final town of this state, Tribune, Kansas. Cute shops line the roads, nestled up next to a large agricultural emporium. Underneath a layer of light dust, the town feels prosperous.

Paul says, "Why do you think this place looks like so unique, compared to some of the near ghost towns we've ridden through?"

"There's no Walmart. No Target. No chain restaurants catering to the interstate traffic," I say. "These cute small businesses can't compete with the big box stores, so they only survive in the towns that are far from the main roads."

"That's a shame. These little places add a ton of color."

"Yeah, I remember back in Missouri, I cycled into a town that felt like little more than an interstate rest stop. Applebee's, and Chili's, and a huge strip mall. I got really disoriented, like I had seen the place before. I actually had to check my map to make sure I hadn't cycled the wrong direction."

"Why do these huge box stores do so well, then? The prices?"

I think back to my time at GrubHub, and one of the lessons I learned there.

"No. It's more than that. Sure, people want low prices. But there's something more valuable."

"Time," he offers.

"Not quite time, exactly. Attention. Mental space."

"What do you mean?"

"There's so much pulling at our attention all the time. Literally everything from Facebook, to commercials, to worries about our health and how we look. Even the apps that we use, which at first make things faster, end up barraging us with constant notifications and requests for ratings. We're bombarded with constant bids for our attention. These big stores, with clean brands are a balm to that. It's a defense mechanism to seek out convenience and familiarity. You don't need to *think* when you walk into Walmart or buy something on Amazon. You don't even need to retype your credit card number."

I continue, "And hitting the auto button goes beyond mere familiarity. When you go into one of these big chains, you don't need to spend energy on interacting with other people, because the uniqueness and peculiarity of those people is washed out to the point of being invisible. All the cashiers wear the same clothes. Even the greeters act in very specified ways. If you wanted to, it would be easy to do a whole shopping trip without saying a word."

"So, did your app do that?" Paul asks.

"I'd like to think it did the opposite, originally. We put the uniqueness of individual restaurants on display, but in a way that lowered the mental barrier, and made it easy to keep coming back. In fact, it's the same thing Amazon did in its early days when they were a portal for individual sellers, rather than competing with them."

Paul notes the regret in my voice.

"But not anymore?"

"No, GrubHub just announced a deal with Taco Bell. I've only been gone a month, and they already signed their first big chain. I thought I had created something that was leveling the playing field for independent restaurants. But there's more money to be made on the chains. And public investors care about exactly one thing: quarterly earnings."

Paul sighs.

"So, people should just avoid the big box chains?"

"There's a pretty strong narrative shaming people for being lazy, promoting the solution of shopping locally, and all the effort that goes along with it. But people are too tired. There's too much competing for our mental energy. It's totally understandable that customers crave familiarity and convenience. I think the only thing that works is to make the unique more approachable."

The pair of us amble into the diner on the main strip and take a seat.

"Take this place, for example. It's unique." I gesture around. On the walls are a bunch of rifles, accompanied by pun-filled labels that proclaim the owner's love of all things firearms. A few stuffed big-game trophies attest to someone's skill at using these weapons. In between all the guns are old, rusted metal advertisements for various brands of feeds.

"Yeah. Unique is right. They love guns here, don't they?"

"But what's on the menu?" Paul picks up the laminated paper. "No, without looking at it. What's on it?"

He puts the menu back down, and without reading it says, "Eggs, pancakes, bacon, hash browns."

"And how do they make the eggs?"

"Any way you like 'em."

"Every diner from Virginia to Oregon will have exactly the same menu, along with a few specials. I love these places. Even as the country changes around me, and the people I'm riding with come and go, these are touchstones of familiarity. I can *relax* at one of these diners."

I go on, "But it's not just a vanilla version of the same place. I haven't seen quite this level of shrine to the Second Amendment so far."

The waitress sidles over to take our menus. We each put in a double order for bacon, eggs, and hash browns. It's the same order that we did at the last place, some seventy miles back.

"You boys riding the TransAm?" she asks, in a Boston accent that couldn't be more out of place. She draws out the last word, sounding like Matt Damon from *Good Will Hunting*.

"Yeah, about halfway through now," Paul says. Picking up on her accent he asks, "How about you, where are you from?"

"Moved here from Boston," she says, drawing out the "Baaaaaastan."

"Really? How come?"

"Kid was getting into gangs. I pulled out a map and found the spot furthest from any big city, smack-dab in the middle of the country. Loaded up my car and drove here. That was four years back."

"Wow! Do you miss the city?"

"Yeah. This place is pretty boring. But I'll take boring. My kid is out of trouble, so it's home. Besides, every summer, we get a handful of you riders in every day, every one of you ordering enough for three people and a bit mesmerized by all the guns. So, that's fun."

An hour later, with our stomachs bursting, we set to pedaling again. I spend an hour or so riding in amicable silence next to Terry as I try to figure out my grand unified theory of uniqueness and familiarity that's key to the success of a small business. But it eludes me. Honestly, it's hard to string all those thoughts together. Mostly, I'm just gobsmacked by the vastness of the American Plains.

Mostly, I'm just present.

Terry says, "That stink is getting worse." Now that he mentions it, I notice it. It's faint, but horrific. Something like manure, but with an acrid chemical tang underneath.

I recognize it.

"That's a feed lot," I say.

"What's that?"

"Out East, there's enough rain that cows can roam about eating grass and pooping until they get big enough to be turned into steak. But out here in the West, there's less water, so farmers use big circle irrigators, harvest the hay, and bring it to the cows to feed them. Hence, feed lots."

"The cows don't walk around?" Terry, the vegetarian, asks.

"Nope—they just stay in their pens their whole lives until it's time for slaughter."

The stink of cow manure becomes all pervasive, and eventually we pass an actual feed lot, where the cows are all pushed together into a small pen. Seeing one in person is far worse than either Terry or I had expected. Each pen is maybe one hundred square feet and holds maybe fifteen or even twenty animals. Bulldozers push the manure into piles—one of the pens has a pile of manure that's at least fifteen feet tall. There's a cow on top of it. She's the Queen of Shit Mountain. That's the most she can ever aspire to be. She's reached the literal pinnacle of her life.

Terry pulls his bike over, and retches. My gorge rises, too, but I manage to hold on to my hash browns. There's nothing for it but to keep riding. A quarter mile upwind of the feed lot, the smell mercifully fades, if not the memory.

Western Kansas has been getting drier by the day. And poorer. Everywhere we see signs of poverty, buildings are neglected, or just as often, abandoned. Towns out here need a reason to survive—mining, perhaps, a university, a train station, or some kind of tourist attraction. Without something, they just fade away. As much as I hate the Walmartification of America, I might have to admit that the economic benefit such monsters bring is probably better than this slow wasting.

The transition into Colorado is highlighted by a progression from arid scrubland to the austere splendor of a legitimate desert, with its browns and tans of parched soil. Drifts of sand and tumbleweeds punctuate the road. The landscape is dotted with tiny pink flowers that stand out vibrantly against the muted surroundings. Then, with shocking suddenness, the blue skies disappear as a shelf of stone gray clouds deliver a cacophony of thunder. There's no rain, but a siren peals in the distance.

The Brits stop at the Welcome to Colorado sign to do a bunch of pictures. But I opt to keep riding. I'm a few miles ahead of them when I reach the town of Sheridan Lake, in Kiowa County, Colorado. This town, like many we've seen recently, has seen better days. The eponymous body of water, down a hill toward the center of town, has long since dried up—the remains of a single finger dock reach from a dilapidated building into the sand. As I enter a convenience store, the woman behind the counter confronts me.

"Didn't you hear the tornado siren?" she asks. "Get to the church, they'll have room for cyclists in the basement. Are there any other riders out there?"

"Yeah, a couple of Brits I'm riding with, probably ten minutes behind me. Oh, and John and Jonathan behind them. And behind them, Jess and Tuan."

"Shit. I'll go get them." With that, she runs to her pickup truck and peels out of the parking lot, not bothering to even lock the door to her shop. For all our differences, America still raises good people.

At the church, I'm the first cyclist to arrive for the night, but eventually fifteen of us huddle in the basement. Paul and Terry arrive under their own steam. Others are rounded up by kindly local folks in pickup trucks—then the trucks head back out again looking for stragglers. Seven of us are west-bounders, the same group that's been leapfrogging most of the way since the coast: Me, Terry, Paul, Jonathan, Jerry, Jess, and Tuan; the rest are heading east.

Outside, the sky is an ugly bruise, green and purple. Wind comes in bursts, each time from a different direction. In between, the air is as still as a crypt. Some of us venture out on the lawn, but we don't see any tornadoes. Without warning, the rain comes crashing in sheets that drives even the most committed peekers and photographers back into the safety of the basement. We quiet as the night comes on and as the storm abates. We've been rescued and treated with incredible kindness.

We'll sleep well tonight, made safe by amazing people in the middle of this amazing country.

PART THREE

I ride into the sunset

14

Brass Ring

I'm sitting comfortably in a leather chair at forty thousand feet. The captain has just told me that he's expecting a smooth flight to New York. He hasn't mentioned this over the intercom. No, he stepped out of the cockpit to let me know this personally. Don't worry, the copilot has everything well in hand.

After some idle chitchat, he assures me that I am in good hands with the stewardess. Oh, by the way, our friends at Citi have arranged a special meal for me.

What follows is the utter definition of decadence. Lobster tail. Steak tartare. Shrimp cocktail. Dom Pérignon. Charcuterie. Delightfully warm chocolate chip cookies.

In time, the private jet lands at Teterboro. I disembark. A jet-black SUV is waiting twelve steps away. The freshness of spring mixes with the sharpness of jet fuel on this exquisite blue-sky day. Attendants stand by with umbrellas, just in case. It would be unconscionable for us to be exposed to the elements.

I embark.

I am whisked to the W Hotel, not far from the intersection of Wall and Broad streets, where the GrubHub initial public offering will be happening in two days. There are sixteen-dollar cashews in the minibar. I eat two cans.

———

I awake, momentarily disoriented before my brain turns on.

I'm in a hotel. The W Hotel. New York.

It is Friday, April 4, 2014, the day of the GrubHub IPO.

The bedside clock reads 4:07 a.m. The room is aglow with ambient light. Cars angrily accelerate in single block bursts on the city grid. Bulldozers chuff their throaty roar and annoying reverse beeps as they dig out the foundation of the new World Trade Center building next door. This early in the morning, there are no tourists out, but I spot revelers on the sidewalk below making their way back home from bars and clubs.

My body strums with nerves and energy. There's no chance I'm going back to sleep. I slap on my Mizunos, grab my iPod, and make my way outside for a dawn run. Navigating the security and construction detours around the 9/11 Memorial puts me in a reflective mood.

According to Google, the distance to Central Park is five miles as the pigeon flies, six if I run along the Hudson River path. Round trip, that's a half marathon. I'm training for this bike trip I'm about to take, so I'm in shape for it, but a run that long will take too much time, and leave me too tired. Maybe I can do a run up there, and take a Bike Share back to the hotel. Though, I'm always self-conscious biking in running shorts. That's a lot of leg.

While I run, I've got money on the brain.

I'm going to become rich today. Well, I'm already rich, with a million in the bank after paying off my debt. But today I'll make another twenty million. That's stupid rich.

I can't get over the thought, *What am I going to do with all that cash?*

My second thought is always, *Make the world a better place.* Then I go into a loop about how.

Step one: Help my family. Since the housing crisis, none of my three siblings nor any of Christine's three siblings have been able to get a mortgage. Since everyone's popping out babies, condos and starter houses are busting at the seams. I'll just buy everyone houses. My nephews and nieces won't have to worry about college. I can set up a fund to handle their other needs too.

Great. So, that's one million spoken for, nineteen more to go.

Once I jog over the pedestrian bridge to the West Side, I consider step two: nonprofits. Twenty million dollars isn't Bill Gates or Warren Buffett money. But I can make a big dent locally in Chicago. Christine and I have already decided we're going to focus on justice and education. But giving lots of money to nonprofits is, in itself, a full-time job. Nonprofits tend to be both ever hungry and prone to overeating. No amount of cash is ever enough. This makes sense, to some degree, as humanity is never without need.

My watch beeps at me as my run passes the one-mile marker. Across the Hudson to my left are the skyscrapers of Hoboken. The early dawn light is just now catching the tops of a few. Below, in the dimness, a dozen boats plow the waves, most notably a commuter ferry bringing hundreds of workers from Jersey into the city.

For-profit companies can be a driver for positive social change just as much as nonprofits. GrubHub made a difference in people's lives, and does even still. I saw it firsthand when Moe from China Doll restaurant on Wells Street, in Chicago, brought me flowers and thanked me for keeping his restaurant in business through the housing crisis. It happened again with Leona's, a Chicago institution, who we enabled to compete with the online ordering tech of the big pizza chains, early on in this adventure. And then there are the smaller, but no less important moments, like the US Army private, stationed in Afghanistan, who used GrubHub to order an anniversary dinner for his wife back in the States.

I pass pier after pier along the Hudson River Greenway. I've been going for three miles. In the water is a mix of charter motor yachts, barges, ferries, shipping, and purely recreational boats. Just about every type of ship you could think of, other than an aircraft carrier. The greenway is beautiful. It doesn't feel like the biggest city in the country. It feels like nature.

The third option, of course, is to found another company. Thirty-six is way too early to retire. So, really, another company is the only option.

My thoughts of the future turn naturally to the past. If I'm going to create another company, I need to take some time to think what I want to do differently. What would I want to get out of a second go-round?

In some ways, important ways, GrubHub got away from me. Financially, it's going to do great. But it seems clear that it's not going to be great for restaurants in short order. Did it get away from me because I checked out, mentally, or did I check out because it got away from me?

When it was just me, I wanted a pizza, but finding a new pizza place was hard to do. So, I made it easier. Simple problem. Simple solution. Simple goal. Then it evolved to online ordering. And my goals evolved too. But it was still just me.

But then I got investors. And that changed the direction of the company. For the better. A good venture capitalist (VC) wants to change the world in a specific way: They're sniffing out innovations that alter consumer behavior. They'll take risks on ideas and people because the upside is huge financial returns. So, they're relatively patient, and they're even fine with some of their bets failing completely. A good venture firm doesn't care much if there's a blip in a company's revenue for a year—they tend to the long view, sometimes prepared to even wait decades for return.

Then we got more investors. And that was a bit of a mixed bag. The private equity (PE) firm that we inherited with the merger wanted something different. PE firms aren't so interested in innovation—they just want efficiency. They want to find the waste in the process and root it out. Since they do this for lots of companies, they get pretty good at seeing patterns: overbidding on vendors, bloated middle management, overpaid top executives, excess physical locations. These investors aren't quite as patient as VCs, but they don't mind a bad quarter, as long as things are generally trending in the right direction.

At mile five, I see an aircraft carrier. Apparently, somebody parked it on the Hudson. It is enormous, reaching up to about mid height of the twenty-story buildings across from it. The gunmetal gray behemoth is adorned with bright metal jets and helicopters that saw service in decades past. It's a museum. New York is weird.

And now we're about to get public investors. And unlike venture capitalists or private equity, they bring nothing to the table. There is no expertise or knowledge that public investors use to benefit a company. Worse, their timeline is very short. A single missed quarterly earnings report means the sky is falling. Individual public investors might each be wonderful, talented, moral people. But as an aggregate group, John Q. Public act like a person. And that person is the most short-term thinking, greediest narcissist that humanity has ever spawned.

I reach Central Park and run a small portion of it before admitting that I really need to get back. The Bike Share is sponsored by Citi, and their branding is plastered all over the station. I chuckle at the serendipity. I grab a bike and start back toward my hotel, letting my thoughts roam free.

Maybe the investors are just half the story—maybe a company has a mind of its own. What if, the second time around, I create a company where the business we are in can't be divorced from the benefit we create? What if we only hire employees who sign up for our social impact? What if we only take investors who agree, contractually, with our mission being an end, in and of itself, rather than just a means to an end for making money? (Spoiler alert. This is exactly what I end up doing in a few years when I create Fixer.com.)

These ideas are as inspiring as they are frustrating. Why the hell couldn't I have thought of this back when I was coding version one of GrubHub?

As I ride down the West Side, I feel a twinge of loss and regret. I mourn for the company that I might have created, knowing everything I now know. GrubHub could have been a permanent bastion for the independent restaurants against the creeping, choking influence of corporate chains. It could have grown to be an amplifier of opportunity for immigrants, who often find their first taste of the American dream by opening a local eatery in their mother country's tradition. It could have been a strong influencer away from single-use plastics and Styrofoam, using its reach and profits to promote more sustainable food packaging.

But GrubHub isn't any of those things.

Not because of investors or the public stock market.

Because of me.

I just aimed to pay off my school loans. And I did. I didn't shoot high enough.

Be careful what you ask for. You just might get it.

Next time, I'm going to get this right.

———

The run and ride helped me shake my funk. Showered, suited, and in a much better mood, I make my way to the corner of Wall and Broad streets. There's the New York Stock Exchange. It looks a lot like an ancient Greek temple with its imposing granite, fluted columns, and broad steps. In a way, it *is* a temple…to capitalism.

Stretched across the four columns, running over two hundred feet from side to side, is a bright red banner emblazoned with the GrubHub logo in two-story-tall white lettering that looks pretty damn cool. Todd Clark, who has been with me at GrubHub for a decade, arrives.

"Well, that's something, huh?" I say.

"No kidding," he says, as we gaze up at the banner.

Todd, cool as ever, glides purposely toward the building and I lockstep with him, doing my best to not look too excited.

A handler picks us out easily—we're 5 percent more confident than tourists, but 100 percent less purposeful than traders. We're waved into a visitor's lobby. The walls here are decked with row after row of pictures of companies that have gone public. Some are from last week. Some are a century old. Today, they'll take pictures of us.

In the lobby, I run into a slice of pepperoni pizza. He's six feet tall and about four feet wide. We hired a trio of actors and dressed them up in ridiculous food costumes for the media frenzy of the day—we went with pizza, a bagel, and sushi. It's hard to make a grown adult-size sushi look appetizing, but, surprisingly, he makes my stomach growl.

The foods join me, the handler, and a few other employees who made their way here early to an enormous boardroom set up with finger food. Eventually, the whole gang filters in—Matt, Jonathan, and a slew of others who've been with us from the start. We all nervously chat and pick at the spread, then we head to the main event.

My first impression walking into the trading room is how *electronic* it is. Monitors and screens are everywhere. Most of the trading happens on computers these days, so there are fewer traders on the floor than there once were. Most of the space they used to take up has been converted to miniature TV studios: I can see Cramer's *Mad Money* and a few others.

We climb the stairs to a small platform overlooking the trading floor. Our stock symbol, "GRUB," is emblazoned on a larger-than-life delivery bag.

The moment comes. This is really it. We're opening the New York Stock Exchange on the day of our IPO. From a bus ride in Chicago, craving pizza, to this. It hardly seems real. Matt pushes the button to start the day.

Bells. Clapping. Whoops and hollers.

On the floor, traders zoom between the trading pits in their bright, color-coded jackets. There are about a dozen pits, circular booths with flat-screen monitors facing outward. There is a row of screens at eye level, and then others overhead, angled down. Underneath and behind the screens are actual humans, though they are largely ignored. All of this digital surface area serves up a dizzying quantity of streaming financial information. I don't begin to understand how they keep up.

One pit, though, is dedicated entirely to GrubHub. Thirty screens display a single word—GRUB—stark in white lettering against a red background, like the huge banner outside. Gone are the days of open trading where people would cry, "I've got soybeans! Soybeans at ten dollars!" This GRUB pit is quiet. It reminds me of a crowded city bus, people all mashed up together, noses in armpits like all those years ago in Chicago, only these guys are staring intently at their tablets, ignoring everything around them.

One person stands out in the clump—the "market maker." He gathers interest for the first trade, aggregating the individual purchase requests for GRUB. Nobody can make individual transactions until after this guru executes this huge initial order. The point of all this activity is to reduce massive spikes and drops in the stock price in the first few minutes.

Ten minutes pass; twenty. I didn't realize how long all this was going to take. Mike Saunders, the founder of Campusfood, is here with me. When we bought the company, three years ago, Mike got a nice chunk of stock. He's just as interested as me in the price that is about to come up on the screens. We're standing around like bums as these multicolored bastions of capitalism flow around us like rocks in a river. An employee assigned by the exchange comes by to tell us everything is normal; it can take up to an hour for this process to play out. But, giving lie to her words, a commotion erupts in the GRUB pit. A few loud voices, crescendoing and joined by others. People are shouting numbers now.

The screens go black.

Then, they're up again.

GRUB: $40.25.

There are reporters circling me, waiting for a response. Somehow, I don't lose my shit. And fortunately, I don't say out loud the math that is coursing through my head.

I had expected $9. Maybe $10 at a pinch. But $40.25? I just made One. Hundred. Million. Dollars.

I still believe that I'm not going to spend it all. I still believe that wealth comes with an obligation to benefit society. I still hate the way we talk about how much people are worth, and how a bigger number somehow implies more intrinsic value as a human being. But I grew up playing *Super Mario Brothers*, and you get another life at one hundred coins. Which feels a lot like what just happened.

Day 36. Mile 1,897.

The thing about a well-loved camp stove is that it stinks. Weeks of heavy use have transmuted the sterile aluminum of my Jetboil into some new thing, a substance not previously known to science.

Steam pushes aside the Jetboil's flimsy lid. I sit hunched over it, bathed in the wafting steam. The flavors hidden in that metal come to me one by one: There's a hint of couscous with raisins; layered underneath that is cheese quesadillas. The vinegar-pepper smell of Cholula that ends up on everything is in there somewhere too. Deeper down, there's breakfast—apple cinnamon oatmeal.

My current meal mixes notes of dishwater and steamed noodles.

I'm reclining in my tent, anticipating the gastronomic masterpiece before me. Once I finish this, I'll make an attempt to read, and then I'll sleep like the dead. I enjoyed my ride with Paul and Terry today, but they are staying in the hostel down the street. Hungry, and tired from a long day of riding, I'm too cranky to be fit for human company, so I'm bedding down solo in a park.

Since crossing the Mississippi, many of these western towns have let me plop my stuff down in the city square and camp out for the night. It isn't entirely clear if I'm allowed to be in this particular park, though. It would've been nice to have a tree or something to set my tent behind, but this far west, the vegetation has started to thin, and while there's plenty of scraggly brush, it doesn't provide much cover.

I'm wearing the same bike clothes I donned at the Atlantic, but they aren't really "bike clothes," at least not the embarrassing spandex type. My shorts, which come down just past my knees, are made from the reinforced fabric motorcyclists prefer. They were black, back in Virginia, but they've been sun bleached, and turned a weird splotchy purple. On top, I'm sporting a long-sleeved wool shirt. It's very thin, working equally well to keep sun off my arms in the heat of the day, and adding extra warmth when I'm pedaling at dawn. Even better, several holes have developed around the collar, improving its ventilation with the increasing heat of summer.

I am hungry all the time—but not usually like this. It was a long day of riding. Finishing before twilight was the goal, so I skipped dinners today—both of them.

Now I've got that bone-deep, ravenous, six-thousand-calories-a-day hunger. It obliterates rational thought.

"Hi there, mister."

Shit.

This kid shows up in every third town—sincere, kind, and generous. He wants to know if I'm hungry. He's got a sandwich right here. And do I, perhaps, know Jesus as my personal lord and savior?

I *do*, now that you mention it. But I've got 680 calories of mac and cheese that is quickly passing al dente on the way to inedible mush. So, could you, perhaps, go away?

I'm supposed to be getting better at this. That was the point, after all. For a start, I *was* this kid, once, a lifetime ago. Before GrubHub, I didn't take myself too seriously. I was sincere and kind and patient. I want to be this kid again.

But here in my tent, with my ravenous hunger, I'm an impatient asshole who wants to be nothing more than the vagrant he appears to be. Such vagrants often invite a visit from the local constabulary, so, let's just keep our shit together here, shall we?

I fiddle with the dial on the Jetboil, grabbing it by its insulated sleeve, forgetting that it slips easily. I burn myself. Again. Holding the lid, gingerly with the box turned potholder, I pour out the gray water. It splashes. The too close, too kind kid jumps back a foot.

I take a bite of my salt-fat-carb-cheese-Cholula. The demon inside me retracts its claws, powerless against pasta.

"You want this sandwich?" the kid asks.

"Sure, that'd be great," I say.

"We've got a Bible study at the church, just over there. You're welcome, if you'd like to join us."

"I might stop by—thanks for the invite."

He's a beautiful person; I'm just so hungry. Still, he shares some choice verses as I grunt and chew.

Blessedly, he walks away.

I make short work of the mac and cheese. My blood sugar rises. My hanger subsides. I am, in fact, still very much an asshole. Mathematically, this is a problem: I have ridden my bicycle across half the country. But I'm still 100 percent asshole. I should have lost half that assholery by now. I should be down to just one cheek's worth.

I unwrap the sandwich. It looks pretty good. The church sprang for the crunchy peanut butter. The free meal couldn't be more of a contrast to the last one I had, sitting comfortably on a private jet, two months back. In all honesty, this one tastes better. I don't think it's the peanut butter. I think it's the kid who gave it to me.

15

Prosperity

Finally, the Rockies are here.

Terry, Paul, and I are in Pueblo, Colorado, at the range's eastern edge. The flats of Kansas are far behind us; now, we're facing the most daunting part of the TransAm: traversing America's great mountain range—purple mountain majesty and all that good stuff. Also, thousands upon thousands of feet of climbing. Over the next two weeks, I'll do over ten times the vertical I did in the Appalachians. I am very scared about this.

We're being joined by Chuck Templeton for a few days. Chuck and I became close friends during the years he was involved with GrubHub. Leading up to the merger with Seamless, he left the GrubHub board, so I'm looking forward to reconnecting.

Chuck is just over five feet tall, but despite his limited stature, he's physically terrifying, a veteran of the 10th Mountain Division, an Army Ranger, and a master sniper. Chuck is not scared about the mountains.

The path out of Pueblo is made of fine-grained, red gravel—soft and pleasant, like the rails-to-trails limestone paths back east. The route meanders through Japanese rock gardens and carefully crafted arid landscapes, showcasing beauty native to the Southwest.

The flat bike path ends unceremoniously at a steeply inclined road with no shade. The climb begins, and it never stops. Over the next three days, we'll climb through the towns of Guffey, Hartsel, and Fairplay, the highest township in the US. After Fairplay, we will go even higher, eventually cresting the Continental Divide. We'll be heading up more than three times the altitude of the Blue Ridge Parkway, which, lest I forget, nearly forced me off my ride.

Back in Wichita, I visited three bike shops on a quest to change the gearing on my bike. Eventually I landed on an extremely small chainring for my front derailleur, giving Persephone the equivalent of three more low-speed gears. I'm hoping with this new gearing the Rockies will be a big improvement over the Appalachians and Ozarks. It doesn't solve the balance issues inherent to a 'bent—I still can't really go below four miles per hour. But instead of a slow pedal stroke, I'll be spinning my crank more quickly. It should be easier on my legs, if not my lungs.

Early in the trip, I was expecting to have lots of time to puzzle things out—about my recent past, about where GrubHub went wrong—morally, if not financially—about where I wanted to head in the future, if I wanted. But the truth is, I've just been too tired. Keeping the bike moving has been an all-consuming task, with no energy left for pondering the great questions of life. But here, on this intense climb toward the Continental Divide, I'm surprised to find myself not even winded. Up I go. One thousand feet. Two thousand feet. Three thousand feet. No sweat.

And so, I ponder.

Back at the start of GrubHub, I had wanted to get rid of debt and be my own boss. Later, my aspirations got bigger, grander: I wanted to equalize the playing field for independent restaurants. But dreams change as you dream them, and by the time I wanted to achieve those bigger goals, I was too far along a different path to make them come true.

I come to an important realization on day one up the Rockies.

First, I can do it again. I'm not too burnt out. I'm not too old. I can start another company, and when I do, I can cast a bigger vision for what I want to accomplish. Second, if I'm going to be any good at it a second time, I need to stop fretting about the missed opportunity that I didn't even know I wanted when I set out on that journey. Current Mike needs to extend past Mike a little grace, so future Mike isn't shackled by regrets.

The second day of the ascent is much like the first. I'm not trying to break any speed records; I climb the mountain at what amounts to just over walking pace. I'm at four thousand feet. Five. Six. The dry air and my elevated breathing cracks my lips—by the time I find some lip balm at a convenience store, I'm just trying to keep them from getting worse, rather than healing. (My lips will remain bloody and raw for the next thousand miles.)

On day two I realize I'm kinda done with meat. Queen of Shit Mountain—that cow back at the feed lot—really did a number on me. But more than that, the last decade has not been a particularly healthy one—for me or my customers. I am directly responsible for a significant increase in the consumption of dairy products and pork in the United States—I have enabled the easy online ordering of millions of pepperoni pizzas for a start. It's hard for me to argue that choosing to forgo meat could balance out the environmental impact my business had on the world. But again, I can't let past choices hold me back from where I want to go next. Somewhere around six thousand feet, I decide I'm now a vegetarian. Weird.

On the third day, the weirdest thing of all happens: I get calm.

The final ascent toward Hoosier Pass runs aside the gentle burble of the South Platte River. I leave the tree line behind, ascending into alpine meadows. A marmot pokes its head out of a rock pile; a golden eagle swoops overhead. I'll get to the highest point in the TransAm in a couple of hours, but for now I'm happy to just be in the moment, pedaling my way up a mountain, watching the flora and fauna.

Is this what contentment feels like? I wish I could bottle this stuff. I laugh out loud at both my moment of serenity, and my brain's inability to just *savor* it.

And then I realize that the slope is leveling out—I guess I sort of expected to just be going upward forever. There's a marker at the top, proclaiming the spot as the Continental Divide. I pull up and let out an earth-shattering yell of triumph.

There's a dudebro and some friends in a Jetta parked off to the side of the road, enjoying the view and sharing some beers.

"Nice work!" he calls. "Want a beer?"

He hands me a Pabst Blue Ribbon, a golden nectar of the gods at the top of the world.

"You just rode up that whole mountain?" he asks.

I nod and drink.

"Damn, dude. That's epic. Where'd you start?"

"Virginia," I say, like it's nothing. (It's not nothing.)

"Holy shit! You rode your bike here all the way from Virginia? That's epic! Guys, this guy just rode his bike here from Virginia!" he shouts to his friends in the car.

As one they exclaim, "Holy shit! That's epic!"

Chuck rolls up. He's smiling ear to ear.

"That was a climb," he says, as I hand him the beer. Is he actually winded? No. Of course not. Chuck ran a marathon in a jungle in Costa Rica once. By himself. Terry arrives and takes a sip as well. Finally, Paul shows up and immediately starts chatting up the locals.

"Hard part done!" I announce. "It's all downhill from here."

Oh, honey. Bless your heart!

A couple days later, in the town of Kremmling, Colorado, at the foot of the mountains of the Gore Range, Chuck and I are reminiscing over an obscene amount of hash browns.

"So, was taking that first investment from Bruce worth it?" he asks.

I say, "You remember when you told me that there were a bunch of reasons that a founder should take investment, but the cash was the least important one? The thing that you said that really nailed it for me was that I'd stagnate, personally, if I didn't push myself to take on investors and a board. But if I did, they'd push me in uncomfortable ways."

"Yeah, I remember that. Did it work?"

"I learned a lot, for sure," I say, "enough that I wish I could go back and do it again. Do things differently. I wish I could go back and change my goals for what I wanted out of it."

"Change them to what?" he asks, ordering our fourth plate of food.

"GrubHub got real big, real fast. It ended up having a huge influence on the restaurant industry, and now that they're (not *we're*) hiring drivers, it looks like it's going to be contributing to normalizing this new gig economy thing in a major way. But I was so focused on getting out when I could have been working toward using it as a platform to create positive change. Problem is, I didn't know I wanted that until I had missed my chance."

"That sucks," Chuck says.

"Yeah, but it's also not the whole story. Restaurateurs brought me flowers and wrote cards to thank me. We did some good. I made a difference in some lives, for a time. Could I have done more? Maybe, but I'm not so sure. The opportunity may have passed the moment I took the investment. But without taking the investment, I wouldn't have learned enough to make the differences I'm talking about. The lessons themselves changed my goals. But I couldn't have learned the lessons without my original goals. It's a bit of a catch-22."

"So, what are you going to do about it?"

"I'm not sure yet. I'm still too burned out to think about the next thing. But my mind has been wandering more the last few days as I've been pedaling. I left GrubHub forty-two days ago and I'm already daydreaming about jumping into another startup for round two. Probably with something new, though. I'm a bit worried if I try something with restaurants, I'll be sour grapes about the missed opportunity with the last company."

"What would be different, if you did something new?"

"I think the key is finding a business where the social impact and the engine for business are the same thing. Instead of having those two things in tension, like they often were at GrubHub, I want running the business to create a positive social or environmental impact because it exists, rather than in spite of it."

"Like an education technology company? Or maybe an investment technology play that educates, or something like that," Chuck says.

"Yeah," I say, "something like that. But I'd want it to be something everyone can use, not just teachers and rich people."

"Well, I hope you find something," he says. "I'd be happy to invest, whatever your next thing is."

"After a break," I caution.

"Fair enough."

In the end Chuck and I murdered six plates of hash browns with peppers, onions, and mushrooms. We would have kept going, but the mushrooms ran out.

Later, Paul, Terry, Chuck, and I ride into the town of Saratoga, not too far across the line into Wyoming, my seventh state (eight if you count the ten miles I might or might not have been in Tennessee but couldn't slow down to check a map on account of the dogs chasing me).

Saratoga is one of the gems. It reminds me a lot of Mineral, Virginia, back on day two. It sports a freshly painted Welcome sign, and a clean swept bike lane. The National Forest Ranger station is painted in familiar browns and tans. Everything speaks of an understated prosperity.

Just into town there is a sign proclaiming the famed Hobo Hot Springs, free to the public. By unanimous consent, the four of us pull off to the side to enjoy a quick dip. They have three different pools: hot, hotter, and Hades. Submersed in the heat, our muscles unclench—the damage done by the mountains of Colorado is soothed by the springs of Wyoming. The heat enervates us, draining whatever energy we might have used to ride further. So, we decide to stay nearby for the night, in a campsite just past the edge of town.

As we meander through Main Street, we see lots of boutiques and eateries, a grocer, and a butcher. Notably absent are Walmart, Dollar General, or for that matter any kind of large chain business. Smiles abound and children frolic in a park. This town is happy. The final bastion of commerce is a promising-looking diner, likely to be replete with mushrooms, peppers, and onions, capable of serving up unlimited plates of hash browns to a group that has, with my recent conversion, three vegetarians. (Paul kindly offers to eat our shares of bacon.)

"What's the difference?" I ask, as we settle into a booth, "Why is this town thriving, while others are dying? This is a thing I've been wondering as I've passed through a number of these gems: Somerset in Kentucky, or Farmington back in Missouri. Compare those to the ones that are desperately struggling, like Ness City in Kansas, or Sheridan Lake, where we hid from the tornado."

"It's not the people," says Terry. "Take Sheridan Lake, for example. That town was on hard times, but the people were brilliant, driving around, picking up bikers with a tornado bearing down."

"Maybe it's not the people," Paul says, "but I think it's a person. Or a small group. Look at this." He points to the pictures on the walls. "That's twenty years worth of group photos from 4-H clubs, baseball teams, the local school, all offering thanks to the owner of this place. That's got to make a difference. I think what happens is you get two, maybe three committed individuals like that, organizing a town for twenty years, and you end up with a place like Saratoga."

Terry chimes in.

"Yeah, at some point, the town council was debating what to do with those hot springs, and somebody stood up and demanded that it be free to all visitors. That takes a lot of guts. It's an investment in the town as a whole. Somebody pushed for that."

I wander around the restaurant looking at the pictures on the walls. In addition to all the school sports teams, there's tons of events that happen in this town. There's a woodchopping jamboree and rodeo. They host a microbrew festival. In the winter, they have an ice fishing competition. The town has less than two thousand people, and it is *thriving*.

In all these pictures on the wall, there's a few familiar faces that show up again and again. Two or three local leaders are holding up a prized fish, chopping wood at the jamboree, or drinking a beer. Tucked behind the host stand, there's a plaque. It's been awarded to the owner of the restaurant for their contributions to the community. I'd bet dollars to donuts that this is one of the people in all the pictures.

The notion feels right to me somehow. The people of this country are great. It's been an experience I've had that's so close to universally true, that the three or four exceptions across three thousand miles prove the rule. But for a town to prosper, it takes more than just great people— something more than just sufficient distance from an interstate, and all the big box stores.

This is the key. It takes a couple of dedicated individuals to lead a community. It takes somebody who cares. Somebody who acts.

Two days later, we experience the exact opposite of Saratoga's prosperity. The town of Jeffrey City, Wyoming, has seen better days. Stunted grass peeks through cracks in a vacant parking lot to the right side the road. Presumably, there were stores or homes or something attached to that lot some years back. But now, there's just a scattering of abandoned debris: tires, an old washing machine, other detritus. Today's ride has been a long one, so we're grateful as we pull into the only restaurant in town, the Split

Rock Bar. Chuck's time with us ended, just after Saratoga, so it's back to just me, Paul, and Terry.

I order three waters from the bar. This earns me a sour look. There's nothing obviously meatless on the menu, but generally that doesn't present too much of a problem since most places serve breakfast all day, and who doesn't love pancakes and eggs? But no, they don't serve breakfast all day, and no, we can't make any substitutions. Terry and I grumpily settle on four orders of french fries between the two of us.

Paul shares an observation about the town: "This place is seeing hard times."

I point to the wall. Pictures adorn it, similar to the ones we saw in Saratoga, supporting the local community. They are smaller in number, and older, but they suggest that there was just as much civic engagement here, some time ago.

"This is pretty good evidence that it's not so simple as a couple of people working to make the community prosper," I say.

Terry points out some information he sees online.

"Looks like this town's economy was built on the nearby uranium mine. Back during the arms race of the Cold War, this was a boomtown."

"So, a town needs some kind of economic hook?" I say. "Hot springs, or a National Park, or an annual motorcycle rally? Barring that, a lot of towns make a devil's bargain with strip malls along an interstate, with Walmart and Applebee's sucking the uniqueness out of the town, in exchange for economic life support."

"Maybe that's why so many people are mad across these small towns," Paul chimes in. "It's gotten a lot harder to be in charge of your own destiny if manufacturing and a bunch of other industries are relocated to places with cheaper labor. There's just not as many options as there were twenty years ago."

It takes nearly an hour for our paltry food to arrive. We endure sour looks and overhear disparaging comments while we wait for the food too. I'm so hungry that my newfound resolve nearly crumbles when I see Paul's burger. As we leave Jeffrey City, Terry says, "I'm not sad to show that town my heels."

The sharp contrast between Saratoga and Jeffrey City isn't the last I see. To travel through Main Street America is to experience a nation of contrasts. Over the following three weeks, Paul, Terry, and I experience a dozen different Americas as we pedal across Wyoming, Montana, and Idaho.

There is the serene beauty of Grand Teton; I swim in its frigid Jenny Lake, without another soul nearby. I get stuck in traffic in Yellowstone National Park, pushed off the road repeatedly by rented RVs, their drivers unable to master their road rage.

I shiver in my sleeping bag outside of Dubois, Wyoming, unable to get warm, camped next to a snowfield unconcerned by the fact that it's July. In Idaho, I spend hours nursing Paul back to health, sitting with him in a mountain stream, trying to cool down from a too hot day that made him faint with heatstroke.

I struggle to sleep, my tent perched upon broken glass in the nearly deserted town of Lamont, Wyoming, drinking water that was trucked in from forty miles away by a dedicated trail angel who goes by the simple initials, JD. Then later, Paul and I enjoy a game of checkers, free whisky, and a serene campsite at Willie's Distillery in Dillon, Montana.

A cyclist-hating trucker blasts his horn and comes within inches of ending my life, just miles away in Madison County, Wyoming. He then involves the police, falsely claiming that the three of us were blocking the road. But less than forty-eight hours later, I'm receiving gracious hospitality and free ice cream at the Adventure Cycling Association's headquarters. I'm even given a tour of the facility by the very same cartographer whose ancestry I cursed as I struggled through the hills of the Ozarks (she had described the inclines as "moderate").

In Wyoming, I meet a woman by the name of Joanna Abernethy, a primary school teacher from Australia, who is doing the TransAm to honor Dr. Martin Luther King Jr. I'm touched by her passion, but also worried about her competence, as she starts the ascent of a dangerous mountain pass at six in the evening. By the time I'm entering Idaho, I read online that she has been killed by a drunk driver as she cycled well past midnight in Ohio.

Paul, Terry, and I ride a thousand miles and meet a thousand people. With each pedal stroke, I get just a little bit better at being present. With each conversation, I get a pinch more perspective. This country is beautiful, and I am lucky to experience it at nine miles per hour, my head toward the horizon, as I ride my lawn chair across it. But that beauty is eclipsed by the warmth of the people in it, who, despite their harried lives and hectic schedules, find time to chat with us, offer pie, or a place to sleep.

Pacific

Day 70. Mile 3,819.

Fun fact: Oregon is mostly desert. Who knew? I thought it was all rain and hipsters. Turns out you have to get through the deserts and Confederate militias to get to the good part.

Also, Oregon is on fire.

The thermometer hasn't dropped below one hundred degrees in eight days. For the last five hundred miles, since Paul's heatstroke in Idaho, Paul, Terry, and I have been splitting our daily ride into two parts: early morning and predusk. We sit out the middle of the day in whatever shady stream, bar, or friendly church we can find, cowering from the heat. We managed to find air-conditioned hotels for two of the last eight days, but the other six have been fever-dreamed, sweat-soaked nightmares.

Hopefully, the temperature will break today, as we steadily climb, leaving behind the three hundred miles of desert we've endured since the Idaho-Oregon border. By 5:30 a.m., we are rolling out. Paul, Terry, and I each managed to eat about a dozen pancakes in the predawn light, compliments of the kitchen of the Dayville Presbyterian Church, where we spent a blessedly air-conditioned night.

The approach to the Ochoco Mountains, where we're headed today, is a gorge carved through mesmerizing rock strata in red and tan—the lines of color are sharply defined, like stacked oval Legos. The mountains and buttes present sharp relief against the clear morning sky.

From a plane, the country is black and white. From a car, it's an old TV. On a bike, at nine miles per hour, it's high definition. With friends, especially visitors from another land, I have fresh stereo commentary.

I've ridden over two thousand miles with Paul and Terry. It's been a solid four weeks of close friendship, occasional bickering, and sublime beauty. We've soaked in the grand peaks and vast skies of the American West, and much like the scenery, the beauty of the people has been breathtaking too—not a single day has passed without generous offers: cookies, pie, a cheese plate, a place in the shade, a toke of weed, a comfortable bed, music around a campfire.

If only it wasn't so damn hot.

Bank signs argue about the temperature, one claiming 104, another 105. A headwind would normally be a relief, but the sirocco pushing into my face feels like a hair dryer. We find shelter in a bar where we sit for four hours, nursing nonalcoholic beverages. Finally, the bartender tells us we need to leave, though he does reluctantly agree to fill my water bottles and even grudgingly adds ice. My bill comes to eight bucks, so I double that with the tip, happy to have rented air-conditioning at that rate.

It's approaching 2 p.m. when we finally leave. The Ochoco Mountains are before us, mounting in a double row with two mountain passes, each ascending over two thousand feet. Four thousand feet of climbing, on the second half of a scorching day, is a terrible idea. It would have been impossible two months ago, but I'm strong now. My middle is small, and my quads are enormous. And there's a reward: I'll finally be done with this desert. Paul and Terry agree. Let's go for it.

The first summit is at Keyes Creek—we find a trio of cyclists atop it. They are not yet twenty, starting their journey across America, like the previous guy, heading east. One of them has a bigger than life American flag, at least seven feet tall, strapped to a fifteen-foot pole zip-tied to the bike. They have a swagger about them, the kind that signifies nothing could possibly stop them—they even casually reveal that they conclude each day with a bit of rock climbing.

One of them says, "Yesterday we climbed one of the buttes back down at Mitchell. We wanted to see the fire."

Excuse me?

"What fire?" I ask.

"They closed the road just after we got through..."

I barely wait for them to fill me in—I utter a quick goodbye and pedal away. We need to get to Mitchell as quickly as possible. The town lies between the two passes, downhill all the way. I fly along the broad downhill road at over fifty miles per hour, not even the slightest temptation to tap Persephone's brakes.

At the general store, the elderly gentleman behind the counter makes no bones about my options. He is no spring chicken—hell, he's not even a *winter* chicken. He's ancient, with parchment-thin, liver-spotted skin. He reminds me of the Witch King of Angmar from *The Lord of the Rings*.

True to form, he intones, *"The way is shut. We do not suffer the living to pass."*

OK, he doesn't actually say that. What he says is, "You need to turn around and go back east."

"How big is the fire? How far would I need to go?" I ask.

"Big. Far," he says, absently wiping down the counter with an old rag.

Paul describes this ghost's noninformation as "really helpful," because he is very polite, and the closest he allows himself to an insult is to praise a person, but with maximum sarcastic intent.

Fortunately, some other folks in town are much more willing to speculate, though no one seems to agree on when the road will open, how far down the road the fire is burning, where the roadblocks are, and which side roads are closed. There are either zero, two, or four cyclists already at the top. Lightning started the fire. Coyotes started the fire. A salamander spontaneously combusted. Every piece of information I receive conflicts with the last. There is only one consistent data point: The road across the mountains is definitely closed because of a very real forest fire. Oh, and the firefighters have taken over every motel room, as well as the local campsite.

Can I get through? No idea. The possibility that I might need to backtrack is becoming depressingly real. A quick look at a map means I would need to climb back up the first pass of the Ochoco Mountains, then back down into the desert, and track as far east as fifty miles before finding a road north around the fires. In total, this could add three hundred additional miles to a trip that is only supposed to have two hundred miles left.

If I need to go around, can I make it to the coast in time to meet up with Christine at our arranged time? Probably not.

There's only one hope: Get to the roadblock and ask if there's a way to get through.

It's a two-thousand-foot climb to the top of the mountain. The road-block could be just as I start out, here at the bottom, but it could just as easily be all the way at the peak. Unfortunately, there's no other options. I can't make a plan without real information, and if a small window to get through the area opens, I need to be in place to take advantage of the opportunity.

As Paul, Terry, and I discuss these options, an ash-covered firefighter walks by.

"Did you come from the roadblock?" I ask.

"Yeah," he says, and pointing to our bikes, "there's no way through. You all need to go back east. You've got to go up north, all the way into Washington to get around, because there's fires from here all the way to the border."

The route he's suggesting is even longer than what I calculated.

"I'm going up to the roadblock," I say, before despair takes over.

"Don't. They won't let you through," the firefighter says, more urgently now.

"How far is the roadblock?"

"About twelve miles. Maybe a little further."

I frankly have no choice—it's past time to finish this ride. Tripling the distance to the end might break me. Paul and Terry agree to join me to scout the situation. Accordingly, I load up six liters of water—for myself, but also for Jerry and Jonathan, who have been ahead of us by half a day. If they got caught unawares up at the top, they'll need it too.

We set out.

The ride up—a two-thousand-foot climb stretched over fifteen miles—is easy for me at this point in the trip, at least physically. But I'm over-whelmed with nerves about what I might find at the roadblock. I find myself scanning the horizon for fire, but all I can make out is a bit of white haze in the sky ahead—there are no plumes of smoke for the first eleven miles up the mountain.

Eventually, I see real smoke, but it's barely anything, just distant wisps. What a relief—maybe this whole situation has been exaggerated. I finally relax a bit, taking in the scenery around me. Forest borders either side of the road. The pine trees are short, but full and healthy. They sit sparsely among golden fields of grass, punctuated here and there by rocky outcroppings. The road snakes its way up gently, every turn revealing a new section of the mountain.

And then, the roadblock suddenly appears from behind a blind turn. Four official-looking trucks sit beyond an orange barricade. Five passenger cars, an RV, and two wide-load mobile home trucks are parked on the highway, too, all waiting for the road to reopen.

I get the real skinny from Jonathan and Jerry who arrived early this morning and have been waiting out an opportunity to get across. The road is closed. One worker told them it would reopen in a few hours. Another said it would be a week. A few hours ago, an Oregon Department of Transportation (ODOT) employee offered them a ride through. They turned it down, wanting to preserve their perfect bike-only trip across the nation.

(I have no such compunction, having already wrestled with that demon and lost, when I was forced to take a ride through the no-bikes Cumberland Gap Tunnel when I was off the official trail, playing with doggies.)

"Hey there," I call out to the ODOT worker.

"Can't get through. Go back."

Undeterred, I say, "I hear ya. But if there's a truck heading through, I'd appreciate a ride. I need to be done with this trip in five days, and there's no way to do that if I need to go around."

"Can't help you," the guy says. "Go back."

"OK, well, if it's all the same to you, I'll just wait over here in the shade."

"No, don't," he says, more forcefully. "Go back."

I don't go back. I head over to the shade.

Paul and Terry arrive.

"What do you think?" asks Terry, "Wait for a ride, or go back?"

"I don't know," says Paul. "We've biked almost the whole country. It would be a shame to get a ride with just a couple hundred miles to the coast. I can smell salt water."

"I think that's smoke," I say.

Sure enough, the horizon is increasingly hazy. This could take a while.

So, we wait. (Which is pretty remarkable—I was not aware that simple waiting, absent any kind of real plan, was a thing I was capable of. Maybe it wasn't before I dipped my wheel in the Atlantic. Maybe I learned something on this trip after all?)

The ODOT worker wanders over to his truck, grabbing his lunch box. This makes me hungry, so I cook up some pepper jack and avocado quesadillas on the flames of my Jetboil. Slathered with Cholula, they're pretty damn good. I wave over the ODOT worker, offering him a quesadilla, which he gratefully takes.

This is not a bribe. Living in Chicago, I know bribes. No, this is what we called "Burrito Arbitrage" at GrubHub. People love food. Here is a partial list of the people who love food: Union foremen. Angry customers. Angry employees. Happy employees. Movers—we had four separate offices. The folks who rented one of the offices before we did and didn't want to be bothered coming back to unhook their audio/video equipment. Also, Oregon Department of Transportation workers who just happen to have space in the back of their truck.

So, not a bribe—merely Burrito Arbitrage.

"Why are those big trucks waiting right there?" I ask him as he eats, pointing to a mobile home transport, along with its flag trucks.

"Their oversize vehicle permits are only for a specific road on a specific day," he explains. "They aren't allowed to detour—it's this road or nothing for them. They're waiting, hoping somebody will take pity on them and let them through."

"Will you?" I ask, out of not-so-idle curiosity.

"Nope," he says, seeing through my ruse. "Fire has jumped the road. Headed north. I live on the other side, west of the fire, over the pass, and even I'm worried I won't be able to get home after my shift ends."

As he's speaking, a huge four-engine jet plane roars overhead. It's flying slow and low. As it passes over the highway a couple miles ahead of me a cloud of red fire retardant erupts from its belly. For all its size, the plane's falling cargo looks utterly useless, dwarfed by the increasingly thick columns of white smoke on the horizon.

Eventually, the ODOT worker thinks of something—food will do that—and heads back to his truck. He comes over to us with a map, spreading it across the sandy ground. He waves over Paul, Terry, Jonathan, and Jerry.

"Look folks," he says, pointing to the map, "there's an unmarked forestry service road…here. A part of it is dirt road, and there's a small stream without a bridge that you'd need to ford, but it's easily passable, even on bikes. It's about half the distance of the next highway beyond, which is all the way up in Washington. But the fire is on the move, and the only reason this unmarked road isn't closed yet is that we know most people don't know about it. If you hurry, you might get through."

This is amazing news. Yet another win for Burrito Arbitrage. But we're not out of the fire yet.

"National forestry service is going to take over this operation once the fire enters national land," the ODOT worker says. "That guy over there [he points to an official-looking vehicle, with an official-looking man standing next to it] told me he's going to kick you off this road the instant he's in charge."

ODOT man heads back to work leaving the five of us to confer.

Jonathan says, "Doesn't look like they'll drive us through—I won't take a ride, in any case. I'm headed back down and going to try the pass the guy pointed out on the map."

Jerry likes this plan, and away they go. Now there were just three.

"I can't go around," I say. "Christine will be in Florence in five days, and I've got plane tickets home. I've got to get through. If I don't, I'll need to just rent a car and drive around this. Or abandon the trip. I'm going to wait and hope I can get a ride."

Paul says, "I'm torn. I really don't want to take a ride in a truck. But I want to finish the trip with you, Mike. And anyway, it sounds like no trucks are going through."

"When that ODOT worker's shift ends, I bet he's driving through," I say. "I'm going to beg him for a ride."

Over the next few hours, the smoke increases as the late afternoon winds feed the fire. We're told repeatedly—by the Oregon Forest Fire Unit, the Bend City Fire Department, the Oregon Department of Forestry, and even by our new pal in the Oregon Department of Transportation—that we should really think about another option, specifically the one that involves going back down the mountain.

Eventually, the big dog from the US Forestry Service wanders over. He hooks one thumb in his belt and places the other atop his gun. My English friends are intimidated by this, though I recognize it as just your garden-variety cop swagger.

"Well," the ranger says, looking off into the distance, "you all put in a good effort to stick around. But I'm afraid that's over now. I've decided it's time for you all to head back down the mountain."

"Yes, sir," Paul and Terry say in unison.

My blood is up. This guy's attitude... I'm from Chicago—have I mentioned that?

"Thanks for the advice," I say, calmly, "but I'm going to wait it out."

"No, you're not, sir. I've decided it's time for you to go."

"Understood. Respectfully, though, that's not your decision to make," I say.

"That's fine," the ranger says. "When my department takes over, you'll be evacuated without your bikes. This is your last chance to leave voluntarily."

I don't sense it at the time, but this is likely the moment my ODOT friend changes his mind. Like the archetypal local cop in a movie, he's annoyed that the feds are going to take over. A few minutes later, just before his shift change, his coworkers head up the mountain and across the pass to get home, and once they are out of view, he wanders over to me.

"Look, I can get you through," he whispers, "but you've got to cover your bike up with a tarp, and duck down when we pass the other side. If my supervisor sees you, it's my ass. We need to hurry—you need to be in the truck with your bike loaded before the next shift gets here."

Paul and Terry watch me load up the 'bent. I'm abandoning them.

"We're going to wait and see if we can ride through on our own wheels. If not, we're going around," Terry says. Paul gives me a big hug. From what I've seen in movies about Brits, this is a very un-Brit thing to do.

"It was great to meet you, Mike," Paul says. "Come visit us after all this."

In other words: after the bike trip, years from now, half the world away.

This is goodbye.

I jump up into the truck, and we peel away. I don't have a lot of time to process this, because, as I may have mentioned, Oregon is on fire.

As we round the very first bend the smoke immediately intensifies.

"Most of the work is about clearing the roadside trees," the ODOT guy says. "Not really about containment anymore. Fire's out of control. The real danger to cars, and bikes, for that matter, is hazard trees. They fall after they burn out."

"How long do they take to fall?" I ask.

"Could be an hour, could be a month. When they fall on the road, they're a lot more work to get rid of. Also, they prevent us from manning the roadblock, keeping crazy bikers like you all from trying to ride through. Usually, we try to cut the hazard trees down *before* the fire arrives. Sometimes we cut them down while they are still burning. Those are fun."

All around us, hundreds of freshly cut trees and stumps line the road on either side. We pass an extended cab pickup truck parked right on the highway, no sign of its crew. A chain saw rests on the hood. My companion adopts a more deliberate pace, winding up the mountain slowly.

Things escalate quickly.

I feel the fire line before I see it—intense heat and a whooshing wind signal our entrance into a very active forest fire. The smoke becomes very dense. Breathing isn't hard, but the smoke is irritating. Then, we are in the flames—fully engulfed trees surround us, bright orange in the premature, smoke-induced dusk. I pull out my camera, hoping to snap a few pictures from the inside of a forest fire. I sincerely hope this is a once in a lifetime opportunity.

"Won't be able to slow down to take pictures," the guy says, not that I wanted him to stop. "Tires might melt."

The road is stained red with fire retardant. Apparently, asphalt can catch fire. I resist the urge to lean over and slam his gas pedal to the floor.

Get me the hell out of this hell.

And then, just as quickly, we're over the top of the mountain flying down the other side. The flames retreat. My new best friend mutters phrases like "lost containment lines" and "insufficient helicopter assets." It's clear this is a very bad situation, just as it's clear that there is zero chance Paul and Terry are biking through that—even if they could get around the roadblock, there is simply too much smoke.

Also, melting tires.

After a mile or two this quiet hero lets me out around a bend, out of sight of his supervisor. I thank him profusely—what he did for me was invaluable, and kind.

And then I'm riding again, like nothing happened. Down at the bottom of the mountain, a perfect campsite waits for me. It's adorably cute, with little grass plots, a store selling ice-cream sandwiches, and laughing children playing in sprinklers. The temperature has finally dropped into the nineties.

I can't enjoy it. I'm gutted. I feel hollow. I've left behind the friends I've ridden with since Kansas. I started the TransAm alone. I'll finish it alone.

I'm not out of the woods yet, either—literally. I call my brother, Steve, so he can check online to see if there are fires to the west of me (I have no internet service here). Yup, he says—and there are fires west, east, north, and south of me.

Oregon is on fire. The whole state.

Still, Steve thinks he can chart me a route through if the information on the state's website is accurate. I jot down the directions for tomorrow morning. I'm to head toward the Cascade Range, with their beautiful sequoias and redwoods. It would have been great to see those with Paul and Terry. This part of America is as new to me as it would have been to them. Exhausted and depressed, I skip dinner. I am asleep before the sun is down.

Sometime around midnight, I'm awakened by my tent being shaken. At first, I think, "bear attack!" until I hear two British accents. Which is confusing, because I didn't think the grizzlies up here had British accents. Paul and Terry decided to break their perfect cycling record across the US and hitch a ride through the fire so we could finish together.

I hug them, crying like a baby.

They don't cry. They're English, after all. They only cry for dogs and horses.

———

My eyes flutter open. In my muddled waking, the first thing I notice is the smell: damp earth. This is not the pine needle memory of my youth, but the more primal Jurassic aroma of wet ferns and giant sequoias. I inhale deeply, pulling in as much air as possible, seeking out a hint of salt water on the air.

Nothing. The coast is still twenty miles away.

The ground through my tent floor is soft and springy, an earthen mattress of untold years of accumulated castings from the ferns and trees. Water rushes nearby. Nobody stirs. It's too early for Paul to be up, and Terry stays in his tent until his much slower striking camp companion is already up for at least half an hour, a smart, friendship-saving compromise worked out over months on the road together. I'm glum that the others in our merry gang won't be with us, here at the end. I don't know if Jonathan and Jerry made it through the supersecret forestry trail or had to take more traditional roads, but regardless, they are now days behind.

I emerge from my tent. It's bittersweet to be close to being done—I'm rested and happy, but melancholy too. Now that its upon me, I don't want this trip to end.

A few minutes of fiddling with my trusty Jetboil results in my morning cup of joe. I sit atop an old wooden picnic bench in the too cool, too damp forest morning, my hands wrapped around the mug, steam wafting into my nose. The warmth seeps through me as I drink a cup, and then a second. This is luxury; this is joy.

"Morning sunshine!" Paul says brightly, his head pushing through the smallest possible rent in his tent wall. "It's a bit chilly, then!"

"Coffee?"

"Oh! All right then!"

Terry stirs, too, and emerges, naked as the day he was born. Off he trots into the trees to relieve himself. This is his daily ritual. Terry's "no clothes while sleeping" policy is unshaken by the reality of camping in the woods behind a church on a Sunday morning. I have never met, nor will I ever meet, a person more comfortable in their nakedness than this bony Englishman.

We take to reminiscing about other parts of the trip. A bittersweet pall overshadows the morning. In time, the conversation trails off, and the bikes are packed. We pedal out of our last campsite, toward the coast. A diner stops us in our tracks, barely five miles out of the barnyard. We sit and reminisce some more. Breakfast blends into brunch. Eventually, we can't find any more excuses to linger.

"I have a request," I say. "When we first get to the coast, I'd like to have ten minutes alone. Sharing this trip with you has been one of the most amazing things of my life, but I started alone, and it's important to finish alone."

No one objects.

The final miles are not the easy downhill glide I had expected—a final set of sharp hills resist my passage. No big deal—I grind away as it seems like I've been doing my whole life. Then, suddenly, I'm out of the mountains, crossing highways and strip malls, like I did on the other coast back behind me. The deep brown earth gives way to sand, and I smell salt. The majestic sequoias have been left behind, replaced by coastal grasses and stunted bushes.

A thick fog surrounds me as I cross the Pacific Coast Highway and glide down a gentle hill into a parking lot in the town of Florence, at the mouth of the Siuslaw River. Florence is known for the gigantic sand dunes on their beaches. Sure enough, the first one, over fifty feet tall, obstructs my view of the ocean. A well-worn trail leads off into the sand—on either side of it discarded plastic buckets show evidence of recent castle building activity. A few feet in, the bike sinks, and then I'm dragging it over the lowest looking dune. Then another. Then a third.

Sweaty and bug bitten, I curse my way down the final slope, which levels out before me. I hear the crash of waves but can't see the ocean through the fog. My world is only thirty feet in any direction. I plunge into the unknown. The sand turns damp.

And then, there it is: the Pacific Ocean.

My feet are in the water. More importantly, my front wheel is in the water.

I did it.

I look out into the foggy sea and feel . . . nothing. Absolutely nothing.

Hmmm. That's not right.

Over the last seventy-five days, I've daydreamed of what the moment would feel like. As I crossed the Mississippi, I experienced a small bit of exuberant joy, a precursor, perhaps, to what I'd enjoy here at the end? As I crested the Continental Divide at Hoosier Pass, a sense of accomplishment foreshadowed what I thought I'd feel as I rolled my front wheel into the ocean. Creeping along under the blazing sun of the Eastern Oregon high desert, I dreamed of the expected relief I'd feel as I finished.

But now that it's here, none of those things happened. Arriving here, after 4,157 miles, none of the emotional fireworks and blazing glory of my expectations comes to pass.

At this point, I'd settle for a solitary tear, poised expectantly on my lower eyelid. No such luck.

I wait. Five minutes, which turns into ten.

And then I realize: Nothing *is* something. Because that nothing is actually peace. I am actually having a very profound reaction. It's subtle, it's hard to spot. It requires stillness. Once I do spot it, though, I can savor it.

I feel at peace. That's the Pacific, and that's what I feel: pacific.

I scoop up a bit of the ocean, sealing it in the empty vial I've had this whole time. It joins its siblings from the Mississippi and Atlantic.

I walk over to Paul and Terry. There is no melancholy, no ecstatic whooping. Just smiles.

Terry says, "Well, that's job done. I think it's time for a spot of lunch."

I linger for a moment, staring out at the ocean, as the Brits make their way back up the beach. My mind wanders to the anticipation of seeing my wife in an hour and continuing on with my life.

I stand for a moment longer, content.

In the end, I started in an armpit and ended in peace.

Epilogue

Creating a multibillion-dollar business was great. Everyone should do it. The victory lap was an amazing time of self-reflection. Everyone should do that too. Instead of ending with an exclamation point, there was a final, quiet moment of contentment.

Problem is, contentment is fleeting. I did get to enjoy a couple of years staying at home with my newborn daughter. It was wonderful, and I will always cherish those years of my life. But, as the months passed, I could not shake the feeling that there was something left undone in my career.

It has been eight years since the GrubHub IPO and the TransAm. I'd love to say that I became a patient person and that I've wrangled my anger and left behind the asshole I'd become starting GrubHub. I didn't. Not much, anyway. Even after a life-changing event, we all revert back to the person we were before we started. Mostly.

And for me, that means I'm back to being a malcontent. Oh well.

So, I put it to work.

I got deeply involved in impact investing. Impact businesses work to be successful while doing good. They take both ideas seriously. This isn't the minor leagues, where some well-meaning, naive entrepreneur is wasting investment dollars on philanthropy. Rather, it combines the reality that businesses are effective levers for change, with the recognition that the best companies look holistically at the world of which they are a part. Impact businesses benefit *stakeholders*, rather than exclusively shareholders.

The best impact businesses reject the concept that there must necessarily be a conflict between profit and purpose. Instead, they are a carefully thought-out combination of the two. The key insight is this: Effective impact businesses create benefit in their communities *because* they profit, rather than *in spite of* their profit.

My first forays into startup investing (both impact and traditional) were disastrous. It takes a unique skill set and temperament to be an investor, one aspect of which is patience, something I have never learned. So, I lost some money, and spent more than a few board meetings grinding my teeth in frustration.

So, I quit my hobby as an investor (there is a theme here) and started something new.

I started with a problem.

One day, I wanted work done on my gutter downspout, installing a rain barrel to catch water for my garden. I tried finding a handyman online, but after a dozen or so calls, I couldn't get anyone to come out to my place. I even looked in the Yellow Pages.

And then I got cranky.

Why do I have to call all these handymen on the phone? Why won't they call me back? Why are they all men? How does somebody even get into the trade anyway? How on earth am I back to looking in the Yellow Pages?

Then, I got the band back together, calling up my old coworkers and brainstorming to see if there was something we could do about it. We decided to build a handyperson business that looks like GrubHub—easy online ordering, good communication, and solid quality control. But rather than employing gig economy workers, we decided to create full-time positions with benefits. And since there are not enough skilled people to do the work, we committed to training our workforce from scratch. We picked a gender-neutral name: Fixer.com.

The idea behind the business is that by increasing the number, skill, and diversity of the tradespeople in the communities we serve, we are also building a huge competitive advantage in terms of the quality that we can bring to customers' homes. The more benefit we create in those communities, the more we generate profit.

The idea has worked, but it hasn't been easy.

It has been expensive to get it off the ground, gobbling up investment dollars with a voracious appetite. Building a training center from scratch with no education experience was surprisingly difficult (to me at least, but not to any teachers I know). It is also incredibly hard to fine-tune policies that make a physical labor-oriented workplace attractive to women, men, and everyone. Then the pandemic hit, just as we started building up momentum. Overnight, I found myself the CEO of a business that operates in customer homes, and all those homes were on lockdown.

It has been hard. Way harder than GrubHub was.

That's OK. Hard things are easier when you have a goal. And we've got a big one.

This time, I didn't shoot too low. We are on a mission to reboot trade education in the United States in a gender-inclusive way.

I did something different this time around. I didn't just set this big hairy audacious goal for myself. Everyone in the company knows it. My investors know it. It is even written into the company's charter.

I already have the victory lap figured out. A decade from now, I am going to quit and sail into the sunset. Literally—I am going to sail a boat around the planet.

Finally, let me leave you with a small piece of advice.

If you see something that is broken, and it bothers you…If you can't shake the feeling that it could be done better…If you look around and realize that nobody else is as annoyed by this thing, and that maybe nobody else is going to fix it, and that maybe, just maybe, you might be the person to do it…

You can.

That's my piece of advice to every would-be entrepreneur. Don't overthink it. Don't write a business plan. Don't hire a lawyer, or a market research firm. Just start.

Make the thing.

Sell a customer.

Start.

Acknowledgments

It is more difficult to get a book published than it is to create a multibillion-dollar business. This is not an exaggeration. I've done both. The book was way harder. Seriously.

My warmest thanks to my lovely, patient, kind, giving, superhero wife, Christine. You were so supportive and patient during the GrubHub years, and then again through the writing about the GrubHub years. Nobody should have to go through that twice. I look forward to another half life-time amusing and annoying you.

To my agent, Alice Martell, thank you. After most of a decade trying to get a science fiction writing career off the ground, you took a chance on me. With patience and encouragement, you helped me navigate the off-route, through the backwoods, up a mountain, chased by dogs trail that is the publishing industry. Always punctuated with your catchphrase, "Onward!"

To my editor, Krishan Trotman, thank you. You insisted this book live up to its potential. Not once did you let an unresolved thread, or confusing metaphor, or unexplained background get past you. You fixed countless errors, pointed out a multitude of blind spots, and, on at least three occasions, saved me from utterly embarrassing myself. I'm incredibly grateful now that I'm done. ☺

To Luke Dempsey, thank you. Thank you for helping me keep my best turns of phrase, suggesting new ones at times, and being a huge support as I churned through revision after revision, trying to get this thing just right. It wouldn't have been the same book without you. Your empathy certainly helped with some of the more head-banging-on-desk moments of this process. It's very un-British, but I send you a virtual hug.

Thank you to Lisa Garon, who managed my social media, podcast, and outreach campaigns. The other part of writing a good book is getting people to read it, and you helped tremendously with this. I would have gone crazy trying to do this without help.

A special note of thanks to my writing family. First, to Abby Geni and Story Studio Chicago, who taught me a solid foundation as I wrote my first science fiction novel. To Piper Drake, who brought me under her wing and introduced me to her writing people at SFWA, and to Smokies. And, who, importantly, told me to quit slaving over the same stalled sci-fi novel, and start something new. Thank you to the Smoky Writers group, who accepted me as a wannabe author, with no judgment or expectation. Specifically, among Smokies, thank you, Alex and MK. Both of you heard early scribblings on this concept on a cold misty day in the Smoky Mountains, and responded with such enthusiasm and joy that I really just had to write the book at that point. Jeff Cebulski, thanks for reading. Ariana Evans, you too. Also, thanks for the perfect epigraph suggestion from *The Hobbit*!

Thank you to the Adventure Cycling Association, who keep the crazy dream of bicycle touring alive in a nation enamored with cars. And, of course, to my cycling mates: Jonathan, Jerry, Jess, Tuan, and my dear friends Paul and Terry.

And finally, a deeply felt thank-you to all the restaurateurs who took a chance on a twenty-five-year-old kid with a website. Without your trust and your amazing pizzas, pad thais, burgers, tacos, chop sueys, nachos, burritos, salads, wraps, sushis, and cookies, I could never have built the business I did, nor kept my ample belly so well supplied. Thank you.

A portion of proceeds from the purchase of this book will benefit the Adventure Cycling Association. Please also consider supporting their great work financially. Or, even better, go on a long bike ride. You can.